A PASSIONATE AFFAIR
The Story of Neeme Järvi and Göteborgs Symfoniker
The National Orchestra of Sweden

A passionate affair

The Story of Neeme Järvi and Göteborgs Symfoniker

The National Orchestra of Sweden

Pia Naurin
Martin Hansson

WARNE FÖRLAG

Graphic design: Annika Lyth
Picture editor: Anders Friberg
Draft translation: Cannon Språkkonsult AB
Factual editor: Lennart Dehn
Music compilation: Martin Hansson and Michael Bergek
CD master: Michael Bergek
Repro: Reproman
Produced by Warne Förlag AB

© Copyright Pia Naurin, Martin Hansson and Göteborgs Konsert AB, Gothenburg 2003.
Printed by Almqvist & Wiksell, Uppsala 2003.
ISBN 91-86425-46-3

Contents

Preface to the English edition · 6

A PASSIONATE AFFAIR · 9
Full speed, full calendar · 14
Neeme Järvi · 16
Love at first sight · 17

WHAT KIND OF AN ORCHESTRA WAS IT? · 21
Järvi and Stenhammar's First Symphony · 24
Wilhelm Stenhammar · 28
What kind of a hall was it? · 30

LIKE A ROCKET · 39
Franz Berwald · 44
Eduard Tubin · 47
A record company director remembers · 48
Fake announcement at Landvetter airport · 49

THE VOLVO SPONSORSHIP · 53
The great sponsorship debate · 56
Five-party motion · 60

MILESTONES · 64

MUSICAL BODY-LANGUAGE · 67
Jean Sibelius · 73
It's wonderful · 78
Hardenberger's most difficult moment · 80

MOST PERFORMED WORKS · 84

AN EMOTIONAL COMEBACK · 87
A raised eyebrow is enough · 88
Edvard Grieg · 96
Do you have church bells up there? · 97

DISCOGRAPHY · 100

BEHIND THE IRON CURTAIN · 105
Dmitri Shostakovich · 112
Conductor anonymous · 116
Arvo Pärt · 119
Järvi and Pärt · 120

CITIZEN OF THE WORLD AND GOTHENBURG · 123
Gustav Mahler · 133
A place in town · 137
Not a dry eye · 143

PERFORMING IS ALWAYS RISKY · 147
About my violin · 161
Revenge in Amsterdam · 162
Personifying traditions · 169

GÖTEBORGS SYMFONIKER 2003 · 176

THE NATIONAL ORCHESTRA OF SWEDEN · 179

THE ORCHESTRA ON TOUR · 187
Carl Nielsen · 196

TOURS 1980–2003 · 204

THE FUTURE · 212

PS – VIENNA 1997 · 218

Contents CD 1 and CD 2 · 222
Sources and picture credits · 224

Preface

This book is about a 20 year journey undertaken by the Göteborgs Symfoniker – The National Orchestra of Sweden (GSO)* – hand in hand with their principal conductor Neeme Järvi. The journey started when the orchestra and the exiled Estonian conductor simply fell in love with each other at their very first meeting. A highly regarded provincial orchestra was transformed into a full-sized, modern symphony orchestra with a world-class reputation thanks to an inspirational conductor, a vast amount of hard work and a controversial sponsorship agreement with Volvo, Gothenburg's largest and most famous corporation. During their 20 year relationship, Neeme Järvi and the GSO have toured the musical centres of the world, winning over audiences and critics alike in London and Lucerne, Amsterdam and Aldeburgh, New York and Nagoya, Tokyo and Tallinn, Munich and Madrid, Helsinki and Hong Kong, Cardiff and Chicago as well as Paris, Berlin, Salzburg and Vienna.

Uniquely for an orchestra based in the second city of a country that most people cannot place on the map, the GSO has recorded on a regular basis for Deutsche Grammophon for most of the twenty years that Neeme Järvi has spent in Gothenburg. The book describes how a farsighted orchestra manager, Bjørn E. Simensen, persuaded the players' union to renegotiate contracts that made recording financially feasible. (At the time it was cheaper to hire a leading London orchestra for a recording.) The new agreement made possible an acclaimed succession of recordings for the BIS label. The collaboration with BIS proved symbiotic, for it not only launched the GSO's international reputation, leading to contact with DG and invitations to perform abroad, but it also helped BIS to become one of the leading independent record labels.

Another milestone in the history of the orchestra was the government's decision – following vigorous lobbying on all sides and annoyance on the part of the musical establishment in Stockholm – to grant the GSO the right to call itself the National Orchestra of Sweden. This has naturally been of the utmost value in creating goodwill for the orchestra abroad.

Success is a fickle handmaid. The GSO is constantly aware of the fact that the triumphs of yesterday do not guarantee success today. And so the GSO and its management, together with the city, regional authorities

---

* The orchestra founded in 1905 was known as *Göteborgs Orkesterförening* (The Gothenburg Orchestra Society). This was later renamed as *Göteborgs Symfoniorkester*. During the 1970s the orchestra took the name *Göteborgs Symfoniker* (Gothenburg Symphony Orchestra). This name is now used internationally with the addition, since 1997, of the title Sveriges Nationalorkester. *Göteborgs Symfoniker – The National Orchestra of Sweden* is now the orchestra's official name both in Sweden and abroad. To help readers of this book, the well known abbreviation *GSO* has been liberally employed.

and the government, are constantly alert to the need for further development.

There is constant investment in the structure and facilities of the Gothenburg Concert Hall. A world class orchestra deserves a world class home! And as Neeme Järvi assumes the accolade of Principal Conductor Emeritus, Mario Venzago has been named the new musical director to ensure the future well-being of the GSO. This book is a tribute both to Järvi and to the musicians. The right chemistry between conductor and orchestra, a passion for music and a great deal of hard work laid the foundations for the orchestra's success. But as Neeme Järvi says: "You're on the wrong track if you see it as work."

Pia Naurin wrote the narrative and the orchestra's Head of Communications Martin Hansson edited the book and wrote the entries on the composers. He also selected the music reproduced on the two CDs that are an integral part of the book. These feature performances with Neeme Järvi conducting the GSO taken from CDs released by BIS Records and by Deutsche Grammophon as well as from live recordings made by the Swedish Broadcasting Corporation.

Our thanks are due to numerous individuals who have contributed to this tribute to the "Neeme Years". Special mention must be made of Robert von Bahr, president of BIS Records, the staff of the Swedish Broadcasting Corporation in Gothenburg and of its music channel P2 in Stockholm, the management of Deutsche Grammophon, Håkan Hardenberger, Frans Helmerson, Peter Schéle, Dai Ya and Nikolaj Znaider. We are indebted to the Friends of the Gothenburg Symphony Orchestra and to the Region of Västra Götaland for their generous financial support. We should further like to acknowledge the invaluable assistance we have received from Tim Ashley, Dvora Lewis, Stefan Nävermyr, the staff of BIS and Andrew G. Barnett in preparing the English-language edition of this book.

June 2003
Martin Hansson, Pia Naurin, Sture Carlsson

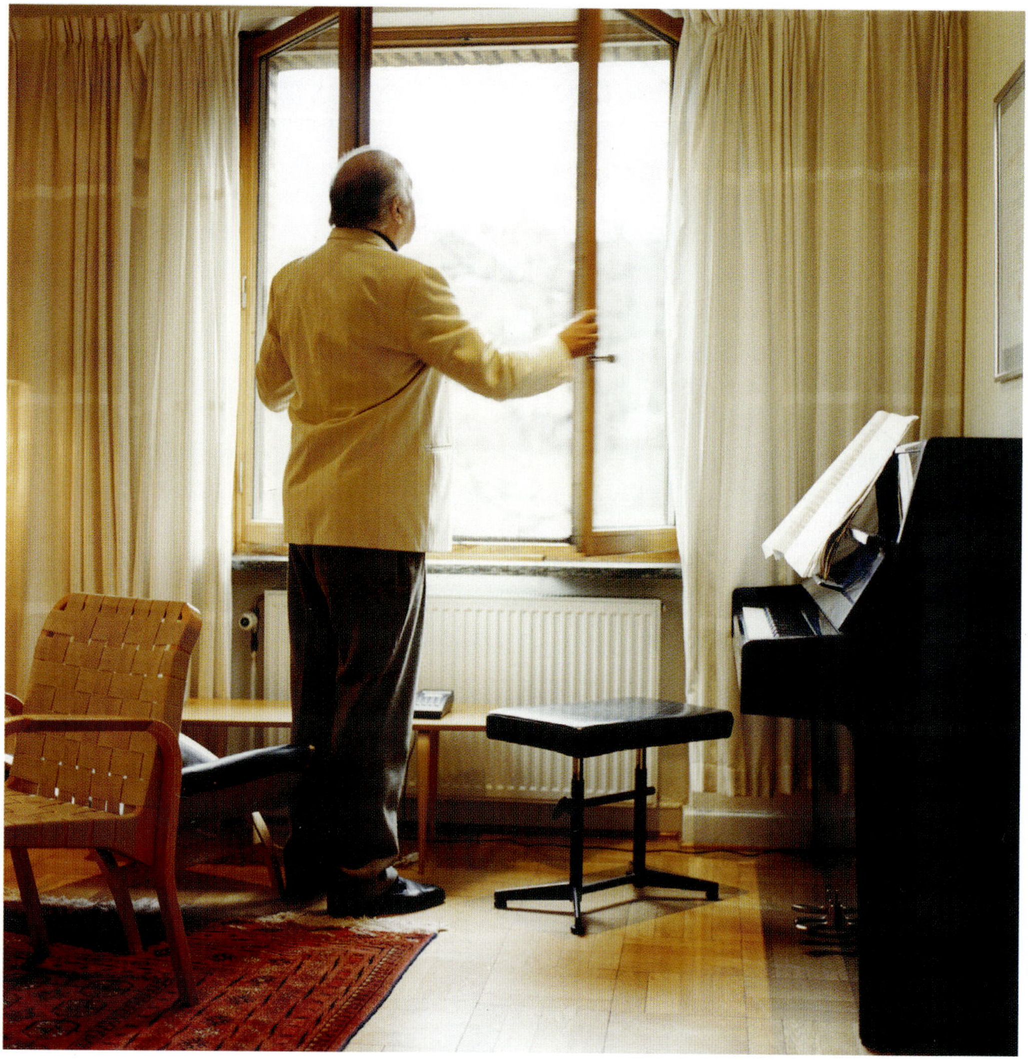

A passionate affair

Neeme Järvi's Gothenburg apartment is directly opposite the Concert Hall, a few floors up in the building on the corner of Viktor Rydbergsgatan and Arkivgatan.

The lights are on in Neeme Järvi's window. The interview is booked for 3 pm and I'm waiting in the Concert Hall. Then he comes, a tall, heavily-built man. Without visible haste he walks the few steps across the street, his dark blue overcoat unbuttoned and his long red scarf flapping in the wind.

He has spent the morning resting, I have learned. Nowadays he takes time to rest after travelling through different time zones. Jetlag is something that never used to bother him.

We sit down in the conductor's room. Between us on the round table are this week's scores: Sibelius, Szymanowski and Tchaikovsky. Above the piano is the honorary doctoral diploma he received from the University of Gothenburg and on the wall by the window there is a portrait of him for visiting conductors to admire.

Symbolically, the window looks out on Gothenburg's beautiful old Music College. The new College of Music, known as *Artisten*, was opened in 1992 with Neeme Järvi in attendance. He is pleased with the view. By no means all conductor's rooms have windows, he says. And he should know because he has seen a large number of the world's concert halls from the inside.

"Music for me is all about spreading happiness. When I look into the eyes of the audience after a concert and see that they have been infected by the joy we feel on the podium when we are playing, then I know that the concert was successful."
Neeme Järvi

But our first topic is his reading glasses. They are a mystery because they are always somewhere else. He has lost them in his apartment and somebody offers to dash across the street to get them.

Everything to do with Neeme Järvi is given top priority. Although his mood is friendly and familiar he is always the maestro. Music is his life, he says. It has been ever since childhood. His own children have followed in his footsteps. En route from the USA to Gothenburg he landed in Stockholm to see his youngest son, Kristjan Järvi, conduct at Berwaldhallen, the Swedish Broadcasting Corporation's concert hall. Kristjan is principal conductor of the regional opera in the northern city of Umeå. Neeme's eldest son Paavo is music director of the Cincinnati Symphony Orchestra and his daughter Maarika is a flautist. In charge of them all is Neeme's wife, Liilia, who ensures that family ties remain close.

Neeme Järvi has now reached retirement age and has started taking things a little easier – he doesn't rush around quite so frantically any more. His illness in the summer of 2001 made him realise that he is mortal. But this hasn't stopped him from booking two busy weeks of rehearsals, concerts and recordings in January 2002 in Gothenburg. Foreign journalists will be flown in, and the press release has finally been drafted: the 2003-2004 season will be Neeme Järvi's last as principal conductor. He will then receive the honorary title of Principal Conductor Emeritus.

Neeme Järvi wishes that he had learned Swedish during his years in Gothenburg, but he just hasn't had enough time. His first language is Estonian and his working language around the world is English. His musical motto is in English: "As much beauty as possible." Even contemporary music, which many of us do not always find easy to accept, "has a lot of beauty," he explains.

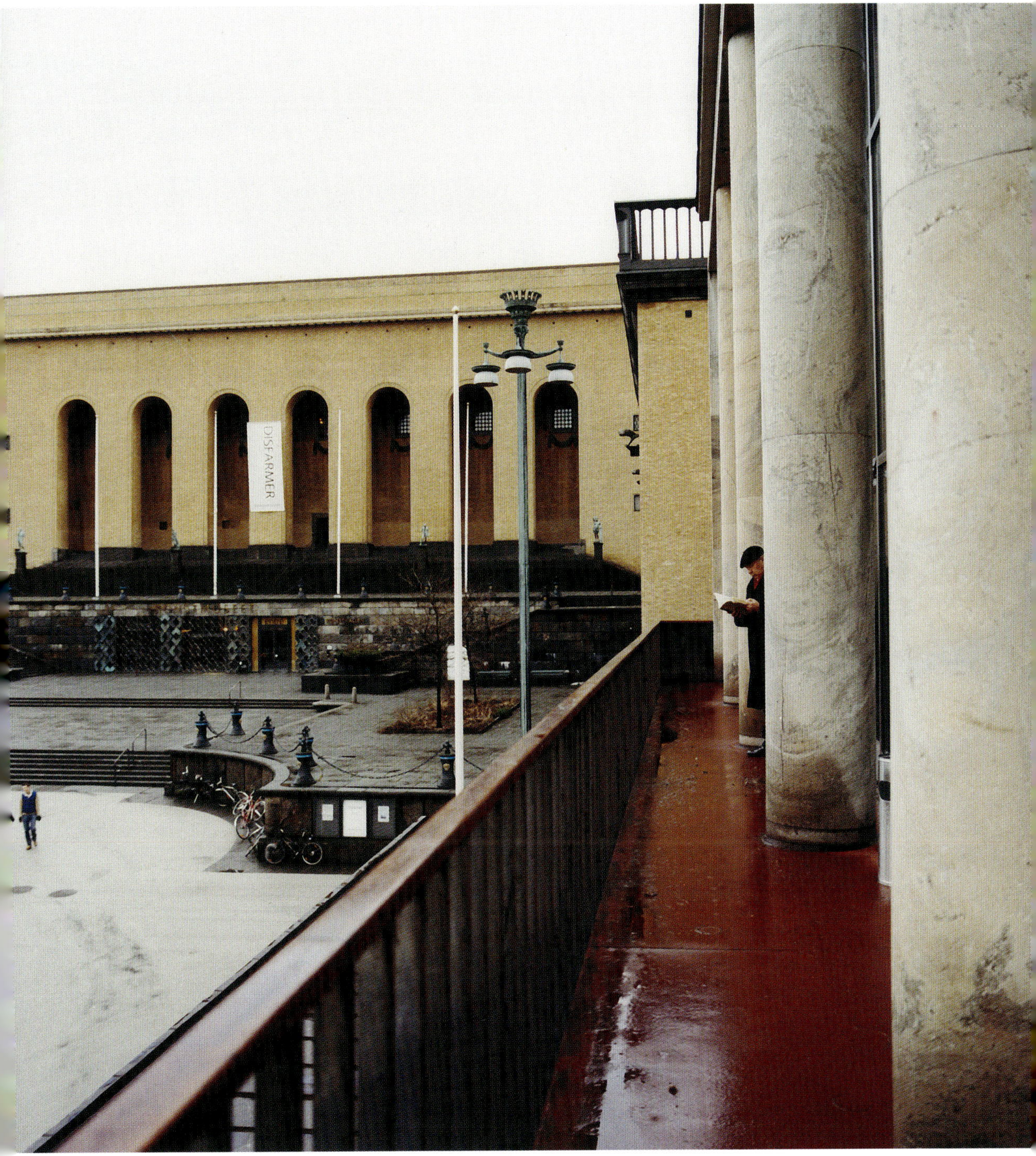
DISFARMER

"GSO is world-class. But the competition is growing all the time, even here in Scandinavia. Ten years ago we had a head start when it came to touring and recording. Then all of a sudden came the Oslo Philharmonic Orchestra. They are strong competitors and have recorded a great deal for EMI. Then there's the Danish Radio Orchestra who record for Chandos and other labels. The Royal Stockholm Philharmonic Orchestra and the Swedish Radio Symphony Orchestra are making records and the Norrköping Symphony Orchestra has also recorded a few good ones, while Malmö is making some headway. It is through competing with the likes of these that we develop. Their successes make us grow."

Neeme Järvi

That's the conductor's job, to bring out the beauty in music.

All the beautiful notes, the phrasing, the remarkable contrasts of tempi, of piano and forte, the tremendous climaxes… that's music, he explains, or rather it cannot be explained, it must be felt.

Where does he get his energy? He puts his hand on his heart. "Here." That's one place. Then there are the role models, such as Carlos Kleiber with his fantastic recordings. "It's not that I want to do it better than Kleiber, just differently. I listen to what other conductors have done, I know them and like them, and then I like to try it my way."

The success of the GSO, he explains, is that they play so wonderfully well, and it is not difficult to say why. It is quite simply that they are professional.

Good technique, good solo players throughout the orchestra, strings, flutes, clarinets, bassoon, oboes and the horn section, there isn't a weak spot anywhere. And that doesn´t just apply to concerts but rehearsals as well, which is very important.

"I have worked with several major orchestras but when I come back to Gothenburg I'm always impressed. The musicians here give their all, even at rehearsals. The orchestra's success is a combination of this, and of me, and the hall, the acoustics, the atmosphere – and of a "good family life together."

Hard work? No, you're on the wrong track if you call it work. That makes it become mechanical. You have to love what you do. "Work is not enough, you have to enjoy what you do", is the principle by which he has lived.

He is now trying to fit more free weeks into his calendar, a new experience for him. "Earlier I have always felt that I must have a full schedule. If there have been any days off then I've filled them as well. Otherwise I would be asking: 'what am I going to do now?'"

He doesn't quite yet know what he will do with his newfound spare time. "I've never had any spare time. But I'm sure I'll find something to do." He seems not to be interested in finding out what he may have missed in the course of a normal life. He has done what was important to him: music.

"Neeme is a complete workaholic. I don't think he regards conducting as work. In his own way he's just having fun. Just look at the number of recordings he's made. Few conductors have made more recordings than he has. Many of them are by composers that few people have heard of. For Neeme it is like an adventure, like entering the jungles of the Amazon with a machete. I think his whole life is just one big adventure."

Kristjan Järvi in a New York Times article.

"Taking on numerous guest appearances was a way of establishing myself, making myself known. That was more important when I was younger. I have been privileged to have conducted most of the world's great orchestras. However, I now find it more rewarding to use my energy to keep developing the orchestras in Gothenburg and Detroit."

Neeme Järvi

Full speed, full calendar

In order to find the time to do all he wanted to do, Neeme Järvi has always worked at full speed. A normal working week at the beginning of the 1980s would look like this: rehearsals with the GSO during the first half of the week, concerts on Thursday and Friday, flying to Glasgow on Saturday morning, recording on Saturday afternoon and Sunday morning, flying back to Gothenburg in the evening and then more rehearsals with the GSO the next morning.

His calendar was just as full ten years later. In October 1991 for example Neeme Järvi travelled on tour with the GSO to France and Germany.

In the space of a fortnight they appeared at 11 venues: Rouen, Le Havre, Stuttgart, Kassel, Düsseldorf, Braunschweig, Hamburg, Frankfurt, Munich, Rosenheim and Berlin. They performed works by Grieg, Sibelius, Pärt, Dvořák, Sandström, Tchaikovsky, Stenhammar, Haydn and Bartók. During that fortnight, Järvi also found the time to travel back to Gothenburg to receive his honorary doctorate.

The day after the Berlin concert with the GSO, Järvi flew to Scotland to conduct concerts in Edinburgh and Glasgow and to record with the Royal Scottish National Orchestra. He spent the following month, November 1991, with the Detroit Symphony Orchestra. They made a recording together and also performed at Carnegie Hall in New York. The same month Järvi also travelled to London for concerts and recordings with the London Philharmonic Orchestra.

The following year, in May 1992, he wrote in his diary:
1 May: Detroit. Rossini's Overture to Semiramide and Orff's Carmina Burana.
2 May: As above.
6–9 May: Music festival in Ann Arbor, USA. Conducted works

> "Being a guest conductor has its advantages. How difficult it is depends on which piece is going to be played and how well you know it. I can't say that I get nervous, that's not the right word. On the other hand, I may feel uncomfortable with the situation. If it's an unfamiliar orchestra and we haven't found enough time to rehearse, one needs to be careful. But if things go well and the orchestra is good, then I feel no hesitation at all when I'm on the conductor's stand."
> **Neeme Järvi**

by Rossini, Mahler, Holst, Beethoven, Schubert, Prokofiev, Rachmaninov, Sibelius, Dvořák and Orff.
10 May: Flight Detroit–Gothenburg.
11 May: Recording with GSO for Deutsche Grammophon. Mussorgsky.
14 May: Concert in Gothenburg. Schubert, Schoenberg, Strauss.
15 May: As above
20 May: Concert in Gothenburg. Mozart, Shostakovich.
21 May: As above
22 May: Recording with GSO for Deutsche Grammophon. Shostakovich and Grieg.
25–26 May: Recording with GSO for Deutsche Grammophon. Shostakovich.
31 May: Opening of Gothenburg's new School of Music, Artisten. Weber, Mendelssohn, Beethoven.

A few days later, on 2 June, he conducted the GSO concert at the Liseberg amusement park, and on 3 and 4 June gave subscription concerts at the Concert Hall. The next day he flew to London to work with one of the symphony orchestras there and also managed to fit in time to make a recording before returning to Gothenburg for yet another recording with GSO.

On 14 June he gave an open-air concert with the GSO in Gothenburg. He then travelled back to the USA and worked a little in Michigan, Detroit and New York – and then in August the tempo increased again. First he performed at the closing ceremony of a grand festival in New York, before returning to Gothenburg for concerts and preparations for yet another tour with the GSO: a festival in Germany and the World Fair in Seville were already booked. Back in Gothenburg he made a recording with the GSO for Deutsche Grammophon. He rounded off August in Glasgow with the Royal Scottish National Orchestra.

**GSO AND NEEME JÄRVI
20 YEARS IN SUMMARY**
- A total of 592 concerts.
- Tours to 21 countries on three continents, 175 concerts in 120 cities.
- 539 different works performed, of which 103 works were done at least five times.
- 62 first performances and Swedish premières with the GSO, of which ten with Neeme Järvi.
- Nearly 40 international tours of Europe, the USA and Asia.
- Guest performances at major musical centres: Carnegie Hall in New York, BBC Proms at the Royal Albert Hall, the Barbican Centre and the Royal Festival Hall in London, Concertgebouw in Amsterdam, Musikverein in Vienna, Philharmonie in Berlin, Théâtre des Champs-Élysées in Paris, Tonhalle in Zürich, Suntory Hall in Tokyo as well as the festivals in Salzburg, Aldeburgh, Edinburgh and Lucerne.
- Concerts at the World Fair in Seville and in Singapore, Hong Kong and Tokyo.
- The first visit by a Swedish symphony orchestra to China, concerts in Shanghai and Beijing in 1999.
- Close to 90 recordings for BIS and Deutsche Grammophon, including major works by Berwald, Borodin, Grieg, Nielsen, Rimsky-Korsakov, Sibelius, Stenhammar, Shostakovich and Tubin plus operas by Prokofiev, Rachmaninov and Tchaikovsky.

Neeme Järvi

Neeme Järvi divides his time between Gothenburg and Detroit. When his contract as conductor of the Göteborgs Symfoniker – The National Orchestra of Sweden, comes to an end at the close of the 2003-2004 season, he will become the orchestra's Principal Conductor Emeritus. Since 1990 he has been music director of the Detroit Symphony Orchestra, a position he retains until 2005, when he will become that orchestra's Conductor Laureate. Between 1984 and 1988 he was principal conductor of the Royal Scottish National Orchestra. The RSNO appointed him Conductor Laureate in 1990.

Neeme Järvi began his career in 1963 as principal conductor of the Estonian Radio Symphony Orchestra and the Estonian Opera, a post he held until 1976. He emigrated with his family to the USA four yeas later. Since then he has been a guest conductor with most of the world's leading orchestras including the Berlin Philharmonic, New York Philharmonic, Chicago Symphony, Philadelphia, London Symphony and the French National orchestras. With more than 350 recordings, he is one of the world's most recorded conductors. Nearly 90 of these recordings were made with the GSO for Deutsche Grammophon and BIS.

Neeme Järvi has received numerous honours and awards. He is an honorary doctor of the universities of Gothenburg, Aberdeen and Michigan, and a Knight of the Order of the Northern Star. Neeme Järvi was also the first recipient of the "Collar of the Order of the National Estonian Coat of Arms".

In 1998 Neeme Järvi was named "Estonian of the century" by his native country.

Neeme Järvi receiving his honorary doctorate at the University of Gothenburg in 1985...

... and in Aberdeen in 1990.

Love at first sight

The first time they met was at the Gothenburg Concert Hall on 8 April 1980. Neeme Järvi was a last-minute replacement and later told a journalist that the reaction was "positive from both the orchestra and the audience." But it was more than that, it was love at first sight. Everything clicked.

In June of the same year a tour of Ireland and the UK was planned. Mariss Jansons, the Latvian principal conductor of the Leningrad Philharmonic Orchestra, was due to conduct but was forced to cancel, having been refused an exit visa by the Soviet authorities. His father, the conductor Arvid Jansons, was also abroad and two members of the same family were not permitted to leave the Soviet Union at the same time.

A replacement conductor had to be found and quickly. Neeme Järvi had just begun his career in the West. He had the same agent as Mariss Jansons, a fact which was much

The first contract from 1980.

more significant in the era prior to internet and e-mail. His diary was still not fully booked and he accepted

A few days before the tour in June, news spread that Neeme Järvi was to "take over the orchestra." In a newspaper interview he gave his recipe for success: Develop co-operation with the musicians, lots of tours and recordings.

On 15 June he conducted the GSO in Dublin. The leader Christer Thorvaldsson recalls:

"The auditorium was a sort of pillared hall with glass-fronted cabinets along the walls. To make more room, the stage had been extended with planks on trestles and it rocked a bit where we sat. But we soon forgot about that. The place was packed to capacity. Elisabeth Söderström sang, and performing with her was a fantastic experience. That evening in Dublin and the final concert in London a few days later are two of my most profound memories of the orchestra."

The Dublin success gave the orchestra self-confidence. Despite sceptical predictions otherwise, the tour started to shape up well. The next stop was the famous Aldeburgh Festival founded by Benjamin Britten.

"Following a short rehearsal we had sandwiches," recalls Lars Nyström, who later held the position as the GSO's orchestra manager for many years and is currently responsible for tours and projects. At that time he was a viola player. "We were sitting on the stage eating when the acting manager of the Concert Hall, Håkan Edlén, came in and told us that all the details had now been finalized. The contract with Järvi was signed. At least 15 concerts a year were scheduled, starting in September 1982."

The tour was to end in London. On the programme was Strauss' *Vier letzte Lieder* with Elisabeth Söderström, Alfvén's *Midsummer Vigil*, and Sibelius' Second Symphony, which was to become the orchestra's signature. Jan Johansson, a double-bass player in the GSO since 1966, says that love struck on 18 June in the Royal Festival Hall:

"Sibelius' Second was drawing to a close. We expected the usual final chord but Järvi surprised us in the actual crescendo. It wasn't what we'd rehearsed. But nobody in the orchestra wavered for a split second. He held it all in his hands, and that's where his strength lies. He can do something quite out of the blue, and there is no hesitation, you just follow him."

"... it is a well disciplined ensemble, producing a brilliant, open sound with a keen edge ... thrilling at its high points, was Sibelius' Second Symphony. Mr Järvi's firm manner secured some full-blooded orchestral sonorities."
From the review in the Times of the London concert of 18 June 1980.

◯ CD 2.1

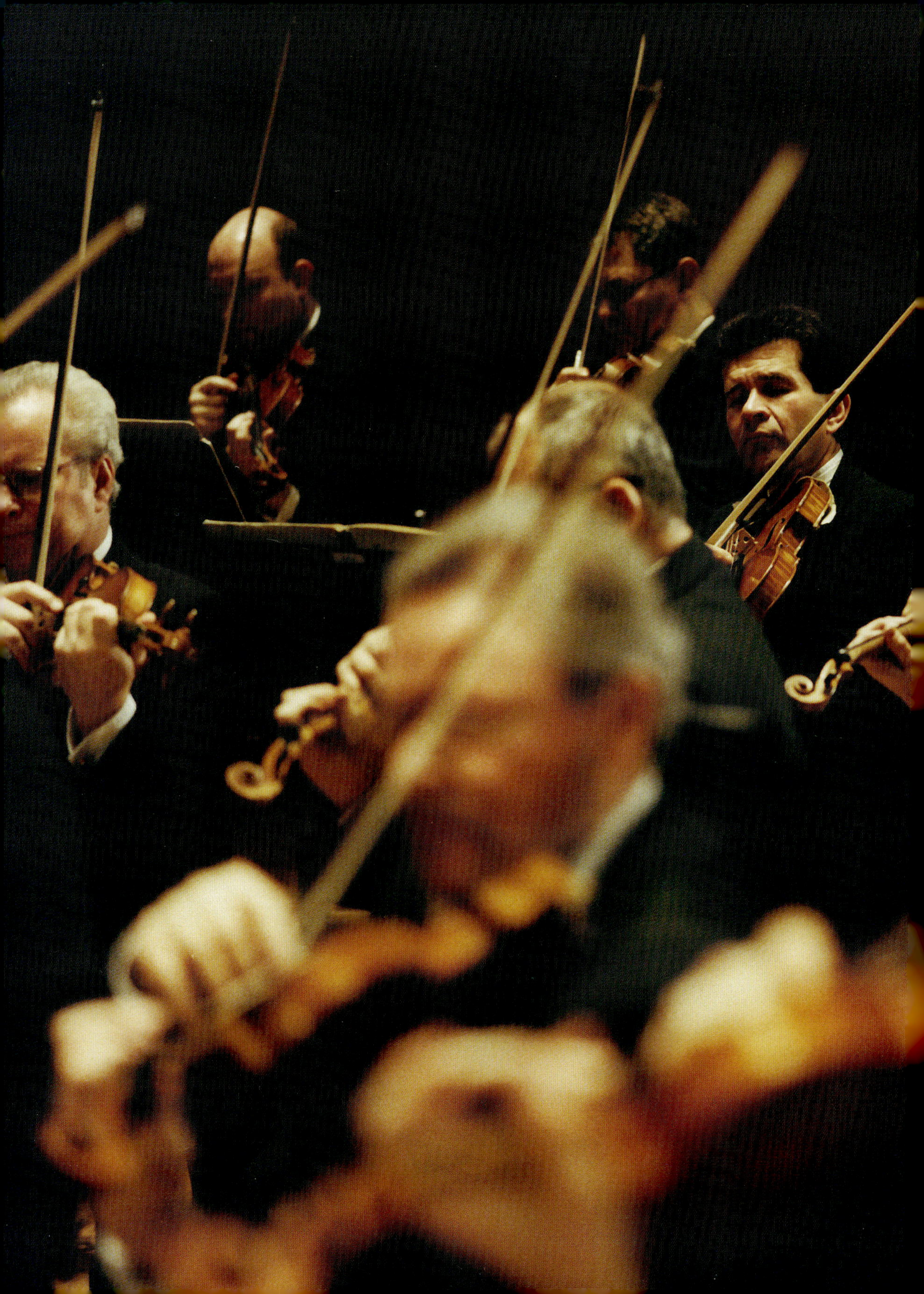

What kind of an orchestra was it?

We know that Göteborgs Symfoniker – The National Orchestra of Sweden is a top class ensemble today. But what were they like 20 years ago when Neeme Järvi came to Gothenburg?

The potential and the tradition were always there. While Wilhelm Stenhammar was building up the orchestra it was ranked highly, just as under Tor Mann's tenure. The Gothenburg orchestra was the main broadcasting orchestra in Sweden for more than a decade including the war years.

The 1970s were also a successful time for the orchestra's artistic development, according to an article published in 1978 by the former manager Sven Kruckenberg. But would this development continue?

During the 1970s the concepts of "elite culture" and "popular music" were pitched against each other. Was there a place for the symphony orchestra in modern society? Not everybody thought so and debate was heated.

Sven Kruckenberg quoted the poet Artur Lundkvist: "What do the dubious expressions *elite* and *elitism* actually mean? They mean contempt for culture and, in turn, a contempt for the people, belittling talent and intelligence, skills and artistic ability… Nowadays anybody can join the cultural consumer elite… Qualified cultural consumers have been around for quite some time in all classes of society."

Conductors replaced one another at a rapid rate at the Concert Hall. In the early 1970s Sergiu Comissiona was followed by Sixten Ehrling and Charles Dutoit, who were all great personalities. However, Sixten Ehrling only stayed for one season and Charles Dutoit and the orchestra seemed not to find the magic required for things to really take off. The Swiss-born Dutoit didn't feel at home with the Scandinavian repertoire and moved to Montreal in 1979, bringing the Montreal Symphony into a top class orchestra, until his unexpected departure in 2002.

After Dutoit the orchestra was without a principal conductor and a series of guest conductors took over the season. "One of the problems that must be solved sooner or later if the orchestra is to maintain the standards set by Stenhammar or most recently Comissiona, is the question of conductors. The number of conductors must be radically cut, otherwise the standard that the orchestra has now reached will be jeopardized. To the uninitiated it might seem as though the management are trying to collect autographs," wrote the music critic Gustaf Hilleström in an article to mark the 75th anniversary of the orchestra in 1980.

Without firm artistic management the orchestra's self-confidence began to fail. Musicians from these years remember tours to small Swedish towns. The trip to the UK in 1980 was the first foreign tour for many years. Some questioned spending so much money. "Why on earth are we going to England to make fools of ourselves," players moaned.

The big question was: who will be the new principal conductor in Gothenburg? Who would consider staying long enough to turn the orchestra's fortunes around? Competition for the best talents was as tough then as it is now.

"The leading orchestras in Europe and the USA now pay

such high fees," Hilleström pointed out, "that a top conductor wouldn't consider tying himself down in Sweden. Despite air travel we are still off the beaten track…"

This is when Neeme Järvi arrived, and Hilleström ended his article with the hope that the orchestra could now lay down the foundations of an international reputation.

Järvi and Stenhammar's First Symphony

Neeme Järvi refuses to name a favourite composer. "There are so many and there is so much fantastic music. It's great music," he says about many composers, a comment he makes about Stenhammar's First Symphony, which was one of the first works he conducted when he arrived in Gothenburg in the autumn of 1982.

At the time Stenhammar's First Symphony was a forgotten work. The composer had himself withdrawn the score. "It only moves on the surface," he explained self-critically comparing it with Sibelius' famous Second Symphony, which was premièred about the same time.

While researching for the 100th anniversary of Stenhammar's birth in 1971 the manager of the Concert Hall, Sven Kruckenberg, found the score in the archives of the Royal Swedish Academy of Music. He asked Sergiu Comissiona to perform it at a concert on Stenhammar's birthday. Lennart Dehn, who was then the GSO's head of communications, says, "I became enchanted by this important symphony and thought it was a shame that it should just sit there collecting dust in the Academy's vaults. I made a tape of the concert and tried, in vain, to interest conductors such as Sixten Ehrling and Charles Dutoit."

As soon as Järvi's appointment as principal conductor was announced, Lennart Dehn was asked to search for as much Swedish music as possible for him. Dehn took the opportunity of smuggling in the Stenhammar tape and this time it ended up in the right hands. "I fell in love," Järvi explains. Stenhammar's First Symphony was scheduled for Friday 24 September 1982. The concert was broadcast live on Sweden's P2 channel. A few months later the recording was released on the BIS label.

"A neglected symphony, warm and romantic, classically balanced," Göteborgs-Posten's music critic, P G Bergfors,

Nielsen, Järvi, Grieg, Stravinsky.

wrote when the record was released in the spring of 1983. "Congratulations!" he added.

Since then the GSO and Järvi have recorded most of Stenhammar's orchestral music. Their most recent recording was a critically acclaimed two CD set for Deutsche Grammophon containing both of Stenhammar's two symphonies as well as the *Serenade* for Orchestra and *Excelsior!* This was released in 1995 and marked Wilhelm Stenhammar's international breakthrough on CD.

Neeme Järvi is proud of being his successor. Maintaining the traditions from Stenhammar's days is one reason for the GSO's success.

"My successor must have a strong feeling for the orchestra's Scandinavian character," he says, and starts counting the years to see which of the two has held the longer tenure as conductor, himself or Stenhammar.

Järvi wins.

PRINCIPAL CONDUCTORS OF GÖTEBORGS SYMFONIKER – THE NATIONAL ORCHESTRA OF SWEDEN

1905–1907 Heinrich Hammer
1907–1922 Wilhelm Stenhammar
1922–1925 Ture Rangström
1925–1939 Tor Mann
1937–1970 Sixten Eckerberg, head of the Gothenburg Radio Orchestra
1941–1953 Issay Dobrowen
1953–1960 Dean Dixon
1960–1967 Sten Frykberg, resident conductor
1967–1972 Sergiu Comissiona
1974–1975 Sixten Ehrling
1975–1979 Charles Dutoit
1982–2004 Neeme Järvi

Saltsjöbaden, 4 jan. 1904

Käre, det är ju
sedan länge sedan vi
hade din symfoni här,
— jag tänkte skrifva
genast dagen därpå,
men däraf blef intet,
och så dröjde jag.
Några rader skall du
i alla fall ha. Ty
du skall veta att du
är i mina tankar
dagligen allt sedan jag
hörde symfonien.
Du härliga menniska,
det är ju hela stora
fång af under du
hemtat upp ur det
omedvetnas och outsägligas
djupaste djup. Det

Saltsjöbaden 4 January 1904

My dear friend, much time has passed since we heard your symphony here. I had intended to write the very next day, but I delayed. I shall write you a few lines at any event. For I should like you to know that you have been in my thoughts every day since I heard the symphony. You are a wonderful person, you have gathered huge armfuls of miracles from the deepest depths of the unconscious, of the fundamentally inexpressible. What I had suspected proved to be true: you stand before me as the foremost, the only one, the inscrutable. And I am now waiting for you to present yourself to the world as a bright and formidable figure – to give body to humanity, to give us drama. You do not need it, I can manage without it, but those numerous people who are now turning away from a mystery that they have been unable to solve, they need it. Raise up the characters from your wonderful world of Finnish tales, show them as elemental symbols for those mystical depths which you will never be able to portray other than in music but will never be able to explain other than by action. I implore you on behalf of all those who unconsciously long for this.

I have also now written a symphony. At least it is called symphony. And according to an agreement, which you may have forgotten, it was to be dedicated to you. But this will not be the case. It is fairly good, but it is superficial. I long to search into my own depths. But you will have to wait until I have found my way in. On the great day when this has happened I shall print your name in bold letters on the title page – whether it be a symphony or something else. Until that time I shall bear your name faithfully and piously in my grateful soul, where it will forever remain. You have so stirred me that I shall not be able to forget.

Your friend
Wilh. Stenhammar

Stenhammar and Sibelius first met in 1900, but it was not until their second meeting in Helsinki in 1902, shortly before the première of Sibelius's Second Symphony that they became friends, a friendship characterized by Stenhammar's deep admiration for his Finnish colleague. In November 1903, roughly a month before the première of his first symphony Stenhammar heard Sibelius's Second Symphony in Stockholm. It was a revelation for Stenhammar who later self-critically withdrew his own symphony. At the beginning of the new year he wrote one of the handful of classic letters in the history of Swedish music.

WILHELM STENHAMMAR 1871–1927
Swedish pianist, conductor and composer, born and raised in Stockholm, studied the piano in Berlin. Toured as a pianist with the romantic and classic masterpieces, conductor in Gothenburg 1907-1922. As a composer he was a romantically inspired classicist and a father-figure for Swedish music of the 1900s.

Major works: Two symphonies (1903, 1911-1915), *Excelsior!* (1896), two piano concertos (1893, 1907) and Serenade in F major (1913). Also the songs *Florez och Blanzeflor* and *Flickan kom ifrån sin älsklings möte* plus the A minor violin sonata, incidental music to *Chitra* (1921), *Ett Drömspel*, the interlude from the cantata *Sången* and the last three of his six string quartets.

○ CD 1.1

Wilhelm Stenhammar

One of Swedish music's most versatile talents. Stenhammar celebrated triumphs as a pianist with Brahms' First Piano Concerto, the model for his own orchestral B minor concerto, a work that gave him an international career as a pianist and which he performed under Richard Strauss in Berlin and Hans Richter in Manchester. (Stenhammar's concerto score was damaged during the Second World War and reconstructed by Kurt Atterberg. That version was used until a copy of the original score was discovered at the beginning of the 1990s.)

As a young composer Stenhammar was inspired by Wagner but in 1904 he suffered a personal and artistic crisis. Feeling inferior to Sibelius, withdrew his first Bruckner-inspired symphony. A visit to Florence in 1906-1907 ended his problems. He finished work on the second piano concerto and started on his brilliant orchestral *Serenade* in F major. Influenced by both Sibelius and Nielsen he developed a mature, classically integrated style, at once rich in temperament, yet restrained.

In 1907 Stenhammar moved to Gothenburg where his pioneering efforts over 15 years had a major impact on the history of the orchestra. A performance of Carl Nielsen's First Symphony marked the beginning of a long friendship between the two composers and provided inspiration for Stenhammar's own masterpiece, his Second Symphony, which is intensely Swedish in tone, revealing powerful emotions beneath a disciplined exterior. Stenhammar conducted a great deal of new Scandinavian music in Gothenburg, especially by Nielsen and Sibelius and he also introduced contemporary orchestral works by Mahler, Bruckner and Debussy. Stenhammar's taste and musical idealism was passed on to future generations through his student, Hilding Rosenberg. Stenhammar's music is played regularly by the GSO.

CD 1.10

Recordings: The major orchestral works and the second piano concerto with the GSO conducted by Neeme Järvi are available on BIS. Neeme Järvi and the GSO have also recorded the symphonies, the *Serenade* and *Excelsior!* for DG.

What kind of a hall was it?

It makes no difference how much at home the GSO feels on the world stage. The Concert Hall in Gothenburg remains the orchestra's favourite venue. "It's our second home," say the musicians. This is where the music is welded together, and it is here that the orchestra rehearses and performs throughout the year.

The musicians claim that the hall's acoustics follow them on tour. The resonance is there, even when conditions are non favourable. This is possibly because the musicians are accustomed to playing in a certain way, and possibly – there are no definites in such matters – that their performances have been moulded by the acoustics.

People who are always forced to practice in poor acoustics learn to play in a certain way. This can result in a rather "raw" sound.

Acoustics is the word used to denote the sound conditions in a room. The acoustics of the Gothenburg Concert Hall are exceptionally good. The main auditorium is considered one of the best in Europe. Another important European concert hall is the legendary Musikvereinsaal in Vienna, from which the New Year concerts are televised. It is one of the best, with an almost religious resonance, as if Mozart might come round the corner, or rather his ghost. The Concertgebouw in Amsterdam is another hall steeped in tradition, and the Japanese are also building magnificent concert halls.

Acoustic excellence is not easily achieved. When Sergiu Comissiona, the principal conductor in Gothenburg 1967-1972, was asked to help build a concert hall in the USA he used the Gothenburg hall as a model. Everything was carried out to the letter, apart from the fact that the new hall seated far more people than its Swedish counterpart. It just was not

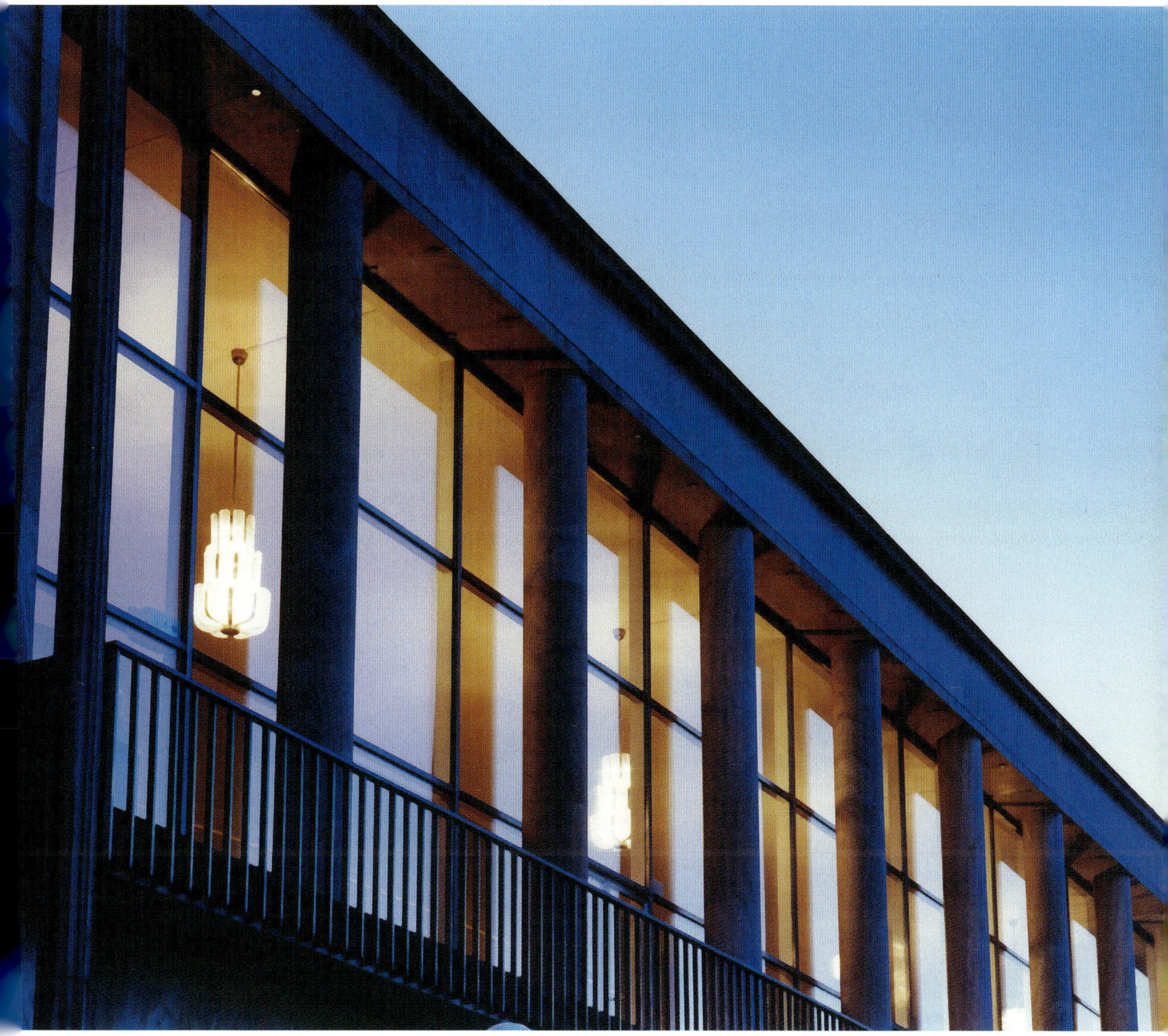

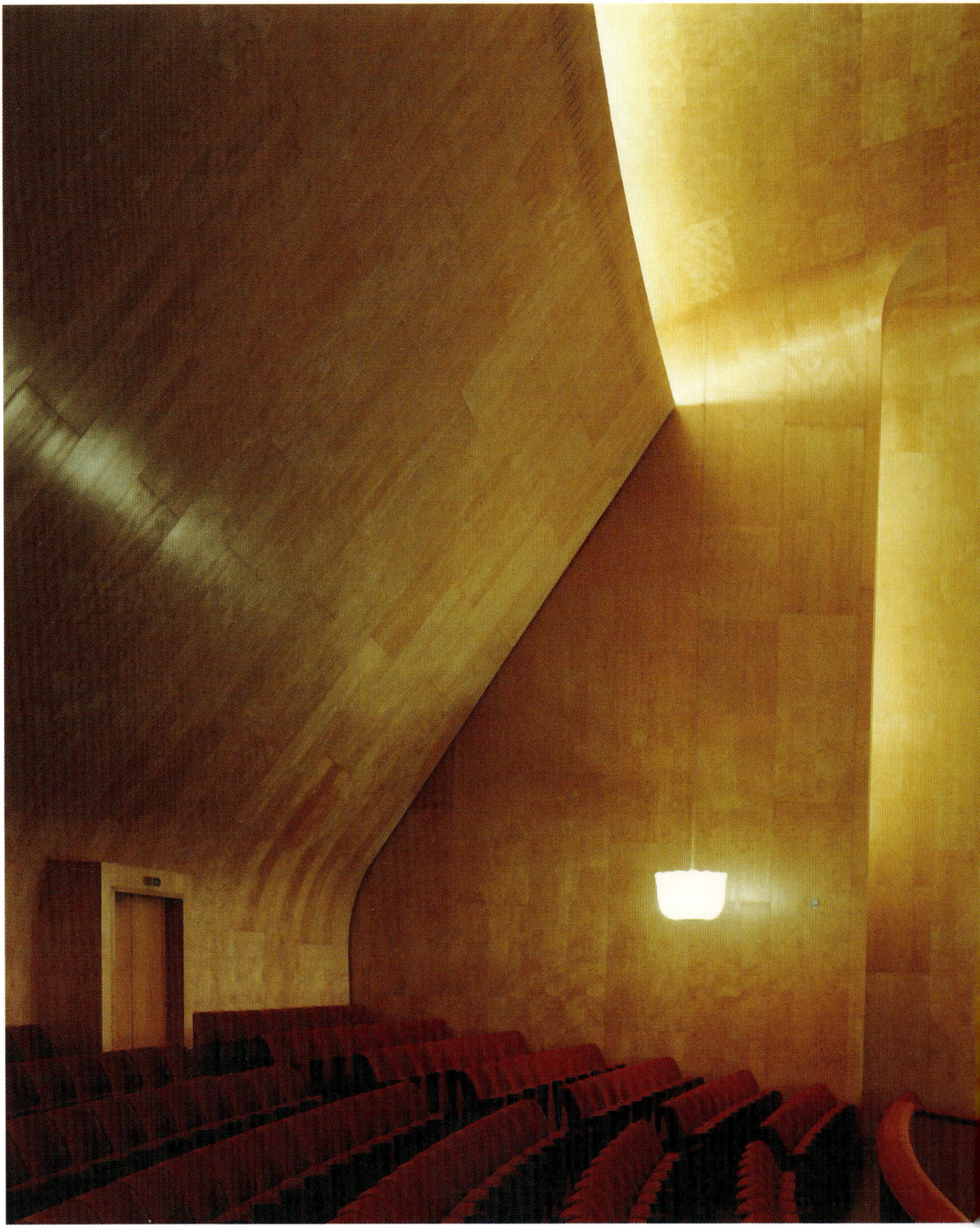

The opinions of visiting experts have always been highly enthusiastic. But few can match Toscha Seidel's enthusiasm. Seidel was one of the great violinists of the interwar period. In November 1935 he said, "This concert hall is unique, it is the most magnificent, the grandest, the most wonderful in the entire world. It is the ideal music hall. You do not need to ask anyone else about this. I have played in the Salle Pleyel and all the other famous halls. Of course they are splendid, or beautiful or pleasant, each in their own way, but what you have here in Gothenburg should not be discussed in the same breath."

Igor Markevitch, the Russian-Italian conductor and composer, was somewhat more restrained: "Gothenburg's Concert Hall is one of the great halls in the world and visually the most beautiful built during the 20th century."

the same. The resonance changed as soon as the scale of the building was enlarged.

What is the secret of the acoustics in Gothenburg's concert hall?

Architect Nils Einar Eriksson described the acoustic qualities in a book called Göteborgs Konserthus (The Gothenburg Concert Hall), published in conjunction with the opening in 1935.

"The main auditorium is shaped so that sound from the ceiling and the podium's side walls is projected over the audience. The rear wall slopes so that sound waves that strike it are projected towards the back of the stage where they are absorbed. The sound pockets on the sides of the hall are there to dissipate the sound, and the angles prevent standing waves. This is a modified form of the irregular walls of a radio studio. One might say that the hall is similar to a fan shape with sectioned side walls.

The walls are made of wooden panels, 20 mm thick, fixed on battens on the concrete framework. The outer surface is of sycamore maple, which is matt-treated with a cellulose varnish. Most materials absorb more high tones than low tones. Wood has been chosen because it gives the most even absorption of tones of different pitches. It also has the ability to amplify sound by resonance. In order to prevent the equally large wooden panels from giving resonance to a particular tone they have been equipped with diagonal wooden battens, which are fixed in different patterns to the rear of the panels."

Sycamore maple is a light wood, sometimes used for making violins. That's why the main auditorium is often compared to a violin. The likeness is not exact because a violin needs to have thin walls in order to resonate, while the concert hall's walls should be thick to preserve the sound.

The hall is completely clothed in sycamore maple. There is no decoration to disturb concentration. The warm colour

CD 2.7

of the walls blends with the tones from the stage. Visual and sonic impressions combine to produce an experience that is hard to describe. Though there have been numerous attempts to explain its special qualities.

"This unusual room can only be described as beautiful. There are no vertical lines, the walls fold and lean inwards, and there are gentle curves that merge into the ceiling which raises its curved vault, in what for the lay person are unfathomable lines," wrote a journalist, following the opening on 4 October 1935. Another writer considered the ceiling as being "a light, well-disposed heaven of sycamore maple, which must be a joy to the sound."

Eriksson's aim was to create the best possible acoustic environment imaginable and he succeeded beyond his expectations. Reactions at the time were rapturous.

The promenade around the main hall.

Tor Mann conducted the inaugural concert of music by Berwald and Stenhammar.

The building was so perfect for experiencing music, claimed the musicologist Julius Rabe after the première performance, that it even ennobled the audience: "It is the free citizen of the world who takes his place with head held high among like-minded individuals to partake of what Beethoven called revelations higher than all wisdom and philosophy."

The Gothenburg Concert Hall is now considered one of the great monuments to Scandinavian functionalism. A "crab in a rectangle," Eriksson once called it, well aware of the fact that there are two buildings in one: one of them built as a shell around the auditorium, the heart of the building, the other as a façade in the city.

One can argue that the Gothenburg Concert Hall reveals its true dimensions as one proceeds through the building. The lobby area and the broad divided staircase leading up to the foyer arouse one's anticipation, and the promenade around the main auditorium affords space for socializing. The walls here are a mild mussel-shell blue. The blue tone and light-coloured woods create a special atmosphere. The furniture was described, as early as the 1930s, as "amicable" and at the same time "functional, but fortunately not like machines for sitting."

Light streams into the foyer. The large window facing onto Götaplatsen is framed on the one side by a monumental painting, *Folkvisan* (Folksong) by Otte Sköld, and on the other side by Sven X:et Erixon's tapestry, *Melodier vid torget* (Tunes on the square) (which includes a portrait of the architect Nils Einar Eriksson playing the banjo). Outside the building, on Götaplatsen, Carl Milles' bronze sculpture of *Poseidon* holds his floundering fish in his steady grasp. He becomes part of the foyer.

The Concert Hall was the last of the grand public buildings to be erected on Götaplatsen. As was usual in Gothenburg, the building was financed by public donation. The donors were Göthilda and Pontus Fürstenberg, and Mrs Caroline Wijk, née Dickson.

The Fürstenberg donation funded the formation of the orchestra association in 1905. A temporary concert hall was built the same year at Heden in Gothenburg.

It was here that Stenhammar spent time with his guests, Jean Sibelius and Carl Nielsen. The concert hall was imposing but built of wood. When it burned down in 1928 the orchestra was homeless. It found refuge in the city's theatres and other public venues for many years while waiting for a new home. Without Caroline Wijk's very generous donation in 1916 the new concert hall might never have been built.

Nils Einar Eriksson designed the building with an orchestra of around 50 musicians in mind. Now, seventy years later, the orchestra is twice as big. To give the musicians and administrators more space, a long awaited extension was built at the end of the 1990s. The public areas have also been restored to their original condition. A modified acoustic screen has been added above the stage which has been extended with a number of adjustable sections. It's function is to improve the famous acoustics and to make it easier for the musicians to hear each other as well as to strengthen the visual impact made by the orchestra.

The extension was opened in 1999. Designed by White Architects, it has received several awards. The Gothenburg Concert Hall is one of the few concert halls in the world to have insisted on maintaining the same high standards on, as well as behind, the podium. Creating the best possible working environment for musicians and guest artists is seen as an important investment for the future.

A design competition was held for decorating the foyer. The editor of *Handelstidningen*, Torgny Segerstedt, wrote at the time: "The finale of the competition for decorating the Concert Hall has been judged. The moaning can now begin. And it has. This is how it's always been, and how it will always be. Works of art are incommensurable. There is no standard by which their innate values can be judged. One person will always think one way, another person otherwise. …In this imperfect world one has to be satisfied with what is good, without letting one's delight be sullied by uncertainty as to whether something else might possibly be better. The Concert Hall has a beautiful interior. Just sitting in the hall or walking up the stairs makes one happy. One would surely be a veritable ass if one were to lose oneself in woeful thoughts about whether something even more beautiful might have been achieved. If you were to wait for an answer to that, nothing would ever get done. At some point you just have to act. And one must be satisfied when the result is as remarkable as that which has been achieved at Concert Hall."

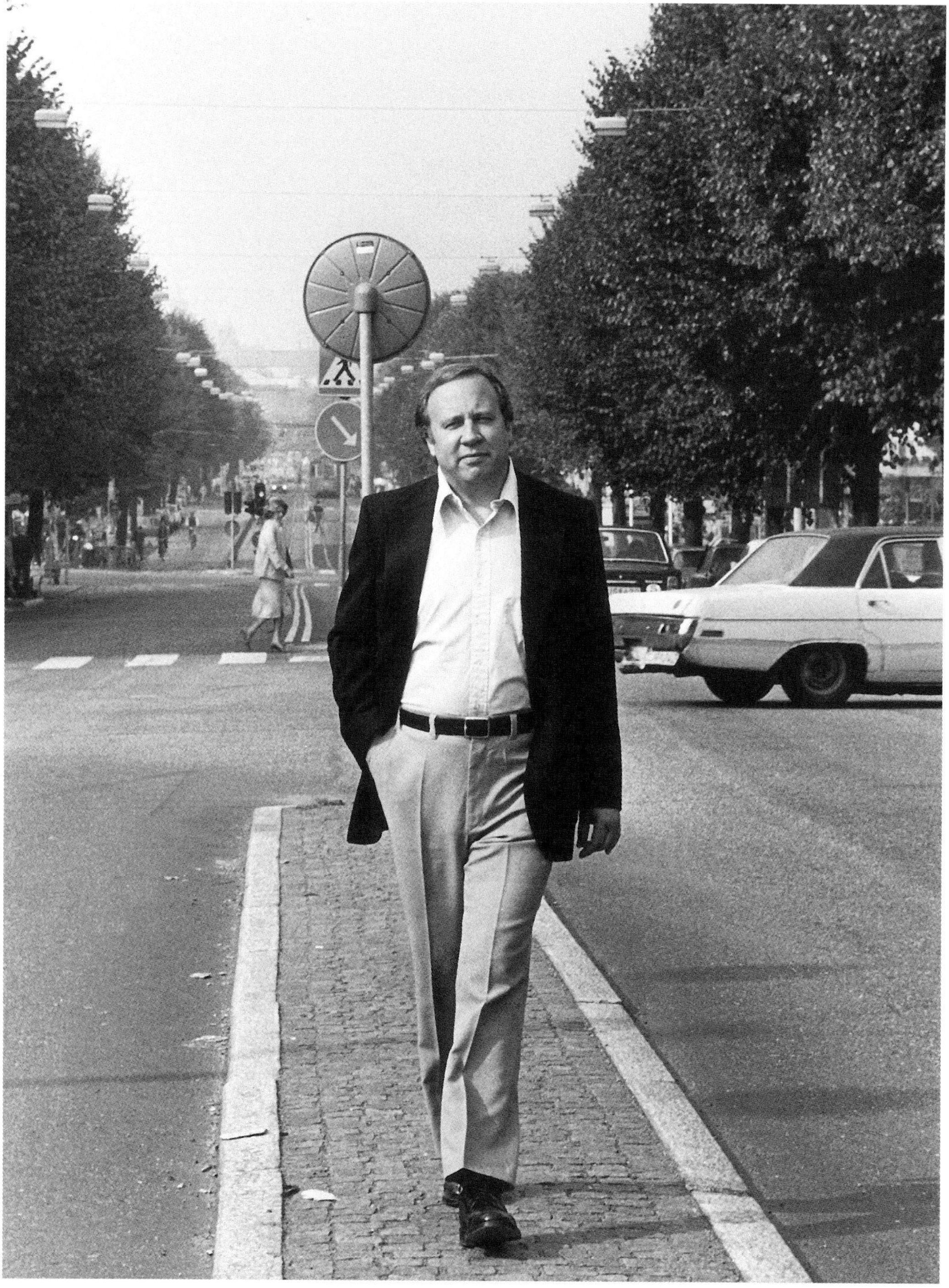

Like a rocket

Bjørn E. Simensen talks about timing. And about dreams:

"Järvi and I often walked down Avenyn, the boulevard that leads down from the Concert Hall, and bought ice cream and chatted and dreamed. He likes ice cream by the way."

"Järvi said, 'Just think if one day I could take this orchestra to my home town of Tallinn. Just imagine, a tour of the USA. Just imagine, if we could grow to one hundred musicians!' And we walked along and laughed. But all our dreams came true!"

Bjørn E. Simensen was cultural director of the town of Sandefjord in Norway when he applied for the job of manager at the Concert Hall in Gothenburg in 1980. In Sandefjord he had organized a concert programme at the cultural centre that attracted a good deal of attention in Norway. In the opinion of the Gothenburg board, this former journalist had no other major qualifications and they delayed his appointment. Perhaps a person with a more solid music training should be appointed? But the members of the orchestra took the Norwegian's side, and just as Simensen was getting tired of waiting and was about to give up, the board decided that PR ability and entrepreneurial skills were more important than musical training.

Neeme Järvi walking down *Avenyn* in the early 1980s.

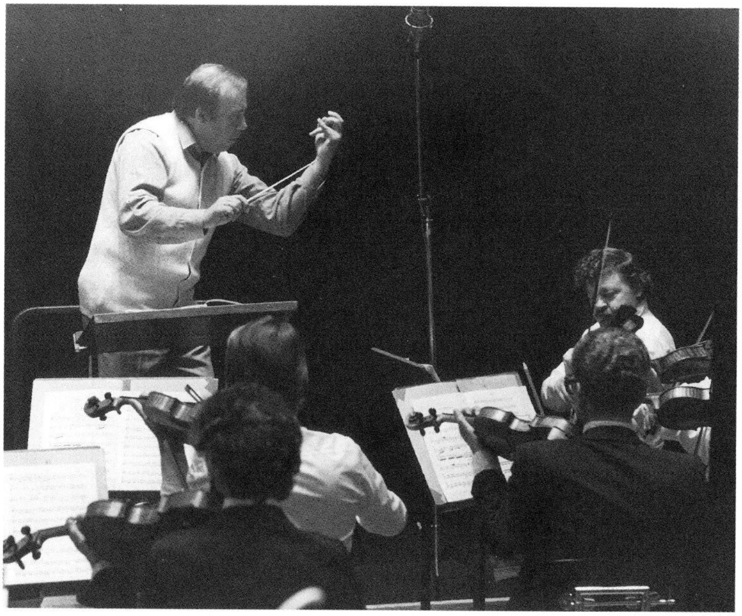

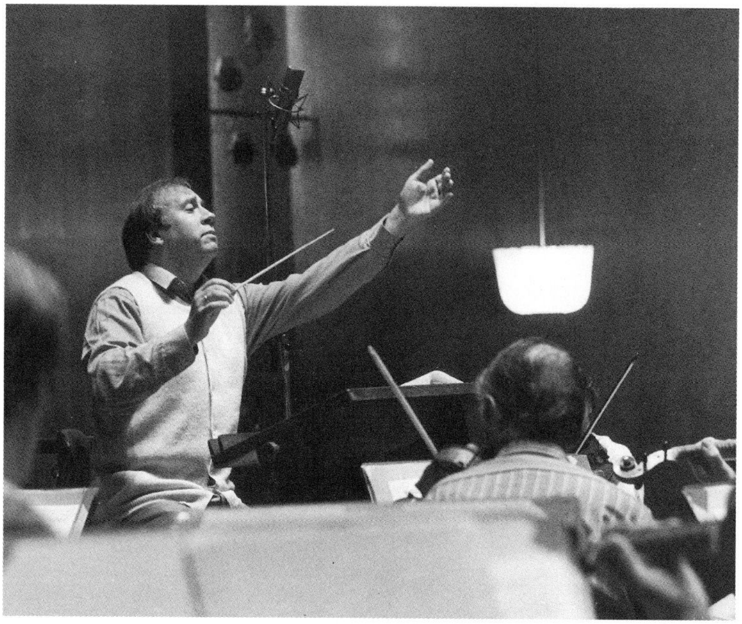

Bjørn Simensen arrived as a question mark and ended up as an exclamation mark, or so people thought four years later when he returned to Norway to become head of the Norwegian National Opera in Oslo, a post in which he remained except for a few years as editor of the Norwegian newspaper Dagbladet.

Four main components contributed to the success of the GSO, explains Bjørn Simensen, as he looks back 20 years later:

The orchestra was hungry.

The new conductor was equally hungry.

The Volvo sponsorship agreement.

The recording contract.

You could add a fifth: Simensen himself.

The first thing Simensen did upon arrival in Gothenburg in the autumn of 1980 was to ask the orchestra what they wanted. Not unexpectedly they wanted good conductors, recording contracts and tours. There were few offers waiting however, and even if a new conductor was contracted it would take two years before he was able to start.

So while waiting for Järvi, the orchestra prepared. Key elements were practice, will-power and a sense of joy in their work. A change of generations was in process, which had a beneficial effect on the energy level in the hall.

"A delight in performing music is crucial, isn't it?" Simensen says.

The orchestra began training. Each section had a famous coach brought in. The concertmaster in Rotterdam, Viktor Liberman, a former leader of the Leningrad Philharmonic Orchestra, coached the strings. The legendary principal trumpet from Chicago, Adolph Herseth, coached the brass section. Esa-Pekka Salonen took charge of the horns, and Karl Leister, principal clarinettist of the Berlin Philharmonic, worked with the woodwinds.

> "Art and culture should be shocking, critical and confrontational. But all art? Always? If it can be, shouldn't it be beautiful? We think so. One of the Gothenburg Symphony Orchestra's goals is actually to play beautiful music, beautifully."
>
> **Bjørn E. Simensen in GSO's season brochure 1984.**

"One hell of a gang," Simensen says, "The crème de la crème."

Simensen went to Stockholm and knocked on Robert von Bahr's door at BIS. "What about recording the Sibelius symphonies?" "Why just the symphonies?" von Bahr replied. "Why not all of Sibelius' orchestral works?" "Right," Simensen said, "It's a deal."

This was a marvellous chance for things to progress in the right direction. For an orchestra there are two options: "Improving or going backwards," says Simensen. There is no such thing as status quo.

Recording sessions are complicated and expensive and there was almost no money available. And because of the way musicians' contracts were set up, it was almost impossible to undertake orchestral recordings in Sweden; at the very least they required considerable government funding.

But the Gothenburg musicians wanted to record. They decided to solve the money problem by taking time off instead of pay. The musicians' union, referring to existing agreements, said that this kind of solution was not possible.

"We had a hell of a time in Stockholm," Simensen remembers. The orchestra gave as good as it got, eagerly backed by Robert von Bahr of BIS. The central union eventually backed down in the face of threats by the Gothenburg musicians to start their own independent union. The fight opened the market for orchestral recordings in Sweden.

"The stubbornness of the orchestra's musicians became a battering ram that changed the entire Scandinavian music scene," recalls Robert von Bahr. Recordings became very important for the spread of symphonic music and also for the cultural scene in general. Other orchestras saw new opportunities opening up and emulated the GSO.

Initially the time spent recording was recompensed as time

in lieu. Nowadays, as musicians' wages have improved, a fixed amount of recordings per year are part of the employment contracts.

"The recordings were just the first step, or to put it more accurately, the realization that we were doing something positive," Bjørn Simensen continues. "We were on our way."

In the spring of 1982 they performed Sibelius' First Symphony, so that they would be well rehearsed when Järvi arrived. On Wednesday 1 September they were clear for take off.

The programme consisted of Rosenberg's *Suite from Journey to America*, Lemba's Piano Concerto No. 1 and Sibelius' First Symphony. To get the right atmosphere, and to mark the importance of the event, the famous Sibelius expert, Erik Tawaststjerna was invited to attend. In his speech to the orchestra he read a letter that Sibelius wrote to Stenhammar, about what a fine orchestra Gothenburg and Stenhammar had.

"And then Järvi got onto the podium... what excitement! What an atmosphere!"

The recording of Sibelius' First was made the very next day. The orchestra was prepared for a number of takes, but Järvi went straight through the symphony's first movement without stopping. Then he went up to producer Robert von Bahr and balance engineer Michael Bergek and listened to the result. When he returned he started up the orchestra again: "Second movement, please." The first movement was in the can. The recording was almost like a live recording.

"It went like a rocket," remembers Simensen. " 'Second movement, please.' Nothing more, but so typically Järvi."

The collaboration with BIS led almost immediately to other recording projects, now with Lennart Dehn taking over as producer. "The GSO plans to record all the orchestral works of Scandinavia's three greatest composers, Sibelius, Nielsen and Stenhammar", Simensen stated at a press con-

○ CD 1.2

Franz Berwald

Scandinavia's leading symphonist of the first half of the 19th century. His father was a violinist and Berwald was tutored at home. He was probably self taught as a composer. Despite producing some promising compositions while still young, he left Sweden in 1829, without any career opportunities, to try and make his way musically in Germany. This venture did not succeed and instead he established a successful orthopaedic institute in Berlin, which he eventually sold in 1841, moving to Vienna where his intention was to work as a physiotherapist. The desire to compose remained strong however, and he eventually received recognition after a concert of his tone poems.

Upon his return to Sweden in 1842 he produced his finest works, including the four symphonies, of which the *Sinfonie singulière* is considered his masterpiece, although he himself ranked the *Sinfonie naïve* as a greater work. Following a further period in Vienna, he returned to Stockholm, poor and disillusioned. He was never granted the musical appointments he had hoped for and, instead, became manager at the Sandö glass works in Ångermanland.

His style was influenced by the classical Viennese school and the early romantic composers but he showed a love of bold harmony and humorous twists. Wilhelm Stenhammar performed his music early on in Gothenburg and, later, Tor Mann conducted concert performances of his operas *Estrella de Soria* and *Drottningen av Golconda*.

FRANZ BERWALD 1796–1868

This Swedish composer and industrialist came from an emigré German musical family. At the age of 16 he joined the orchestra of the Royal Stockholm Opera as a violinist. He made two lengthy journeys abroad, where he found it difficult to make a living as a musician. Late in life he was elected a member of the Royal Swedish Academy of Music (1864) where he later taught composition. Recognition came late and Berwald died in 1868.

Important works: Four symphonies: *Sinfonie sérieuse* (1842), *Sinfonie capricieuse* (1842), *Sinfonie singulière* (1845), *Sinfonie naïve* (1845); the overture to the opera *Estrella de Soria* (1862); and the Septet and String Quartets Nos. 2 & 3.

Recordings: The GSO and Neeme Järvi have recorded the four symphonies for DG.

Lennart Dehn of the GSO and Aman Pedersen, Deutsche Grammophon in 1989.

ference. 40 recordings for BIS were planned over the next ten-year period. The GSO was gaining ground that no other Swedish orchestra had yet managed to occupy: a place in the international recording circuit. Simensen however, was not fully satisfied.

"Järvi and I agreed that we needed a second record company."

They set their sights on Deutsche Grammophon, one of the world's leading recording companies for classical music.

DG's prestigious yellow label was appealing. The Berlin Philharmonic, the London Symphony and the Vienna Philharmonic orchestras are all proud of their yellow badges.

"So I took it upon myself to call Deutsche Grammophon and began the conversation in German. The voice on the other end of the line said: 'You can speak Norwegian if you like.'"

Simensen was fortunate. "Very fortunate," he says. The head of the classical music division at DG was a Norwegian, Aman Pedersen. He had the same feeling for Scandinavian music as Simensen, and no, he didn't think Simensen's idea of

The recording of Franz Berwald's four symphonies began in the spring of 1985. By the autumn of the same year the album was finished and in 1986 the awards appeared one by one: Grand Prix du Disque for the best symphonic recording of the year, awarded by the Académie Charles Cros in Paris, and a Swedish Grammy. The album also received a number of nominations from music critics.

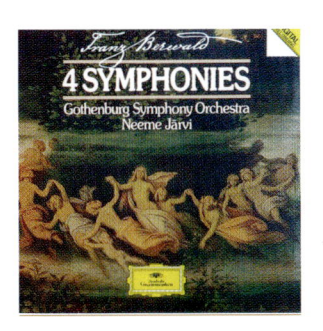

CD 1.4

the GSO performing Franz Berwald was madness at all.

"The wrong person on the other end of the phone could have resulted in them hanging up on me. 'Berwald and Gothenburg! What sort of nonsense is that?' they might have said."

The excellent reviews of the BIS recordings and the US tour in 1983 had aroused public interest. Opinions at Deutsche Grammophon and market research in the USA and UK proved to be decisive.

The GSO is still the only orchestra in Scandinavia with a DG contract. Aman Pedersen visited Gothenburg in the spring of 1984 to finalize the contract. It was signed on Thursday 10 May and a month later Bjørn Simensen moved back to Norway. He could look back on several victories: the Volvo agreement, the tour of the USA, record deals and the open-air concerts in Slottsskogen. "It was a good time, the best I've experienced in my life," he says.

Bjørn Simensen, Neeme Järvi and Robert von Bahr.

Eduard Tubin

Tubin's music is dark in temperament and often contains powerful, driving rhythms, spiced with irony and fragments of his native folk music. He was a contemporary of Shostakovich and he, too, lived under a totalitarian regime; an experience echoed in his ten completed symphonies.

The Third Symphony was written shortly after the Soviet Union occupied Estonia in 1943, and was first performed during the Nazi occupation. It was then banned for 40 years. When Tubin fled to Sweden in 1944 he was regarded as Estonia's leading composer, but he lived in seclusion in his new home without much contact with musical life in Sweden. He was a champion of contemporary music introducing it in his native Estonia. A meeting with Bartók and Kodály in Budapest in 1938 sparked his interest in Estonian folk music.

Tubin gained real recognition only after his death, mainly due to his countryman, Neeme Järvi, who showcased his music, both in recordings and on tour. Tubin was the focus of the GSO's second appearance in Vienna in 1997.

EDUARD TUBIN 1905–1982

Estonian composer, born in Kallaste, Estonia, died in Stockholm. Studied for Heino Eller at the Tartu College of Music between 1924 and 1930 where he later also taught. Conductor at the Tartu Civic Theatre between 1931 and 1944, when he escaped to Sweden. For 30 years he worked as a music archivist at Drottningholm Theatre in Stockholm.

Important works: Eleven symphonies, the last one uncompleted, *Suite of Estonian folk songs* (1931), the ballet *Kratt* (1940), *Requiem for fallen soldiers* (1979), two violin concertos (1942, 1945), balalaika concerto (1964).

Recordings: Tubin's most important works are available on BIS with Neeme Järvi conducting. A number of the recordings feature the GSO: the two violin concertos, double-bass concerto and the balalaika concerto plus symphonies 7, 9, 10. The tenth symphony was commissioned by the GSO.

CD 1.5

A record company director remembers

The BIS recordings made the Göteborgs Symfoniker, GSO, the best known orchestra in Scandinavia. Meanwhile BIS, too, was establishing its reputation.

As Robert von Bahr recalls: "The GSO earned us the respect of the trade. BIS is now the biggest company in its field in Scandinavia and one of the four or five leading independent classical record companies in terms of the annual number of releases, around 80 a year."

Robert von Bahr's mission is to present rarely performed, or unperformed, works to a larger audience. He believes that many composers are unfairly neglected and there are soloists, who despite being very talented, need support in their careers.

"I started out on my own because I became frustrated," he explains. It was in 1973 and Robert von Bahr was married to the flautist Gunilla von Bahr. In those days it was almost impossible for Swedish musicians to make a recording career, and musicians without records don't often get very far. BIS was formed to solve this problem.

During the 1970s BIS was run single-handedly and produced a great deal of chamber music. Collaboration with the GSO furthered the development of the label, and Robert von Bahr found a friend in Neeme Järvi. They have also recorded with other orchestras, and von Bahr especially remembers the recording of Tubin's fourth symphony with the Bergen Symphony Orchestra, which was kept a secret from the composer, who was to receive it as a surprise. Unfortunately Eduard Tubin died shortly before the record was released.

"That taught me that you should tell people about what's going on, so they can appreciate and enjoy it as long as possible," says von Bahr.

The GSO's recordings for BIS in the early 1980s received

excellent reviews, paving the way for the contract with Deutsche Grammophon. After that, the GSO made only the occasional recordings with BIS, von Bahr recalls .

"In retrospect I can of course understand why the management at GSO approached DG. At the time I was quite disappointed and sad. I had placed a large part of my heart in Gothenburg."

"But life went on," he says. Now, with new GSO recordings of Tchaikovsky and Rosenberg coming up, it feels as though we are closing the circle with the GSO renewing its ties with BIS."

An important gap in Swedish music will be filled when the GSO records all of Hilding Rosenberg's symphonies for BIS.

◯ CD 2.12

Fake announcement at Landvetter Airport

Everyone in Sweden was to know that the GSO had a new principal conductor and that important developments were taking place. Bjørn Simensen took the view that things needed to get off to a flying start and he brought the entire orchestra out to Landvetter International Airport to welcome Neeme Järvi. At lunchtime on Sunday 29 August 1982 the orchestra took their seats in the entrance hall. There was a group of fans with welcoming banners and numerous journalists. Järvi finally arrived and the orchestra played Glinka's brilliant overture to *Ruslan and Ludmila*. Bjørn Simensen handed over the baton "the moment Neeme Järvi got off the plane" as the newspapers reported the next day.

That's how the media describes it. But Simensen had been forced to make some last minute adjustments in order to get everything to work according to plan. "When all the arrangements had been made it transpired that Järvi had been obliged to take a different route. Suddenly he was not arriving at noon as scheduled but early in the morning. I drove out to the airport to meet him and explained the situation. Then we went into town and had breakfast. Some hours later we returned to Landvetter and sneaked in the back way."

When the orchestra was assembled and Järvi's arrival was due, the manager of the airport faked an announcement that flight number something-or-other from New York had just landed. Järvi then made his entrance. He walked down the stairs and, looking mightily surprised, accepted the baton and began conducting."

"Everybody fell for it", says Bjørn Simensen. "It's OK to tell a white lie, but not to take it too far, so I revealed the truth to a few members of the orchestra. I said, OK this is how it is. He arrived early this morning, but it was too late to change plans."

"Later on I called the news on TV and asked: Will you be broadcasting this? Maybe, they said, if nothing more important comes along. If they hadn't broadcast it then the orchestra would have travelled to the airport in vain on their day off, and that would have been tough. But the cameras were there and the news of GSO's new conductor was relayed out on national television."

"Surprise concert at the airport"
Newspaper headline, Monday August 30 1982.

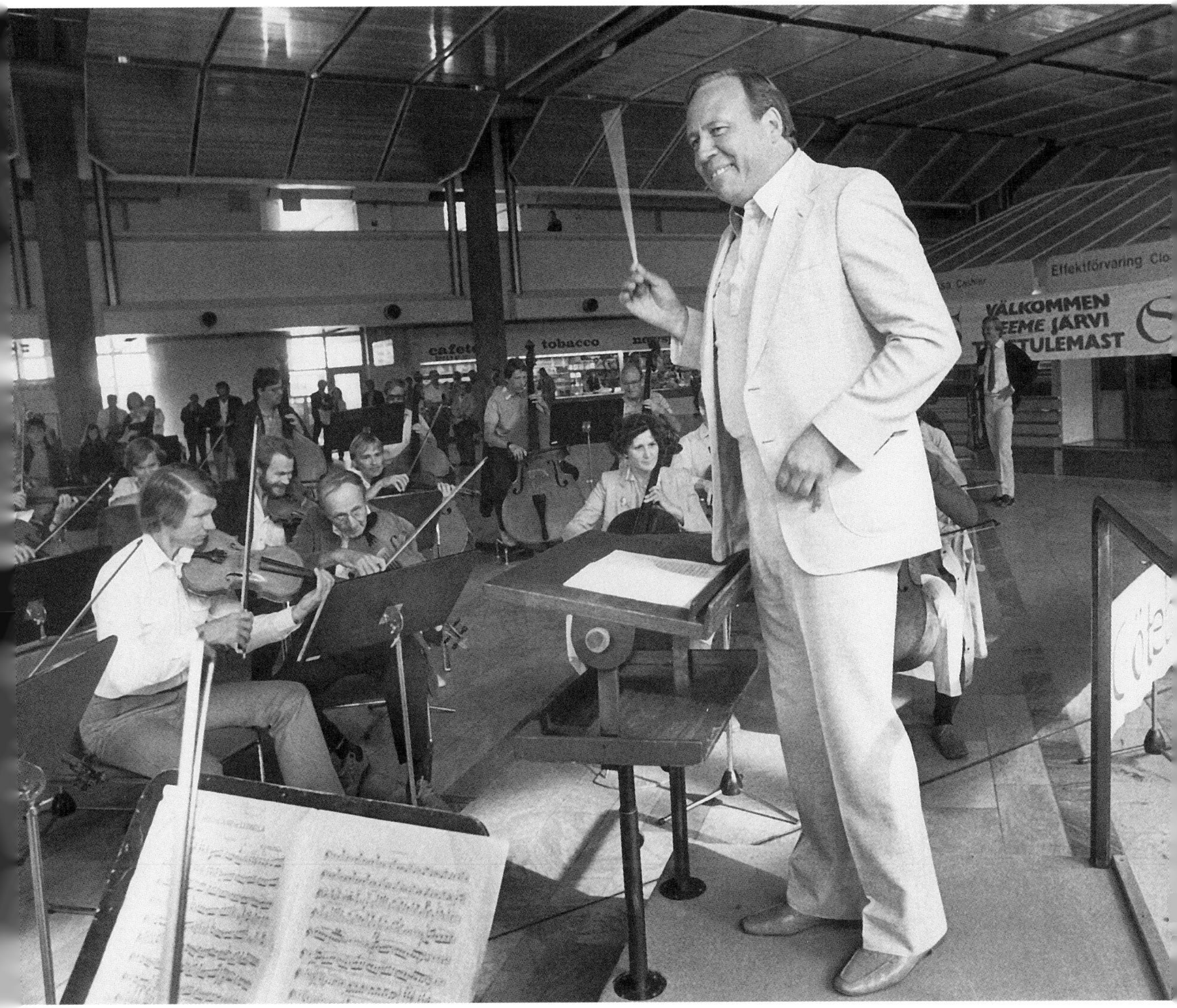

tobacco
VÄLKOMMEN
JÄRVI

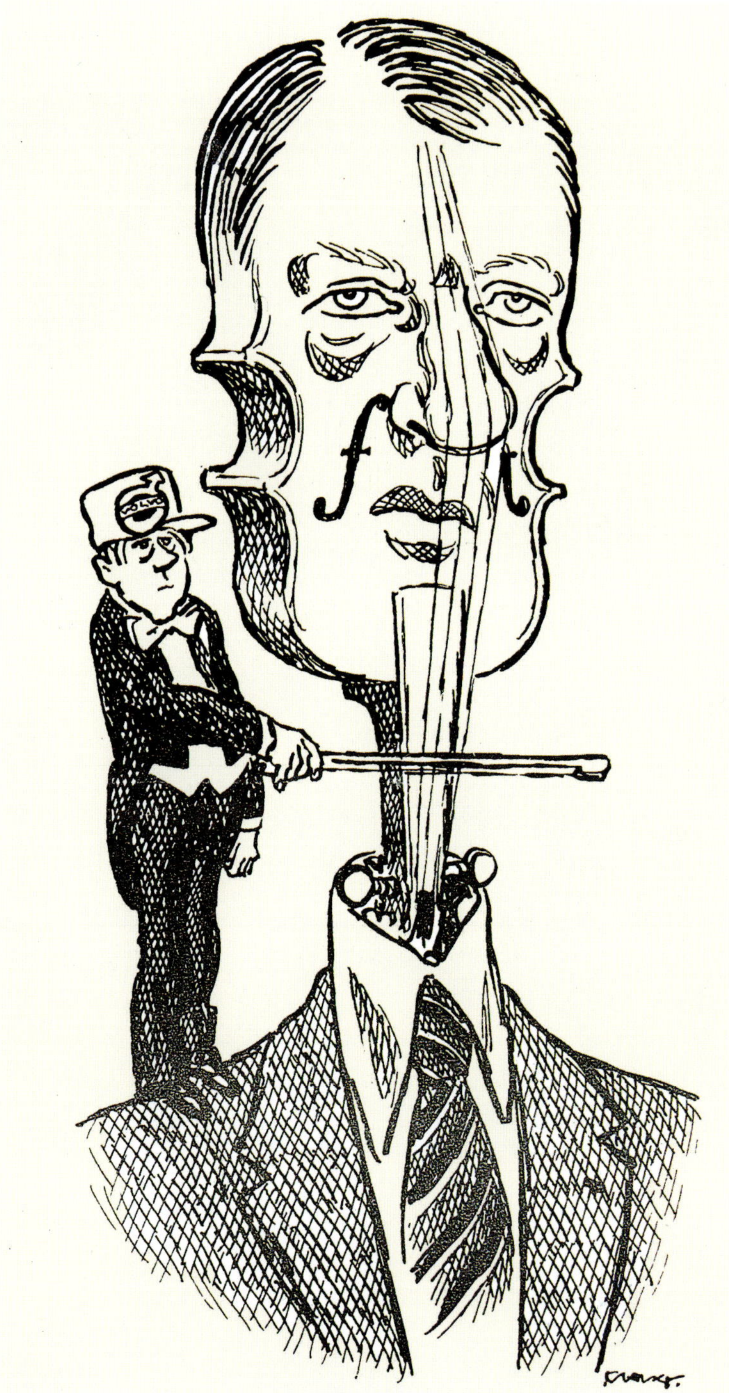

The Volvo sponsorship

Some time at the beginning of the 1980s, one of the directors of Volvo, Bo Ekman, decided to learn the flute. He went to Waidele's music shop to buy a suitable instrument and the assistant asked him how old the child was he was buying it for. Ekman decided to find himself an understanding teacher and contacted Kenneth Wihlborg, a flautist with the GSO.

The two were practising at the Concert Hall one spring Sunday in 1982 and as the lesson came to a close Ekman asked why the orchestra never played any Mahler.

"We can't," replied Kenneth Wihlborg. "Mahler's symphonies require a full symphony orchestra and there are not enough of us. And we can't afford to employ any more musicians." Bo Ekman likes Mahler – the music goes straight to his heart. Immediately after the lesson, he had a meeting with his boss of many years, P G Gyllenhammar. "Instead of talking about plans for the Volvo group, I suggested that the company should sponsor the orchestra. With Neeme Järvi as the new principal conductor they had every opportunity to become a world-class orchestra."

P G Gyllenhammar responded positively. The idea would be mooted immediately at the management meeting the following Monday.

> "Music and theatre were in crisis in Gothenburg. I brought up this issue with my management at Volvo and gave them my views about what constitutes a thriving society, namely that all areas in society should thrive, not least cultural life. We presented our position to the city and to the government. There was a terrible commotion. Had Gyllenhammar gone completely mad? Should a private company get involved in the cultural policies of the wellfare state?"
>
> **P G Gyllenhammar in his book Fortsättning följer (To be continued), Bonniers, 2000.**

At the time the GSO consisted of 78 musicians, or 80 if part time players were included.

No new positions had been opened in the GSO since 1969, while in Stockholm there were two full symphony orchestras, the Swedish Radio Symphony and the Royal Stockholm Philharmonic orchestras, or three if you also include the Royal Opera Orchestra. Reinforcements were needed if the GSO wasn't to risk dropping to a second class level.

The manager of the Concert Hall, Bjørn Simensen, pushed the issue but was cold-shouldered by the politicians in Gothenburg and Stockholm. "Forget it!" they told me abruptly. "There isn't enough money and no political interest either." But negotiations had already begun at Volvo.

Double bass player Jan Johansson, who was the orchestra's union chairman, remembers: "I usually passed Bjørn Simensen's room every morning. We used to chat a little. 'Sit down,' he said one morning and he went on: 'Yesterday, Ernst Knappe was sitting in that chair. Volvo is offering to sponsor us.'"

Ernst G Knappe was Volvo's Director of Communications & Public Relations, and like Bo Ekman, a member of the management. He was appointed by P G Gyllenhammar to negotiate with the orchestra. The issue was to be dealt with at top level.

"I was very pleased to get this assignment," says Ernst Knappe, who is now an honorary member of the orchestra. Initially he talked to the manager of the Concert Hall. What would a partnership between Volvo and the orchestra entail? What was at the top of the agenda? What did the manager and the orchestra think?

"The natural thing would have been to start talking about tours and recordings," says Bjørn Simensen, but instead I went out on a limb: 'We need another 20 musicians'."

The proposal was highly controversial, he says, because what would happen when the Volvo sponsorship reached its end?

Everybody knew what sporting sponsorship was all about, but cultural sponsorship was completely different. It was common in Europe and the USA but was unheard of in Sweden. And never before had a company sponsored new positions.

Work on an agreement began. A major condition was that the government and the city must promise to take over the costs of the extra 20 musicians when the five-year period ended. Other than this Volvo did not make any demands.

"In the end I had to ask Knappe", Simensen remembers, "what does Volvo want in return?"

The answer was one concert a year for Volvo's employees, a few free tickets for company representation, and an advert in the main programme. Brand exposure or demands for artistic involvement never entered the discussion.

"We were very careful at Volvo to avoid being accused of stepping over the line," Ernst Knappe explains. "A discrete approach is still an absolute condition if this type of cultural support is to work."

Simensen and Knappe persuade the municipality to accept the plans and travelled to Stockholm to speak to Jan-Erik Wikström, secretary of cultural affairs at the Department of Education. "He arrived an hour late for the meeting and, of course, couldn't promise anything. But he was positive," remembers Simensen.

"After a while a letter arrived. Wikström explained that he had brought up the issue with the government."

"We felt that we could continue."

FRIENDS OF THE GSO

The Friends of the GSO is a non-profit organisation consisting of around 1 000 individuals and 80 companies. The aim of the Friends is to provide funding and public support to help further the development of the GSO, one of the main cultural institutions in Sweden, and a musical ambassador.

From the beginning the Friends decided to finance the purchase of the musicians' concert evening wear. Since 1989 around 50 musicians have received grants for further study. The Friends also support tours and recording activities and contribute to educational studies abroad. The conductor and soloist fund has made it possible to attract major international performers. Each season the members are invited to meet conductors and soloists. The Saturday coffee break concerts and the lunchtime chamber music recitals are also part of the Friends' activities, as well as arranging an annual gala concert.

The first chairman of the Friends was Bo Ekman. He was succeeded by Ernst G Knappe who handed over to Tore Daun in 1997. Jack Forsgren has been chairman since 2000.

"The expansion means 20 new positions, an increase in tax revenues for the municipality. Almost a million dollars are paid annually to unemployed musicians according to the union publication. The music colleges train many musicians. The training is very expensive and few of the students find work (36 musicians applied for the post of principal horn)."
Quote from a letter from Bjørn Simensen to Secretary of Culture Bengt Göransson on 3 January 1983.

From *Arbetet* 1983.

The great sponsorship debate

In October 1982, the Gothenburg Concert Hall went public with the sponsorship plans. Volvo had agreed to sponsor the GSO over a five-year period with almost a million dollars to allow a further 20 musicians to be employed, with the provision that the government and/or the municipality would take over the costs when the five years were up.

This was shortly after the general election and the parlamentary majority had moved from the liberal conservative coalition to the social democrats. Jan-Erik Wikström, a member of the liberal party who was favourably disposed to the Volvo agreement, was replaced by the social democrat, Bengt Göransson, who was sceptical about cultural sponsorship. The Volvo agreement was in the balance.

During spring of 1983 the great sponsorship debate erupted. Was private sponsorship of the arts acceptable? This is a fundamental question, which is still debated, 20 years on. The Volvo agreement was the first and largest sponsorship agreement of its kind in Sweden and attracted a great deal of attention, not only in Gothenburg. Both Volvo's intentions and the policies of the Concert Hall were questioned. How could the GSO jeopardize its artistic integrity in this way? Would Gyllenhammar take over the baton at the Concert Hall?

Large sums from the industry would distort government support for the arts, said the critics. The GSO would slip a long way down the scale of public priorities. The opinion of Bertil Jansson, cultural spokesman for the Swedish Trade Union Confederation, was that various other matters of musical policy would take precedence over the needs of the GSO. Business should stick to caring for its industrial heritage and

"I'm a car city conductor. I like to be a car city conductor."
Neeme Järvi on being principal conductor both in Volvo's Gothenburg and USA's Motown, Detroit.

workplace culture. It would be better if Volvo did something about pollution before embarking on cultural politics.

Cultural activities give energy to both society and industry, according to the advocates of sponsorship, and why would the state as such be good, and its cultural policies have a more legitimate purpose? Why are artists and cultural institutions so afraid of money that doesn't come from public funding?

Cultural policy is threatened when Gyllenhammar opens his wallet, countered opponents, quoting the main aims of parliament's 1974 cultural act: more and better culture for geographically and socially neglected groups. Large companies were hardly interested in this kind of development, nor in advanced, creative, experimental culture. And even if Volvo

> "The birthday concert was grand. Volvo workers were invited to fill the hall, along with dinner guests. Neeme Järvi conducted and all the members of the orchestra were present. The concert began with Hugo Alfvén's *Festspel*, played with great vivacity…
>
> It was a marvellous introduction to the evening and I felt a certain degree of pride seeing the orchestra in full flight, following the battles I had fought for their future. Two people who contributed to the success of the orchestra were Bo Ekman and Ernst Knappe. Both of them enthusiastically helped the orchestra and they succeeded each other as chairman of the Friends of the GSO."
>
> **P G Gyllenhammar remembers his 50th birthday on 28 April 1985. From Fortsättning följer, Bonniers, 2000.**

agreed not to influence artistic decisions, the actual choice of the sponsorship meant some form of influence.

Bjørn Simensen fought for his orchestra. "It's not Volvo that wants to enlarge the GSO. It's the GSO that wants to enlarge the GSO. The issue of enlarging the orchestra is old and will remain, whatever happens with Volvo's involvement. The difference is that with Volvo's help the expansion can occur now, quicker and with a saving of about 600 000 dollars. It's not a question of 'refined extortion', neither from Volvo nor from us, it's a question of a helping hand in solving a problem that was going to be solved anyway," he wrote in an article published in the Gothenburg daily, Göteborgs-Posten.

Accepting money from Volvo was a complicated matter for the municipally owned Teater and Konsert AB which had financial responsibility for the Concert Hall and the GSO. It was ideologically wrong to let Volvo run the development of the orchestra, claimed leading cultural politicians in Gothenburg.

They were glad to have more money for culture, there was a great need for it, but in that case it should be put into a general cultural fund in order for the elected politicians to decide where it was most needed.

A general cultural fund was not what Volvo had in mind, "but we don't view the municipality's no as irrevocable", said Ernst G Knappe. Bjørn Simensen diplomatically stated that if only they could find an ideologically acceptable formulation everything would sort itself out.

What did the general public think? Volvo's Bo Ekman asked for a consumer survey to be carried out by SIFO: 85 percent of the participants questioned were in favour of the agreement, while 3-4 percent were opposed to it. Opposition was strongest in the arts pages of the newspapers. The orchestra's union chairman, Jan Johansson, was not politically active, but had left wing ideals. This might have made his conversations with the leftist party regarding the orchestra's future a little easier. Late one Friday evening Jan Johansson arrived home from a concert, turned on the radio and listened to an interview with Gothenburg's arts councillor Berit Jóhannesson of the leftist party.

"She had misunderstood the situation. I called her straight away and said that we had to talk."

He met Berit Jóhannesson on the Saturday and explained the union's and orchestra's views. He then continued to lobby by going to a few party meetings: Gyllenhammar wasn't going to decide who was going to play in the orchestra. Volvo employees would be invited to one free concert a year, he explained.

Pehr G Gyllenhammar became an honorary member of the GSO in 1995.

> "1989/90 was an important time for the Gothenburg Symphony Orchestra. We received fantastic reviews from concerts in London, Helsinki, Tallinn, Stockholm and Gothenburg. Financially and politically, the decision of a unanimous Swedish parliament to considerably increase our public grant was naturally the most important event."
> **Sture Carlsson in the programme for the 1990/91 season.**

Meanwhile, a new opera house was being discussed once again. "I asked them to wait a while before making this public until we had finalised the sponsorship agreement and they agreed. There was a risk that the GSO would otherwise end up in a backwater."

Opinion swung slowly in favour of the orchestra. The debate subsided and when it was time for the authorities to make a decision there was only one member of the council who voted against sponsorship. On 15 December 1983 the local authority voted 75-1 to accept the SEK 8 million that Volvo were offering. This meant that the city was guaranteeing the musicians' employment after the Volvo agreement ran out in 1988.

State involvement was not forthcoming however. To win over the government required a further fight five years on.

The five-party motion

It would be no exaggeration to say that the publicity generated by the sponsorship deal exceeded the Volvo management's wildest dreams. The prestige that it brought with it was enormous.

The agreement, signed on 14 November 1983, is still in force and is often used as an example of cultural sponsorship at its best, both in Sweden and throughout Europe. Many articles have been written about it and about the GSO's triumphal progress and each time Volvo has received invaluable publicity.

But there was uncertainty as to what would happen when the first five-year period came to an end. "P G's money has run out" wrote the local paper and speculation concerning the orchestra's finances gained momentum.

There had been a change of management at the Concert Hall. Bengt Hörnberg, once replacing Björn Simensen, had now been succeeded in his turn by Sture Carlsson.

Sture Carlsson arrived from Stockholm's Concert Hall where he had been deputy manager. He had also been a senior official at the Ministry of Finance. His combined musical, financial and political know-how would now be put to good use.

"I arrived on the scene as the Volvo contract was due to be renegotiated. The atmosphere was tense, but I soon realised that the Volvo management were interested in extending the agreement," he says.

The only problem was that the money for the salaries of the 20 new musicians was going to disappear. Paragraph 3:3 of the sponsorship agreement clearly stated: "Volvo's involvement is valid under the proviso that… the Municipality of Gothenburg and/or the government will resume responsibility for the newly employed musicians' salaries after 31 December 1988." Both the GSO and Volvo agreed that the musicians should in future be financed by public funding.

At this time the Royal Stockholm Philharmonic Orchestra was receiving almost half a million dollars more in public funding than the GSO, despite the fact that both orchestras were of equal size. But the GSO's application for increased public funding was once again declined. The Department of Cultural Affairs was not swayed by the positive reviews and critically acclaimed recordings. Volvo takes care of cultural matters in Gothenburg, was the implication from the capital, and if Sture Carlsson wanted more money he should approach P G Gyllenhammar.

"We were quite provoked by these ideas. Only because we once had received money from Gyllenhammar we shouldn't be branded forever," says Sture Carlsson.

He decided to concentrate on getting support from politicians in the western part of Sweden. The bitterness about what was seen as an unjust allocation of cultural funding was

"All concert halls throughout the world are economic rats' nests to some degree."
Sture Carlsson 1989, responding to a question on the state of the Concert Hall's finances.

WHO WILL PAY THE FIDDLERS?

Financial responsibility for the GSO is in the hands of *Göteborgs Konsert AB*, which is wholly owned by a subsidiary of the Regional Authority. The company's budget is in excess of 10 million dollars a year, 40% of which is generated by ticket sales and suchlike.

Revenue: contributions from Västra Götaland Regional Council (SEK 55.8 million), government contributions (SEK 21.8 million), sponsorship contributions (SEK 8 million), ticket sales (SEK 12-15 million), rental income (SEK 4.5 million) and other income (SEK 5 million).

Expenditure: Salaries (SEK 80 million), artist fees (SEK 12-15 million) and other operating costs, such as marketing and local productions (SEK 5-10 million). Each year the GSO performs around 100 concerts, including 24 children's concerts, and does 2–3 tours as well as several guest appearances. Concerts and recitals at the Concert Hall attract more than 100 000 visitors each year. In addition, 90 000 visitors listen to the orchestra on tour.
Figures from 2001 and 2002.

clearly evident among the politicians and the result of the campaign was that all parties signed a five-party motion on which parliament finally acted. The Department of Cultural Affairs had to concede, just as in the case of the National Orchestra title in 1996. The GSO received the support of parliament and in this case, unlike 1996, it was also given money.

"There was an alteration to the budget. Nowadays parliament can no longer effect such changes." This was one of the cases that led legislators to block this kind of option", says Sture Carlsson. The city of Gothenburg had already taken its financial responsibility and after a while confirmation finally arrived that the government would pay 30 percent of the costs.

The Volvo millions could be kept for tours and recordings as well as for artistic development. Göteborgs Symfoniker, GSO, had hit the jackpot.

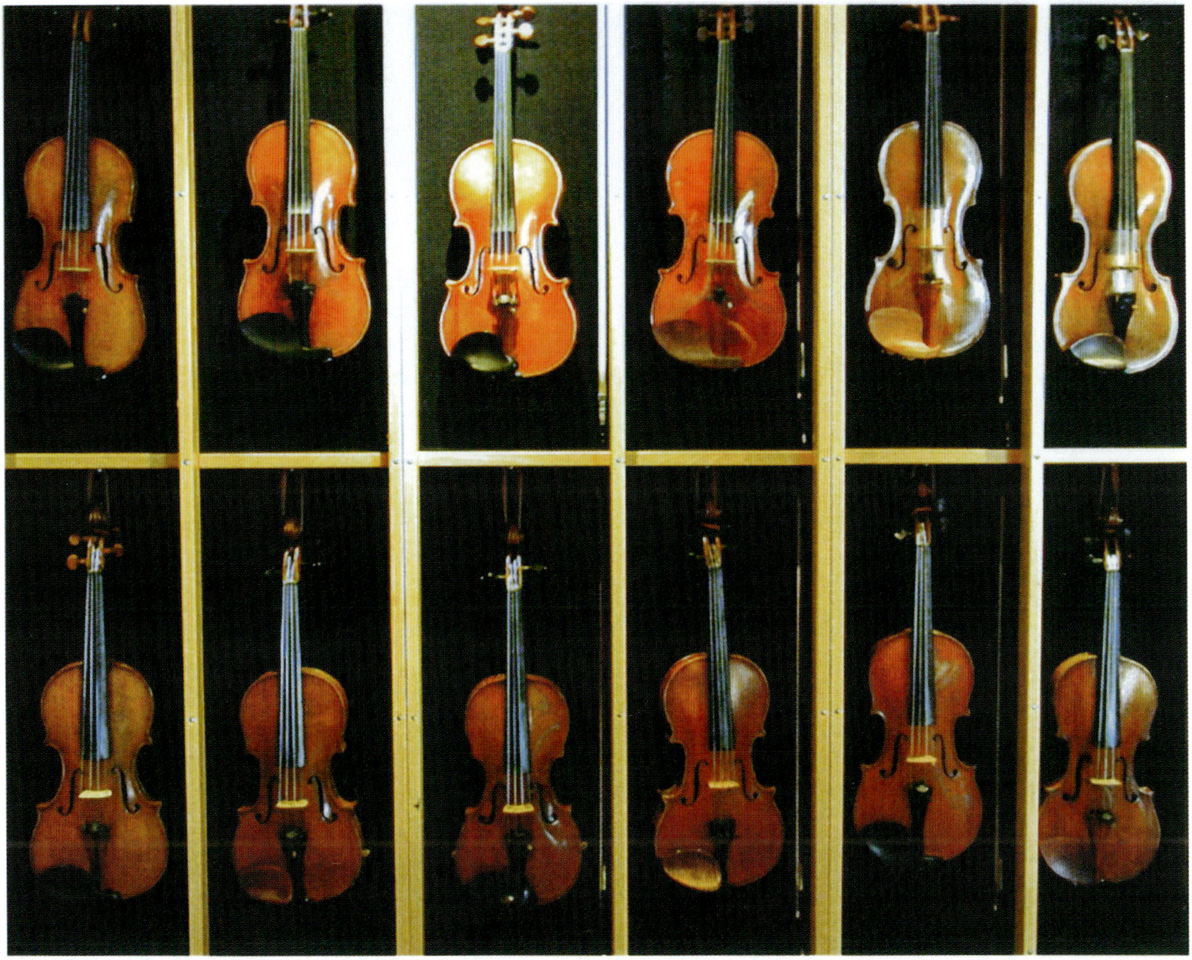

Milestones of the GSO – Neeme Järvi Partnership

1905	Foundation of the Gothenburg Orchestra Society.
1937	Neeme Järvi is born in Tallinn, Estonia.
1963	Järvi begins a thirteen year period as principal conductor at the Tallinn Opera and later becomes head of the Estonian National Orchestra.
1971	Järvi wins the prestigious conducting competition at the ancient Academy of St. Cecilia in Rome.
1979	Järvi is guest conductor at the Metropolitan Opera in New York.
1980	The Järvi family emigrates to the USA. Järvi makes his debut with the New York Philharmonic Orchestra. In April he conducts the GSO.
	Tours the UK with Sibelius' Second Symphony, and signs a contract as principal conductor of the GSO starting in 1982.
1982	Start of co-operation with BIS records with the world première recording of Stenhammar's First Symphony.
	Järvi takes over as principal conductor of the GSO and begins recording all Sibelius' symphonies and other orchestral works for BIS.
1983	GSO's first visit to the USA, including Carnegie Hall in New York.
1984	Volvo provides sponsorship – 20 new musicians are employed 1984–1988.
	Renovation of the Concert Hall.
	Järvi begins working with the Royal Scottish National Orchestra.
1985	First recording for Deutsche Grammophon of Franz Berwald's four symphonies.
	Friends of the GSO is formed.
	Tour of the USSR, without Järvi, who is denied a visa.
1987	February–March: Tour of the Far East and the USA.
	March: Tour of the UK.
	June: Guest performance at the Sweden Jubilee in Minnesota, USA.
1989	August: First guest performance at the BBC Proms with two concerts at the Royal Albert Hall, as well as concerts in Edinburgh and Aldeburgh.
	September: Järvi travels to Tallinn for the first time since emigrating (Estonia still a part of the USSR).
1990	September: Guest performance at the Flanders Festival in Ghent.
	First opera recording for DG – Prokofiev's The Fiery Angel.
	Järvi appointed music director of the Detroit Symphony Orchestra.
1991	February: Scandinavian Music Festival at the Gothenburg Concert Hall.
	March: Tour of Japan.
	Järvi awarded an honorary doctorate by the University of Gothenburg.
1992	August: Guest performances at the Schleswig-Holstein Festival and the World Exhibition in Seville.
	September: Järvi celebrates 10 years as the principal conductor of the GSO.
	November: Tour of the UK including the Barbican in London (complete version of Grieg's Peer Gynt) and Birmingham.

The GSO rehearses in Tallinn 1989.

MILESTONES **65**

1993	February: Paris 1920 Festival at the Gothenburg Concert Hall.
	May: All of Nielsen's symphonies released by DG.
	October: First guest performance in Paris at the Théâtre des Champs-Élysées. Second guest performance at the Barbican, London, with the rendition of the complete Peer Gynt.
1994	October: First guest performance in Vienna at the Scandinavian Festival with focus on Sibelius – Håkan Hardenberger (Pärt) and Maxim Vengerov (Sibelius) are soloists.
	November: Mahler's Symphony No. 8 performed at the Gothenburg Opera – recorded by BIS in memory of the victims of the Estonia ferry disaster.
1995	February: Guest performance of Stravinsky's Symphony of Psalms in the Canary Islands with the Gothenburg Symphonic Choir.
	August: Concert at Nya Ullevi arena for the opening of the World Athletics Championships.
	Herbert Blomstedt returns to conduct after 20 years.
	Local newspaper Göteborgs-Posten becomes the second major sponsor.
	Tour of Germany and Spain, including first guest performance at the Philharmonie in Berlin.
1996	March: Vienna 1900 Festival at the Concert Hall.
	April: Sibelius Festival and performance of all Sibelius' symphonies in Birmingham and at London's Barbican.
1997	March: Second guest appearance in Vienna with a festival dedicated to the GSO at the Musikverein.
	May: The GSO is named The National Orchestra of Sweden by the Swedish parliament.
	June: Järvi celebrates his 60th birthday at the Concert Hall.
	June–July: Tour of Japan.
	September: Second guest performance at the BBC Proms with Oedipus Rex by Stravinsky.
1998	The GSO has its own subscription series at the Stockholm Concert Hall.
1999	March: The GSO is the first Swedish symphony orchestra to visit China. The GSO performs concerts in Shanghai and Beijing, sponsored by local government and industry in Gothenburg.
	May: European tour – Tallinn, Riga, Glasgow, Manchester, Birmingham and London.
	September: Guest performances at the Lucerne Festival and cities in Italy.
2000	February: US tour – Ann Arbor (Detroit), Washington and New York.
	November: Guest performance in Paris with Anne Sofie von Otter and in Amsterdam with Nikolaj Znaider.
	June: Concerts at Expo 2000 in Hannover with Mikko Franck.
2001	February: Two new recording contracts secured: Sibelius' seven symphonies for DG and the symphonies of Tchaikovsky and of Hilding Rosenberg for BIS. Tapiola, a CD featuring compositions by Sibelius, is nominated for a Grammy.
	July: Järvi suffers a stroke and cancels the August guest performance at the BBC Proms and performances in Salzburg with the complete concert version of Grieg's music to Peer Gynt. Manfred Honeck steps in for Neeme Järvi.
	September: The rebuilt stage, ticket office and ventilation of the Gothenburg Concert Hall are inaugurated.
	November: Järvi conducts a rapturous comeback concert with the 65th performance of Sibelius' Second Symphony recorded live and in the studio for DG.
2002	September: GSO and Neeme Järvi celebrate their 20th anniversary
	November: Fourth tour of Japan.
2003	March: Tour to Rotterdam and cities in Germany.

Royal Albert Hall in London, where the Prom concerts are held.

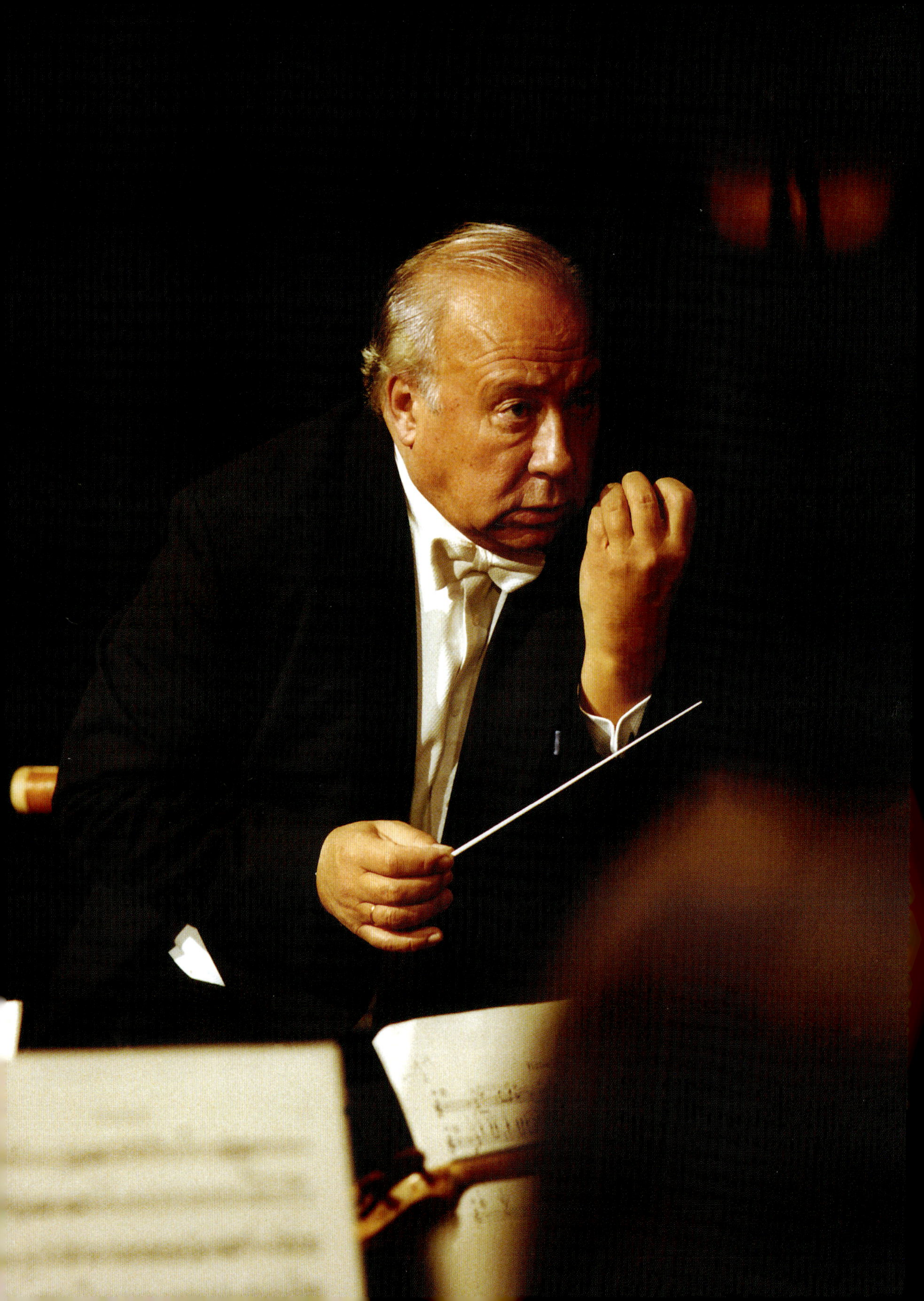

Musical body-language

It seems easy to begin with: "Day one we meet and play the piece through. Day two we meet and make music", says Neeme Järvi looking intensely at the interviewer. Does she understand?

He has tried to explain this to many interviewers. The magic necessary to make music take off is difficult to explain. Schooling and technique are all well and good, but not enough. Järvi often calls it chemistry. Team chemistry is very important. Only if the chemistry between orchestra and conductor works will there be a successful team.

It's the job of the conductor to create a unity of all the parts, to make the music into a whole. Or as the dictionary puts it: "a conductor is a person who, with the help of special arm movements, leads a choir or orchestra in a musical performance. For this to work, educational and psychological skills are needed."

"Each individual in the orchestra must feel that he or she is important and that each moment, each tiny part rehearsed, is important," Järvi explains. The conductor must create an amiable atmosphere if his or her intentions are to be accepted.

Maestro Järvi is greatly respected in the concert hall. Rehearsals can however sometimes be very relaxed occasions:

"He is anything but reserved on stage. Quite the opposite. He is continually saying that you are wonderful and that you play so well.

> "There is a lot of music that is right at the back of the cupboard and rarely gets played – and there's a reason for it. But sometimes a curiosity is picked up and put in Järvi's hands and all of a sudden it turns out to be something good. Neeme Järvi has an enormous musical heart. There is nobody quite as good at making good music out of second-rate music. This is a great talent."
>
> **Lars Nyström, tour and project manager and former orchestra manager.**

CD 2.6

Besides which he has a sense of humour... sometimes there are situations that just make you crack up with laughter."

"Let's make some good music" is often his opening line. "The musicians must feel the majesty of the music from the start and that they play fantastically." It's not sufficient just to play the notes, music must live, it should vibrate.

There have been occasions when Järvi has returned to Gothenburg after a break and has noticed a lack of intensity in the orchestra. "But we start focussing again and we are soon back on track." The potential and professionalism are there all the time: a good sound and balance in the orchestra plus good acoustics.

Conductors are sometimes called baton artists. The best of them receive star status and are in demand all over the world. Their technique and personal styles are analysed. Technique means for example how their beat varies. With hard jerky movements the conductor can bring forth a sharper sound, while calm movements provide a more rounded sonority. The baton is there to make the beat clearer but it's mainly the conductor's body-language and gestures that control the performance. Everything must be expressed in body language – contact with the orchestra, the audience, the music – and it must come naturally. The plasticity should be as interesting as possible. "How you make things happen is decisive," Järvi emphasises.

A large part of a conductor's work lies in preparation. Studying scores can be demanding. But that is when the conductor technically and artistically builds up his interpretation. The aim is that all ideas as to how the music is to be performed should be expressed by the body language from the first rehearsal.

"It is *so* musical, *so* simple," is how Järvi's body language is described.

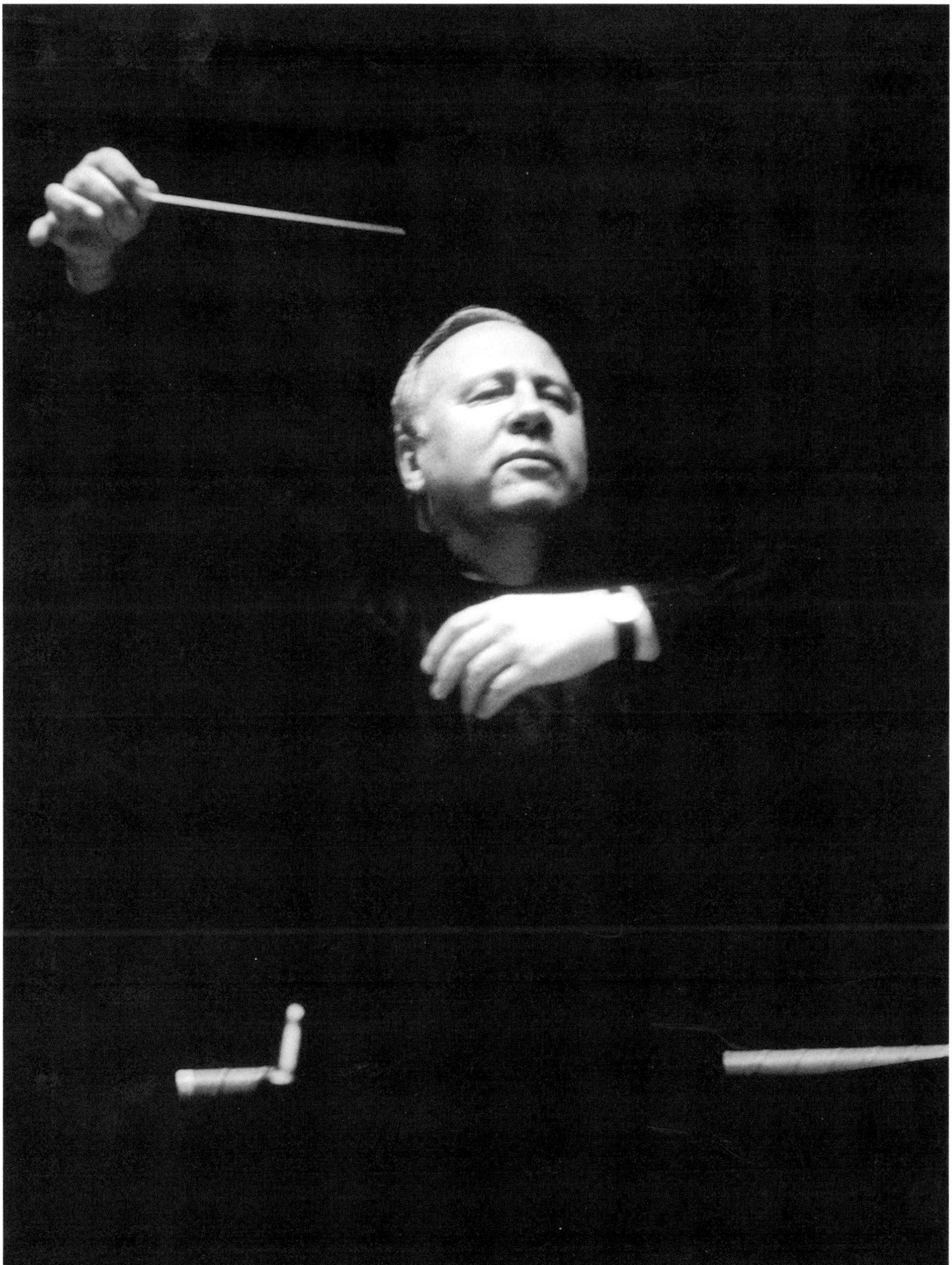

CONDUCTOR
(from latin *conductus*, 'to bring together').
The leader of an orchestral, choral or operatic performance who, with visible signs and gestures, leads and controls the performance of the recreated work. The conductor beats time and determines the tempo, indicates entries and also determines the rhythmic, dynamic and timbral nuances and therewith has the overall artistic responsibility for the performance and the resulting interpretation of the composer's intentions.
A large part of the conductor's work is made up of conveying to the musicians his artistic intentions during rehearsals. The conductor is expected to be highly receptive and to have a capacity for emotional insights into the styles and compositions of different eras. He or she should have the power of creating character and have technical musical skills, as well as educational and psychological abilities.
From the Swedish National Encyclopaedia.

Because it's difficult to explain Järvi's 'lightness of touch', admirers instead use gestures to show what they mean. "This is how Neeme Järvi would do it, and like this…it's so beautiful."

How can this be described? His hands never move more than necessary. However, suddenly the big movements come. Sometimes he leaps up and down, sometimes he dances and sometimes he just stands motionless, like a block of stone listening to the musicians.

The motion of the music should be visible in the conductor's entire body, he says. Symphonic music should swing as well. The conductor therefore should be a master of rhythm and dance. Järvi's background as a percussionist gives him an infallible feeling for the importance of rhythm. Childhood practice on the xylophone is one of the keys to his later success.

"Music is like an act of love," he says. "That should not prevent the brain being in complete control. The brain must be aware of everything in the piece, then it's the heart that governs." Added to this is Järvi's vast repertoire. He learned everything he conducts years ago, apart from the new works of course. The great heritage of classical music is stored in his mind. His colosal experience helps, as does the security he gets from playing for many thousands of people all over the world, and as he says himself, "making them happy."

Some conductors specialize. "They have fixed ideas, they may do 15, 20 or 25 pieces." Not so Järvi. He has a grasp of a much wider field. He doesn't just perform individual works, but entire outputs, both known and unknown works. And he is often among the first to perform these unknown works. Most people in Europe viewed Stenhammar, Sweden's best known composer, as inferior to Finland's Sibelius, Denmark's Nielsen and Norway's Grieg – until Järvi proved otherwise.

"Somebody has to be a pioneer," he says, "and good music is always welcome."

Järvi is like a living encyclopaedia of music. He is probably the most recorded conductor since Herbert von Karajan. "It's important that you never play the same piece the same way twice," he says. He studies the score anew for each concert, looking for new aspects of the music. It is almost impossible to perfectly repeat a performance because music lives its own life and is affected by surroundings and the passage of time. New generations of listeners come forward. Each time a piece is performed, the musicians and conductor have matured and alternative ideas are born. The work can be performed with greater ease. "You rushed through it when you were young, now you can take more time to feel it."

The conductor often uses the score as a memo of his own notes but Järvi knows the standard pieces by heart. He and the GSO have, for example, performed Sibelius' Second Symphony more than 65 times. Järvi is however not one of those conductors who make a show of conducting off the cuff. "Without a score the conductor becomes less free," he explains, "you become tense and have to constantly think, am I doing it right now?"

A few conductors close their eyes when inspiration starts flowing. "There is a risk in this," Järvi explains, "because eye contact with the conductor is fundamentally important to the musicians. A story is told about the legendary von Karajan who had great charisma and who never hesitated to immerse himself in the music. With eyes closed he raised his hands and began conducting, but the orchestra was silent. When he opened his eyes all the musicians were sitting with their eyes closed. They were probably smiling a little as well."

It isn't always easy to know whether an orchestra and a conductor will get along together.

Why is one conductor right for a certain orchestra and not for another? There is no really good answer. Sometimes they just love one another, and sometimes it's just good craftsmanship. "It's just good conducting," as Järvi says, but not love. But if the orchestra's management really wants the conductor they achieve a worthy relationship.

In the case of the GSO and Järvi it was love at first sight. Of the first meeting in April 1980 Järvi says, "We all felt good vibrations straight away, everything felt really good."

Their collaboration is described by all those involved as a long marriage. At their best they are hard to beat – and they can fall out with one another from time to time.

It's unusual that the love affair has lasted for as long as 20 years in this turbulent industry. The maestro, despite his repeated emphasis on the importance of joy for the creation of music, is not always in the best of moods and the orchestra consists of more than 100 artists. Of course, there have been conflicts. "Sometimes Järvi has an over-simplified view of life and about the lives of musicians," someone has said. "Be happy, things will work themselves out, that's easy for him to say. But it's not always so simple. Sometimes he could have possibly helped us over the brink in a less dangerous way."

The main source of problems is the clash between the conductor's impulsiveness and the musicians' need for control. Järvi has the ability to make things happen during a concert that have not been rehearsed. This unpredictability can raise the temperature, but it can also give rise to insecurity. These impulses do not always enhance the value of an interpretation.

There are many ways of looking at a musical performance – for some it's more important to play "correctly", and be precise, than to improvise during the concert. "The ideal is

Jean Sibelius

Sibelius is considered the greatest Scandinavian composer and is one of the 20th century's leading symphonists. He trained as a violinist but gave up his career as a virtuoso to study composition. His main work from his youth was the *Lemminkäinen legends* and he was inspired early on by the Finnish epic poem *Kalevala*. In 1900 the first performance of *Finlandia* made him a national hero.

Sibelius smoked, ate and drank to excess and was well known for his extravagant lifestyle, which was moderated somewhat later in life due to ill-health. He stopped composing in 1929 but lived for a further 28 years.

At the start of the 20th century Sibelius was seen as the guarantor of the symphonic heritage, which he developed in his seven symphonies, all of them completely different. Numbers 2, 5 and 7 along with the violin concerto are his most popular works. Sibelius has a typically Scandinavian voice and an immediately recognizable orchestral sound.

The GSO has a unique tradition of performing Sibelius. The composer became good friends with Stenhammar, who gave the Swedish première of Sibelius' Fourth Symphony in Gothenburg. Sibelius also conducted the orchestra in Gothenburg on three occasions (1911, 1915 and 1923) and dedicated his Seventh Symphony to his friend Stenhammar.

This inheritance has been passed on to Neeme Järvi who has performed a number of complete symphony cycles as well as performing the orchestra's "signature tune", the Second Symphony, more than 65 times.

JEAN SIBELIUS 1865–1957

Finnish composer of Finland-Swedish descent, born in Tavastehus. Grew up poor as his father died young. Began playing the violin aged seven, studied composition and later studied in Vienna. He made his break-through early and lived most of his long life as the most famous celebrity in Finland.

Important works: Symphonies 1-7 and some ten tone poems, among them *Lemminkäinen legends* (1895), *Finlandia* (1899), *En Saga* (1892), *Oceanides* (1913) and *Tapiola* (1926). In addition, the Violin Concerto (1904), the string quartet *Voces intimae* and numerous songs.

Recordings: The symphonies and most of his orchestral music are available from BIS with the GSO and Neeme Järvi. Another symphony cycle is being recorded for DG.

> "While most star conductors focus on a small selection of Brahms and Beethoven scores, Neeme Järvi has continued the tradition of conductors such as Sir Adrian Boult, whose universality and freedom from prejudice enriched listeners to the BBC.
> I cannot think of any present day conductor who, like Järvi, explores everything from Mrs Beach to Bartók, Dvořák, Prokofiev, Shostakovich, Stenhammar, Franz Schmidt, Reger, Sibelius and, above all, his countrymen Eduard Tubin and Heino Eller. His efforts in this area are unsurpassed and his artistry likewise. He has placed all music lovers in his debt. May he continue to strike his own path for many years to come."
>
> **Robert Layton, BBC producer 1959–1990, former reviewer for the Gramophone and author of books about Berwald, Sibelius and Dvořák (1992).**

to have sixteen first violinists performing as one," as someone once said.

For that goal to be reached the conductor must be extremely precise. Neeme Järvi is spontaneous and consciously adopts a different approach. He wants thicker brush strokes and can accept one violinist sticking out, because it's all over very soon and his goal is a strong overall experience.

It's not Järvi's style to do the same thing twice. "This encore," musicians will ask, "what does the maestro intend doing with this?" "We'll see," says Järvi, "Look at me."

It's part of Järvi's greatness, that he dares to take risks. Few conductors have the courage or ability. Things can fall apart – or the performance can rise to new heights. Whatever happens, it's rarely routine.

Rehearsals can be a little succinct, some will mutter. Perhaps the maestro hasn't always managed to find time, it is said, to look at the score carefully before the first rehearsals. Over the years his schedule has been full to the brim and the day still only has 24 hours. But there are those who say that those occasions are manageable because he rarely needs time to think. He reads the score with his body; the signal travels straight from the score to his wrist. It is also said that he has "A hell of an ability to give the musicians an adrenaline kick." On important tours – when everything has to be proven – the following scenario may take place. Upon arrival at an unfamiliar hall, the acoustics must be tried with parts of the programme. Järvi can establish a tempo that is slightly too fast, at which point everyone becomes nervy, and walks around swearing about the unpredictable maestro.

But the end result is that the musicians are highly alert when it's time to play, because anything can happen. Järvi then reverts to the tempo they had been rehearsing and the musicians relax and let go.

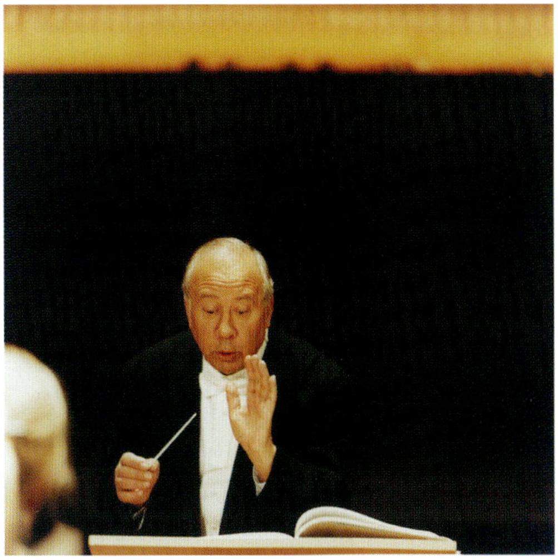
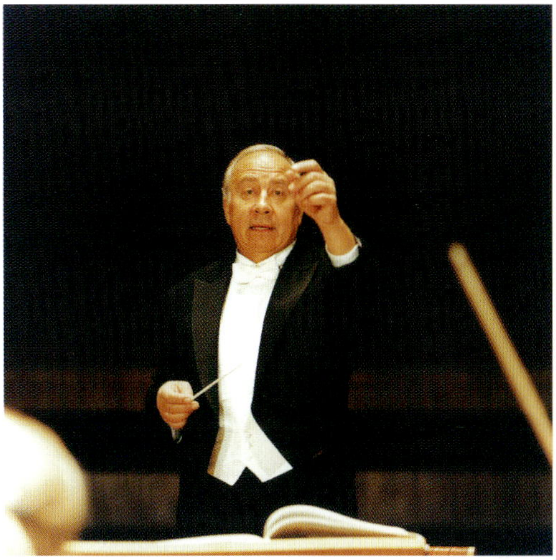
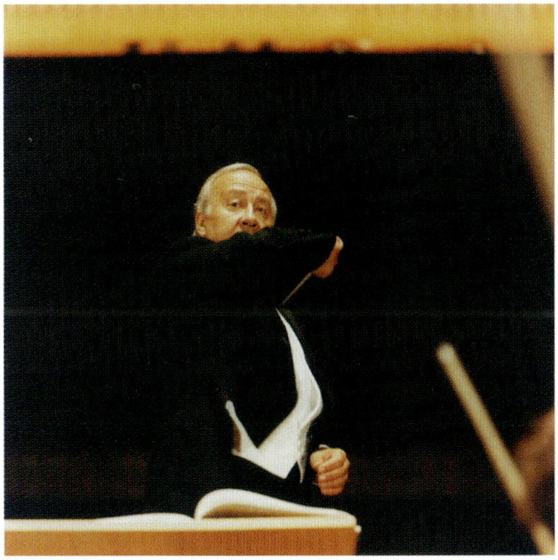
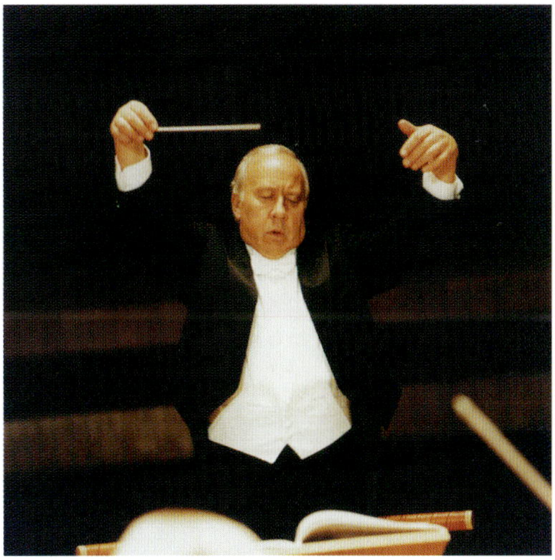

The fact that a conductor automatically is regarded as "he" is because almost all conductors have been and are men. This, in turn, is dependent on the fact that, long into the 20th century, orchestras were a male preserve. But times change, and the GSO has almost as many women players as men. Women conductors are still rare but numbers are growing.

The concert often becomes a great success, with resounding applause and enthusiastic critics.

"And we fall for it every time," says one of the musicians. "He knows exactly what he needs to do to trigger us."

A conductor isn't just at the mercy of the audience's opinion, but also of the musicians he is leading. The orchestra can be critical of a conductor and then full of admiration for him within a matter of minutes. What are the critical issues, then? Tour and project manager Lars Nyström, with thirty years' experience of conductors, as a musician and as orchestra manager, talks about natural musical authority.

"Everyone sitting in front of the concuctor has an enormous amount of professional know-how. Despite this, there is someone standing on the podium who dares to tell you how to play something that you are actually very capable of doing on your own. It's like sitting in the classroom, despite the fact that you possess all the know-how. And if the conductor doesn't really know what he's doing, it's only logical that he's cut down to size very quickly."

But there are other sides to this complex subject.

Judgements about a conductor can vary depending on whether the critic is on the stage or in the audience. "You shouldn't really ask a musician about the result of a concert. The musician may not have a clue about it," Lars Nyström believes. "Sure, he or she might have a general impression, but it's difficult to know how the music sounded in the auditorium."

The musicians' judgement of a conductor is very personal, they talk too much during rehearsals, they are out of time, or they take themselves too seriously. But a conductor who is disliked by the musicians can still make fantastic concerts. Contradictory? "Of course," says Lars Nyström. "Sometimes you have to persuade the musicians and tell them that they should work with this person, because the concert has the potential to be very good."

Average conductors are more likely to struggle. Celebrity conductors are often accepted straight away, partly because they are quite simply very skilled, and partly because they have a psychological advantage to their reputations.

No orchestra likes a conductor who talks too much.

"I remember," says Lars Nyström, "the first time I performed with Yevgeny Svetlanov. He only spoke Russian. He had to have a fan on the stage so as not to fall asleep. He would arrive at rehearsals, say 'Brahms', and then say nothing for one and a half hours. After the break he would say 'Shostakovich', and that was it. He was a fantastic conductor and he did wonderful concerts. He conveyed everything to us without a word."

Järvi is of the same school. He can also perform an entire symphony during one rehearsal. It is an enormous gift to be able to show one hundred people what you mean without saying a word.

"If you use words to explain what needs to be done," Järvi says, "in the end you'll lose," and he flourishes his much talked-about hands – his technique.

To summarise, it's about technique, and about chemistry, and probably also about the creative process sometimes called flow, and which is described as a condition of complete concentration and determination, accompanied by an all-engulfing feeling of euphoria. When the conductor's flow rubs off on the musicians, great art is created.

It's wonderful!

Trumpeter Håkan Hardenberger has performed around 30 concerts, including tours, together with the GSO. Some pieces have been really important for his artistic development. One which he especially remembers – because it was so typically Neeme, he says – was the first performance of Swedish composer Rolf Martinsson's Trumpet Concerto No. 1, *Bridge*, in 1999.

"There was an air of tension when I arrived for the first rehearsal. Neeme and the orchestra had probably had a falling out," he says.

"If you've lived together as long as the GSO and Järvi have done then you easily tend to fall foul of each other from time to time, it's unavoidable," he explains. "Moods and nerves tend to get frayed when so many artistic temperaments are involved. Even renowned conductors have their less attractive sides, and musicians are the way they are." That was the case on this particular day – and to top it all Hardenberger came with a new, difficult piece:

"You could really hear how the score creaked when Neeme opened it."

Järvi got the orchestra going and Hardenberger began playing. "It sounded really odd to begin with," he recalls.

But there was soon an orchestral tutti: "a really wonderful piece of music, almost like Arnold Schoenberg's *Verklärte Nacht*. Neeme then stood up and said: "It's wonderful!" The composer was sitting in the auditorium and I know that he can point out the spot in the score where Neeme shouted. After that the performance was saved, big hugs for all, this is definitely something we are going to do. Neeme does not hold grudges."

Hardenberger speaks highly of Järvi's good nature, about his technique and feeling for music. Many conductors can put a 110-man orchestra in full flight and get the earth to rotate faster, but nobody can silence the orchestra with a single gesture like Järvi.

Hardenberger takes a deep breath and makes a sweeping movement with his arms to describe the technique: "Just like this."

It's exciting working with Neeme Järvi. And sometimes it's frustrating. There have been occasions when they have clashed.

"You might have rehearsed in a certain way, and gained a

Years ago music was often conducted by the composer himself, who sat in the middle of the orchestra and marked the tempo from a harpsichord or organ, playing with one hand and beating time with the other. At the beginning of the 19th century conducting developed into an art form all of its own. The modern conductors' role is not just to beat time but also to communicate his own conception of the composition to the orchestra and the audience.

> "... Stenz also had other talents. In a single gesture, with the help of H K Gruber's *Aerial* trumpet concerto, to unite everything in the way of style and musical expression that the 20th century had to offer. An amazingly humorous, dizzy and impressive illusionary number with Håkan Hardenberger as the wizard.
> Gruber seemed at home in every genre, rhythm and sound, but in the midst of all this there was his own personality, calm and confident.
> Hardenberger and Stenz danced their way with the orchestra through the difficulties as if there were no limits to what could be achieved. That is how great art is created."
> **Håkan Dahl in Göteborgs-Posten 25 January 2001.**

○ CD 1.13

certain image that you would at least like to stick to... but with Neeme you can never be sure. Anything can happen when the inspiration comes."

That's the one side of the coin. The other is Järvi's willingness to accept new pieces and new challenges.

"Certain conductors simply don't want to take on anything new, but not Neeme Järvi. I've learned so much from him."

After Rolf Martinsson's concerto in Gothenburg, Håkan Hardenberger was going on to Birmingham with the GSO and Järvi. The programme for soloist Hardenberger was long since booked: Hummel's Trumpet Concerto in E flat major, and Pärt's *Concerto Piccolo über B-A-C-H*.

But Neeme Järvi had become besotted with Martinsson's new concerto. He wanted to perform it in Birmingham and it suited him and the orchestra. The Gothenburg Concert Hall's manager Sture Carlsson objected that Birmingham wouldn't want any new Swedish pieces and that the programme should remain unchanged.

"Hardenberger, Järvi and the GSO – we do what we like," Järvi decided. Birmingham finally decided to add one piece. But as they didn't want to withdraw any piece, and Håkan Hardenberger played three trumpet concertos in one evening.

"Complete madness of course but it was all down to if I was willing to try it. Järvi then took Martinsson's concerto to the orchestra in Detroit and we played it there as well."

Hardenberger's most difficult moment

Many top soloists have performed with the GSO over the years, on tours around the world and at the Gothenburg Concert Hall. Håkan Hardenberger is one of the soloists who has performed most frequently with the GSO.

Håkan Hardenberger, a world-class soloist who has performed with the GSO on many occasions.

"The first time with Järvi I was still a youngster whom he was generous enough to allow to perform," he explains. It was the middle of the 1980s. A few years later, Hardenberger, Järvi and the GSO travelled to Hong Kong and Singapore.

Haydn's Trumpet Concerto was on the programme during the orchestra's world tour in 1987.

Since then Håkan Hardenberger has performed just about every classical piece written for the trumpet many times over, and he has commissioned and performed many contemporary

"It was a great musical experience listening to the GSO under the guidance of Neeme Järvi in Tallinn in 1989. And not just because I had the opportunity to listen to a wonderful performance of my own trumpet concerto. Ever since my very first encounter with Neeme Järvi I have been fascinated by his ability to find his way through a complicated score, his dramatic instinct, his ability to grasp music in its entirety and his natural way of performing it. He doesn't try to find things that don't exist in the score, but he awakens the most hidden elements, that may have been less clear also to the composer."
Eino Tamberg, composer, Estonia. The photo shows Tamberg with trumpeter Håkan Hardenberger in Tallinn in 1989.

trumpet pieces. It is much to his credit that the modern trumpet repertoire has blossomed over the past few years. He needs challenges, he says, the concerto repertoire for the trumpet is limited.

It's January 2002 and the Swedish première of H K Gruber's trumpet concerto with GSO, *Aerial*, specially written for Hardenberger for a Prom concert in 1999. The BBC wanted him to bring along a new piece of music and the commission went to the Austrian, Gruber, "a brilliant composer," he says. Neeme Järvi conducted the first performance in London with the BBC Symphony Orchestra.

He's looking forward to performing *Aerial* again in Gothenburg, especially as the conditions are the best imaginable. He knows the guest conductor Markus Stenz well, the atmosphere in the Concert Hall is congenial and many of the musicians are his personal friends.

"I whistled all the way here in the car. They've always believed in me here. Not even in my youth did they see me as an upstart."

Markus Stenz has just taken a break from rehearsals. The musicians crowd around back stage and relax during the coffee break. A sign on the soloist dressing-room door this week reads "Håkan Hardenberger". This is where he comes to recharge.

"*Aerial* is not only the best, but also absolutely the most difficult concerto I have performed," he says. If you were to compare this to something outside the world of music it would be worse than a marathon.

He describes the piece: "Have you seen the film The Fugitive with Harrison Ford? The scene where he is being pursued through the tunnel, and when he finally comes to the end of it a huge expanse of water appears and there is a long drop down to the surface, there's no turning back, he just jumps – that's how it feels."

"Why do it? Why expose yourself to such things? Because it's necessary," he says. "One has to."

Hardenberger began playing when he was eight and realised immediately that he would be a trumpeter. He gave it everything from the very start and at the age of 15 he performed his first solo concert. That was 25 years ago. He has played around 60 concerts a year for a long time. During the tough years in the beginning of his career he performed around 90 concerts a year, but he has slowed down and cleaned up his calendar. He is in a position where he can afford to only perform the concerts that he favours, with musicians he respects.

Privileged? Of course. And nervous. A star soloist cannot afford to have a bad day. The trumpet is also an especially demanding instrument to play. One must be in perfect shape, and the long hours of practice are not always fun. There are times when he wonders how long he can keep going, 10 or 15 years? And what would he do instead, conduct, write music, open a restaurant, or what? Reflecting upon the alternatives he always decides to keep going for a while longer.

"If I don't play I feel really awful," he says as he looks at his trumpet sitting next to him on the sofa, a Vincent Bach that has followed him throughout his career.

It sparkles in its dark case.

"I'm nobody without this, that's just how it is."

"A.S. In Memoriam was written to honour the memory of Arnold Schoenberg and his masterpiece *Verklärte Nacht*, now over 100 years old (1899). In bar 49 there is a musical quotation from Verklärte Nacht paying homage to Schoenberg. This version for string orchestra of A.S. In Memoriam is dedicated to Neeme Järvi."
Limhamn December 1999, Rolf Martinsson.
A.S. In Memoriam went on tour to Japan in the autumn of 2002.

● CD 2.11

Most frequently performed works by the GSO and Neeme Järvi

This list includes the 2001-2002 season. Encores and non-programmed pieces are not included. Among the encores are Sibelius' Andante festivo and Alla marcia from the Karelia Suite, which would have appeared high on the list.

Composer	Work	Performances
Jean Sibelius	Symphony No. 2	65
Hugo Alfvén	Midsummer Vigil	46
Antonín Dvořák	Cello Concerto	26
Jean Sibelius	En saga	25
Wilhelm Stenhammar	Excelsior!	22
Edvard Grieg	Peer Gynt: Suite No.1	21
Lars-Erik Larsson	Pastoral Suite	19
Jean Sibelius	Violin Concerto	18
Carl Nielsen	Symphony No. 4, "The Inextinguishable"	18
Joseph Haydn	Trumpet Concerto	18
Gustav Mahler	Lieder eines fahrenden Gesellen	17
Johannes Brahms	Double Concerto	17
Dmitri Shostakovich	Symphony No. 5	17
Arvo Pärt	Symphony No. 3	17
Edvard Grieg	The Last Spring	16
Jean Sibelius	Finlandia	16
Jean Sibelius	Symphony No. 5	16
Franz Berwald	Sinfonie naïve	16
Pyotr Tchaikovsky	Symphony No. 5	15
Jean Sibelius	Symphony No. 1	15
Franz Berwald	Sinfonie sérieuse	15
Edvard Grieg	Piano Concerto	13
Jean Sibelius	Tapiola	12
Béla Bartók	Concerto for Orchestra	12
Eino Tamberg	Trumpet Concerto	12
Wilhelm Stenhammar	Symphony No. 1	11
Sergei Rachmaninov	Piano Concerto No. 2	11
Carl Nielsen	Symphony No. 2, "The Four Temperaments"	11
Franz Berwald	Overture to Estrella de Soria	11
Edvard Grieg	From Monte Pincio	11
Carl Nielsen	Symphony No. 5	11
Anders Hillborg	King Tide	11
Jean Sibelius	Karelia Suite	10
Antonín Dvořák	Carneval	10
Johannes Brahms	Symphony No. 1	10
Edvard Grieg	Norwegian Dances	10
Edvard Grieg	A Swan	10
Carl Orff	Carmina Burana	10
Alessandro Marcello	Trumpet Concerto in C minor	10
Wilhelm Stenhammar	Piano Concerto No. 2	10
Wilhelm Stenhammar	The girl returned from meeting her lover	10
Carl Nielsen	Aladdin Suite	10
Sergei Prokofiev	Sinfonia Concertante	10
Hugo Alfvén	The Forest Sleeps	9
Manuel de Falla	The Three-cornered Hat	9
Edvard Grieg	Peer Gynt: Suite No. 2	9
Antonín Dvořák	Symphony No. 7	9

MOST FREQUENTLY PERFORMED WORKS

Richard Strauss	Ständchen	9
Edvard Grieg	Solveig's Song	9
Richard Strauss	Ich wollt' ein Sträusslein binden	9
Igor Stravinsky	The Rite of Spring	9
Igor Stravinsky	The Firebird	9
Jean Sibelius	Lemminkäinen in Tuonela	8
Jean Sibelius	Suite: King Christian II	8
Jean Sibelius	The Oceanides	8
Jean Sibelius	Lemminkäinen and the Maidens of the Island	8
Johannes Brahms	Violin Concerto	8
Wilhelm Stenhammar	Serenade	8
Wilhelm Stenhammar	Symphony No. 2	8
Richard Strauss	An Alpine Symphony	8
Jean Sibelius	Symphony No. 7	8
Jean Sibelius	Symphony No. 3	8
Hector Berlioz	Symphonie fantastique	8
Ludwig van Beethoven	Triple Concerto	8
Modest Mussorgsky	Pictures at an Exhibition	8
Nikolai Rimsky-Korsakov	Scheherazade	7
Einojuhani Rautavaara	A Requiem in Our Time	7
Dmitri Shostakovich	Symphony No. 6	7
Richard Strauss	Four Last Songs	7
Jean Sibelius	Symphony No. 6	7
Eduard Tubin	Symphony No. 5	7
Arvo Pärt	Concerto piccolo über B-A-C-H	7
Rolf Martinsson	Bridge, Trumpet Concerto No. 1	7
César Franck	Symphony in D minor	7
Jean Sibelius	Symphony No. 4	6
Franz Schubert	Symphony No. 5	6
Bedřich Smetana	Ma Vlast: Vltava	6
Benjamin Britten	Four Sea Interludes	6
Richard Strauss	Don Juan	6
Robert Schumann	Piano Concerto	6
Jean Sibelius	Lemminkäinen Legends	6
Richard Strauss	Wiegenlied	6
Johannes Brahms	Piano Concerto No. 1	6
Carl Nielsen	Maskarade Overture	6
Jan Sandström	Éra	6
Carl Nielsen	Symphony No. 6, "Sinfonia semplice"	5
Antonín Dvořák	Slavonic Dances, Op. 46, 5-8	5
Hugo Alfvén	Dalecarlian Rhapsody	5
Carl Nielsen	A Fantasy Journey to the Faraoes	5
Modest Mussorgsky	Songs and Dances of Death	5
Arvo Pärt	Fratres	5
Richard Wagner	Ride of the Valkyries	5
Arvo Pärt	Cantus in memory of Benjamin Britten	5
Richard Wagner	Overture to The Flying Dutchman	5
Jean Sibelius	Pohjola's Daughter	5
Wilhelm Stenhammar	In the forest	5
Richard Wagner	"Die Frist ist um…" from The Flying Dutchman	5
Richard Strauss	Morgen	5
Camille Saint-Saëns	Cello Concerto No. 1	5
Jean Sibelius	Andante festivo	5
Lars-Erik Larsson	God in Disguise	5
Franz Lehár	Gold and Silver	5

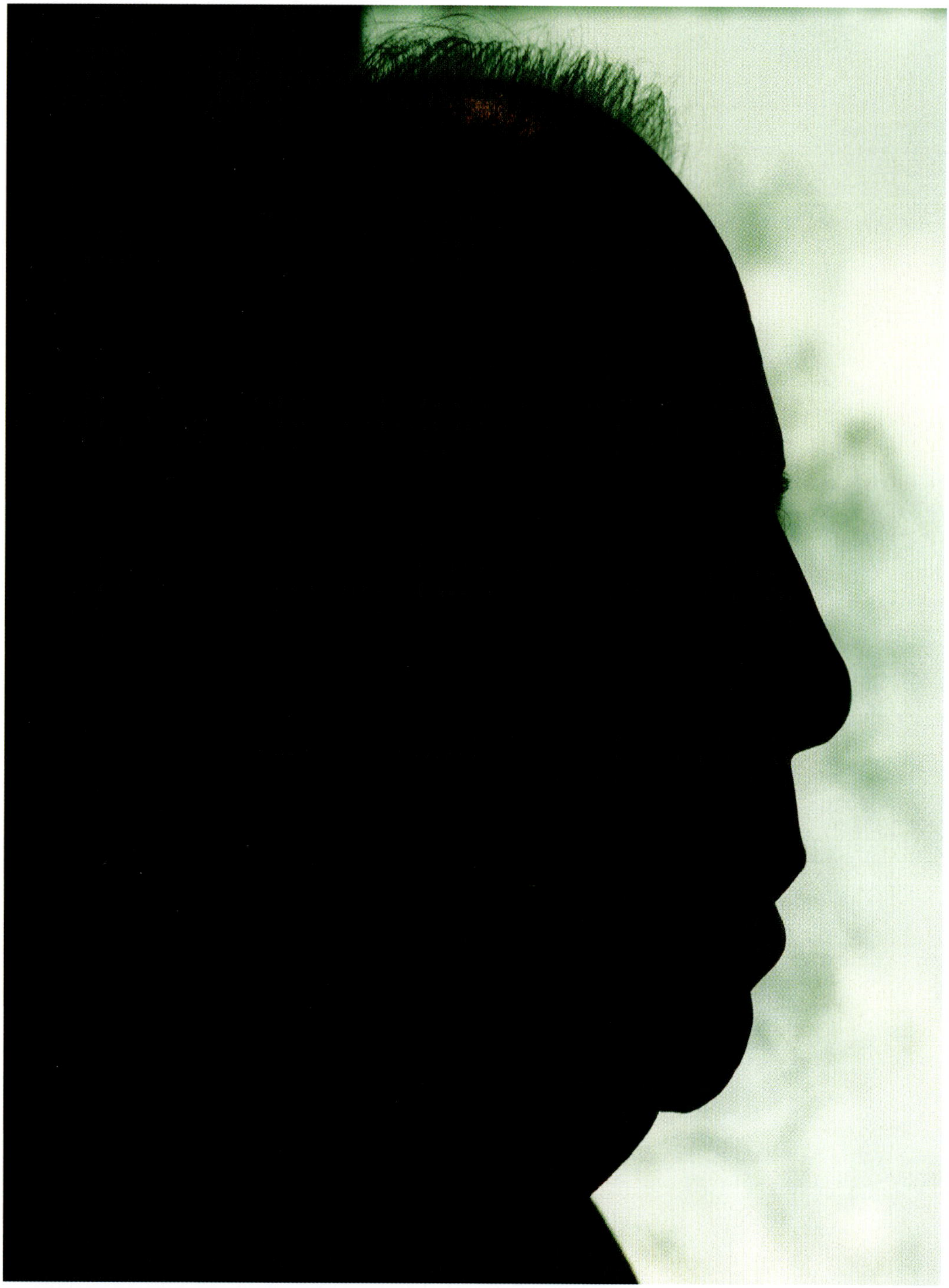

An emotional comeback

Two weeks before the major Grieg tour in 2001, Sture Carlsson, the manager of the orchestra, called Lennart Dehn, the artistic adviser for the tour. Dehn, who was in Paris at the time, had worked intensively for a few months to get the complicated performance to work. Grieg's concert version of Ibsen's Peer Gynt requires actors, vocal soloists, choir and a large symphony orchestra. The concerts were booked for the Proms at the Royal Albert Hall in London and in Salzburg. This was the orchestra's first invitation to the Salzburg Festival. In addition, both live radio and television broadcasts of the concert were arranged for London.

"A problem has turned up," said Sture Carlsson, in his cautious manner.

Neeme Järvi had suddenly been taken ill and had been taken from Pärnu in Estonia, where he was teaching, to Helsinki for an operation.

"I was lying on my bed, resting between recording sessions, when the call came, and that was probably a good thing," recalls Lennart Dehn. Neeme Järvi is very difficult to replace and the planned schedule included a very limited number of rehearsals because Järvi is so familiar with the work.

The doctors said he had had a mild stroke. He recovered surprisingly quickly, but was ordered by his doctors to take things very easy in the immediate future.

That was the first time he had to cancel a performance with the GSO since his bout of gall stones in 1984, which came at a bad time as well. There is never a good time to be ill, especially not for people like Neeme Järvi.

The prestigious tour could be carried out thanks to one of the orchestra's favourite guests, the Swedish Radio Symphony Orchestra's principal conductor, Manfred Honeck, who stepped in at short notice. Everything worked very well. But this didn't stop there being a considerable void left by Järvi. The musicians missed their conductor. Someone once said that, "With Järvi there is more emotion and less control." A few months passed and 5 November 2001 came around with rehearsals at the Concert Hall and a celebratory atmosphere. Neeme Järvi was back. First violinist Nicola Boruvka was also there: "I usually like eye contact with the conductor but at the beginning of the rehearsals, Neeme wore sunglasses, possibly to protect his eyes from the lights. It then became far more obvious how beautifully he conducts. Colleagues said afterwards that they hadn't heard that kind of sound from the violin section during the entire autumn.

After four months' convalescence Neeme Järvi stood on the conductor's stand again. It was an emotional occasion in many ways. The question everyone cautiously asked themselves nervously was: could he still conduct?

A raised eyebrow is enough

"This was an evening where the orchestra and audience could have stood upright for the rest of the night. So expectant was the atmosphere at Neeme Järvi's comeback in Gothenburg," wrote Dagens Nyheter's Martin Nyström following the concert on Wednesday 7 November 2001.

It was the 65th time that the GSO performed Sibelius' Second Symphony with Neeme Järvi. The concert was recorded

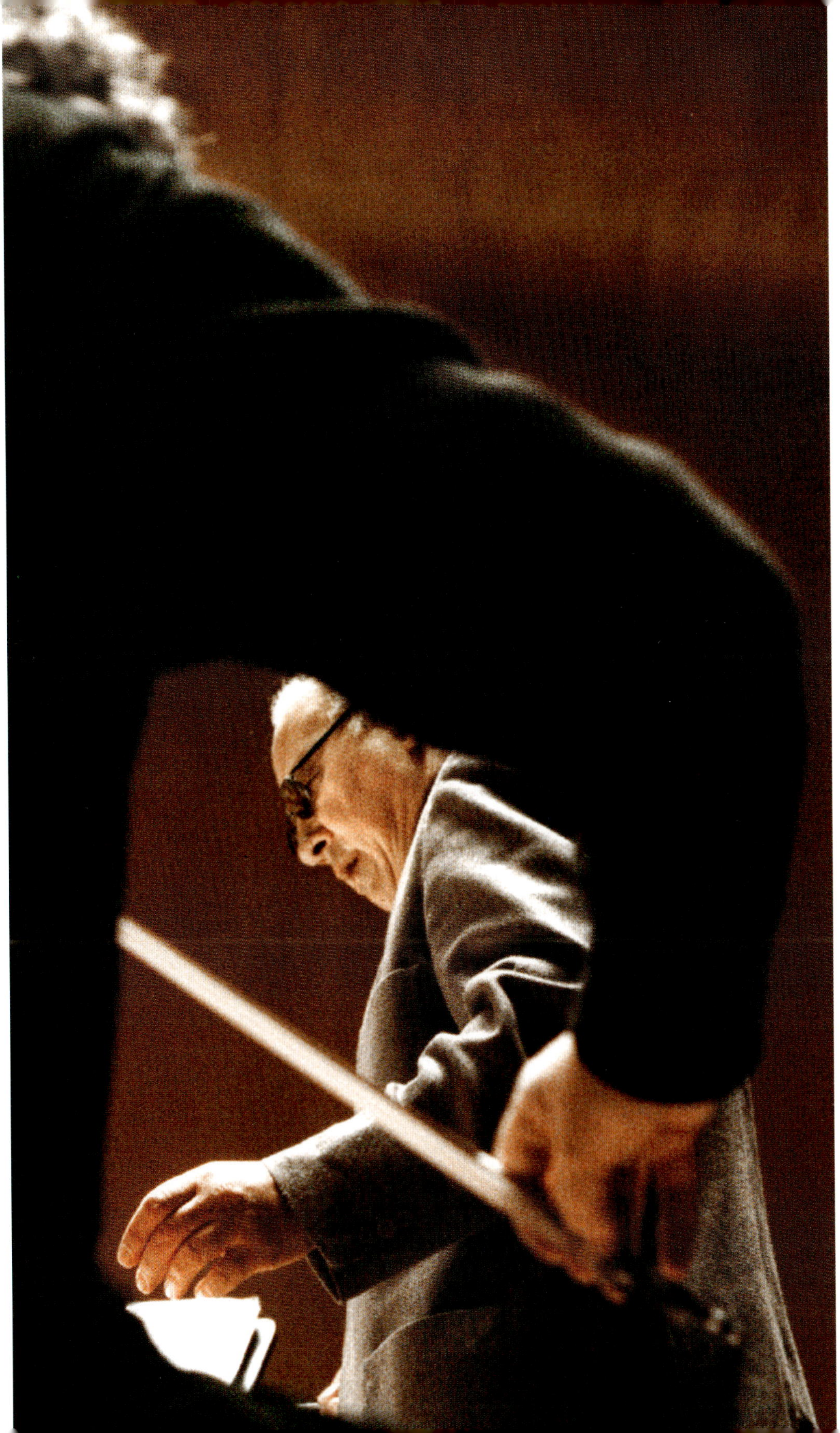

Jean Sibelius sketched by his friend Albert Engström.

"During Sixten Ehrling's brief period as principal conductor, serious efforts were made to interest Deutsche Grammophon in Carl Nielsen's six symphonies. A brilliant recording of the Rite of Spring made no impression at all on the people in Hamburg. The lack of interest was because the GSO lacked credibility beyond the boundaries of Gothenburg. If the GSO hadn't received a helping hand from BIS so that Deutsche Grammophon re-evaluated its stance, then the GSO would still be an undervalued group of musicians.
The ice was broken with the orchestra's willingness to risk their artistic capital when Robert von Bahr decided to record all of the orchestral works of Eduard Tubin, Jean Sibelius, Wilhelm Stenhammar and Carl Nielsen in Gothenburg."
Carl-Gunnar Åhlén, musicologist.

live for a new compilation of Sibelius' seven symphonies to be released by Deutsche Grammophon in 2004.

Other major recording projects under way (2003) are cycles of complete symphonies by Tchaikovsky and Hilding Rosenberg for BIS. The recordings take place at the Concert Hall and are produced from the small control room, visible to the audience on the left above the podium.

Up here sit two discrete talents who are highly valued members of the team. They are well known in the music industry. But their names only appear in the fine print on the record sleeves:

Balance engineer: Michael Bergek.

Recording Producer and Supervisor: Lennart Dehn.

Michael Bergek is the technical director of the Swedish Broadcasting Corporation in Gothenburg and has won a number of prestigious awards for his recordings. Lennart Dehn works in many countries and is based in the UK. He has produced recordings with orchestras such as the Vienna Philharmonic, London Symphony and the Concertgebouw in Amsterdam and is a member of the Grammy jury in the USA.

These two have been partners since their first joint recording twenty years ago, and they liken their relationship to a long marriage; and a happy one at that. The engineer, Bergek knows exactly what the producer, Dehn, wants, and Dehn has learned nearly everything about the limits of technology. Or as Dehn puts it: "We have the same will to express ourselves."

The recording contracts, firstly with BIS and then with Deutsche Grammophon at the beginning of the 1980s, were of central importance to the GSO's development into an orchestra of international renown. Recordings are the entry ticket to the major concert platforms.

Without recordings there would be no reputation, irrespective of how fantastically the orchestra might perform. Close to 90 recordings have been made so far with Järvi conducting, leading to favourable reviews and prestigious awards. The BIS recording of Sibelius' Second Symphony sold over 50,000 copies and was awarded a gold disc. Deutsche Grammophon's recording of Rimsky-Korsakov's symphonies featured in Time Magazine's list of the ten best classical releases of 1988. This marked the orchestra's international breakthrough.

The GSO is among the busiest Scandinavian orchestras in the recording studios. Järvi is even more diligent. Has any other conductor made more records? In 20 years he has managed to make something like 350 recordings; a staggering figure.

○ CD 1.3

"My most vivid memories are from the US tour of 1983 when the GSO first made a real impression abroad. There were unforgettable evenings with the orchestra performing in Chicago and Carnegie Hall in New York. Special for me was performing Dvořák's cello concerto night after night. Neeme doesn't like routine performances, so anything could happen. What's so special about Neeme is his spontaneity, and he knows the orchestra will follow. His hand is incredible. I probably haven't experienced such rapport between hand and sound with any other conductor. His hands are music."
Frans Helmerson 18 June 2002.

Robert von Bahr, Frans Helmerson, Michael Bergek and Neeme Järvi 1984.

The GSO received a gold disc for the recording of Sibelius' Second Symphony in 1988.

Recording sessions are physically demanding. The GSO's working atmosphere, where everybody knows one another and what to do, has contributed to the success.

When conducting, Järvi has visual contact with producer Lennart Dehn through the studio window. Dehn is sitting next to the balance engineer Michael Bergek. A gesture or a raised eyebrow is enough to signal their intentions.

They have never fallen out, apart of course from the time when a really angry Järvi stormed up to the technician's room and shouted, "This is no Kindergarten!" He was forced to concede in the exchange of words that followed and when the producer Lennart Dehn asked Järvi a little later if he was still angry he stated, "Angry? Me? No, no, it was a very artistic discussion on a very loud level."

In truth the teamwork has been exceptionally smooth, despite a great deal of pressure. Recording a symphony orchestra is no easy matter.

Technical precision is required in order to capture the full range of musical expression in a way that does justice to the orchestra, conductor and the music.

Sibelius and Nielsen require a different kind of microphone placement than Beethoven or Brahms, for example. There can be difficulties in trying to achieve a good balance between the different sections. The brass must not be too heavy in relation to the strings. A single entry marginally out of tune or a little bit early is unacceptable in a recording. Tiny imperfections that would pass almost unnoticed during a concert, where the listener is affected by the occasion may sound awful on record. Each time the disc is played the imperfection stands out, which in the end completely ruins the listening experience.

Modern technology allows for detailed editing and for some construed magic. But too much editing can destroy the musical content and the vitality of the music can be lost: the structure of the piece, the long lines and the way the music breathes. Aspects that are more felt than heard.

There is usually a relaxed atmosphere in the control room, as was the case on the Friday evening, when Sibelius' Symphony No. 7 was to be recorded for DG's Sibelius box. They are recording it live. As usual, Bergek and Dehn are in charge of the project from the recording to the production of the finished master.

The producer needs to know the score just as intimately as the conductor. During the week's rehearsals he has formed a view of what Järvi is thinking. And Järvi, in turn, has listened

The GSO received a gold disc for the recording of Sibelius' Second Symphony in 1988. "There was a joyous atmosphere at the Concert Hall the other day when five elegant copies of the Sibelius Symphony gold disc were being presented to the people responsible. In addition to the orchestra, represented by its chairman, principal clarinettist Olle Schill, four other people who had contributed to the project also received their gold discs: Conductor Neeme Järvi, Producer Lennart Dehn, Balance Engineer Michael Bergek and, of course, Robert von Bahr in Stockholm, the man who is BIS, the label on which Sibelius' complete orchestral works have been released."
P G Bergfors of Göteborgs-Posten 2 September 1988.

to what the producer is able to contribute from a listener's point of view. Bergek has been present during rehearsals as well, listening to the sound and solving any technical difficulties that might arise.

"What makes a recording is not technology, but rather the people and instruments on stage, and how the microphones are placed," he explains.

The recording equipment has been adjusted and the microphones placed on stage and in the hall. Dehn has the score in front of him while little green lamps flash in front of Bergek. The concert is about to begin and the audience is informed that the concert is recorded. So silence please, ladies and gentlemen!

Live recordings are not very common in Gothenburg. Stenhammar's first and second symphonies, recorded at the beginning of the 1980s, are the only ones previously released by the GSO, not counting live broadcasts. The reason is, of course, that there is no leeway for mistakes in live recordings.

Everything needs to be right from the start. Even if two concerts are recorded, there still might not be enough material to produce a good disc. There may be disturbances from the audience or background noise that is not compatible between the two performances – the city doesn't sound the same on a Saturday afternoon as on a weekday – and so on.

So why make a live recording at all? The reason is simple. If everything works the way it's supposed to then the result can be tremendously exciting. "Järvi is the same kind of person as Bernstein and a few other conductors who have the ability to make something extra special of a concert," Lennart Dehn remarks.

The GSO performs Grieg's Peer Gynt at the Proms in the Royal Albert Hall, London 2001.

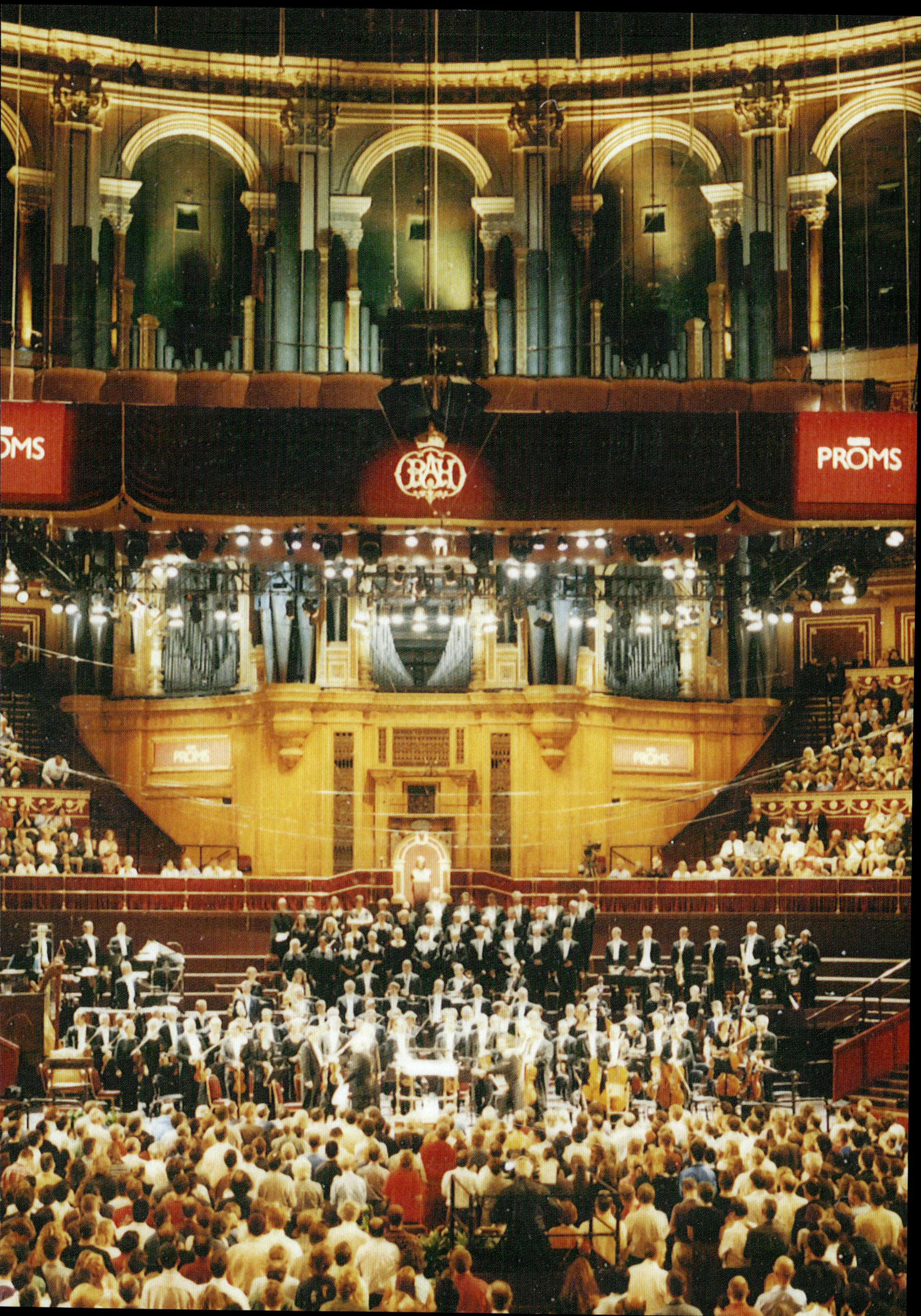
PROMS
PROMS
PROMS
PROMS

Edvard Grieg

The Norwegian composer was previously considered a rigid nationalist. Debussy scathingly said that his music was "a lozenge filled with snow". Grieg's music embodies everything that is Norway – from fjords to church bells and mountain pastures. With his colourful instrumentation he is considered a precursor of impressionism.

Grieg was given lessons early on in life by his mother, who was a trained pianist. His talent was apparent and as a teenager he was sent to Germany to be educated in the German romantic school. However, he later said that he learned nothing in Leipzig. He married his cousin, the distinguished singer, Nina Hagerup, and most of his 150 songs were written for her.

Grieg is the master of the miniature. He wrote his most important works before the age of 35. Some of his best-loved works are his renditions of Norwegian folk music and his *Lyric Pieces* for piano. He became internationally renowned for his piano concerto written at the age of 25. Liszt sight-read it from the score and contributed to the piece becoming a success. Grieg became famous in Europe and continued to tour throughout his life. The piano concerto is still one of the most performed works in the genre.

His other great masterpiece is the music for Ibsen's drama, *Peer Gynt*. The two orchestral suites are world famous. The complete concert version was premièred by the Gothenburg Symphony Orchestra, with Neeme Järvi, Barbara Bonney and Håkan Hagegård in London in 1992.

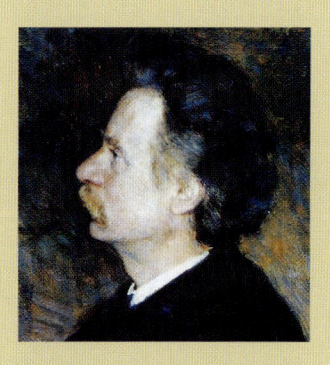

EDVARD GRIEG 1843–1907

Norway's most important composer, born in Bergen. Grieg began composing at the age of twelve. After studying in Leipzig he achieved international success. At the time of his death from a lung condition at his house, *Troldhaugen,* outside Bergen, he was regarded as Norway's leading composer.
Important works: Piano Concerto (1868), *Holberg Suite* (1885), incidental music for *Sigurd Jorsalfar* (1872) and *Peer Gynt* (1875), two suites from *Peer Gynt* (1888, 1891) and *Lyric Pieces* for piano. The songs *The Last Spring, Solveig's Song, A Swan, From Monte Pincio* and *I Love You,* plus a cello sonata, three violin sonatas and a string quartet.
Recordings: The GSO and Neeme Järvi have recorded Grieg's complete orchestral music, issued as a collection by DG, containing a number of first performances.

Do you have church bells up there?

The 2001 tour programme included Edward Grieg's music to Peer Gynt, performed the way Grieg had once imagined it, with choir, soloists and actors.

Grieg never actually saw his concert version performed. His publisher wasn't interested. Instead, the first Peer Gynt suite was printed, and after a number of years, as Grieg still didn't get a go ahead for the concert version a second suite followed. To Grieg's great annoyance, hits such as Anitra's Dance, In the Hall of the Mountain King and Solveig's Song were performed all over the world in every conceivable arrangement. "If I get to live a little longer I will make sure that the music to Peer Gynt is published and performed the way I have always wanted," he wrote to a friend some years prior to his death in 1907.

80 years elapsed before Grieg scholars found and restored the original score. The GSO was approached by Deutsche Grammophon to record the music to Peer Gynt. Lennart Dehn convinced them to follow Grieg's score to the letter, with Norwegian-speaking actors, a fiddler and everything else. The legendary Norwegian actress Wenche Foss was entrusted with the role of Peer's mother Aase and world renowned Barbara Bonney sang Solveig's song. They both performed at the Prom concert and in Salzburg in 2001.

The recording in 1987 was very exciting.

"At that time we mixed everything live. Everything. It was really wonderful when it all worked," says engineer Michael Bergek.

The Grieg recording was the GSO's most advanced production to date. The orchestral music was interleaved with sung and spoken parts. There were even church bells. Järvi stopped conducting and pointed to the score:

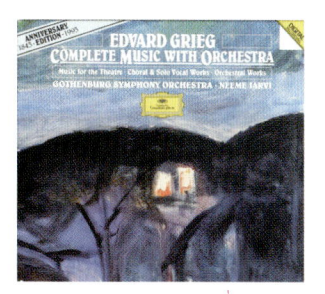

CD 1.6

"The orchestra distinguishes itself in two ways. It has its own sound, a blond, Scandinavian sound that is quite special. Many good orchestras sound much alike but the GSO has a sound of its own. Just listen to their Grieg for example! In addition it's a friendly orchestra. I feel a tremendous support from them when I'm standing on the podium."
Barbara Bonney, the GSO's honorary soprano.

Barbara Bonney and Bo Skovhus in Grieg's Peer Gynt at the Proms in 2001.

"Church bells? Lennart, it says church bells here in the score."

"Don't worry, we've got church bells," Dehn said.

"What? You have church bells up there?" asked the perplexed Järvi.

Bergek and Dehn had been searching the city with a tape recorder for church bells. Now they only needed to press a button on the recorder.

For optimal efficiency the recording was split into numerous sections. The sections requiring actors and orchestra were taken care of first, followed by the choral music. The spoken parts were recorded during breaks and when the orchestra was finished for the day. The sections requiring full orchestra were done first allowing musicans to leave when they were no longer required. The soloist playing the Hardanger fiddle was recorded at a later date. The recorded material consisted of several hundred fragments on a large number of tapes and were very carefully checked against the score. After the sessions, Bergek and Dehn travelled to Stockholm, to the only high quality digital studio in Sweden at the time and pieced the material together. In fact they were the first persons to hear Grieg's original version in its entirety.

For a later recording of Tchaikovsky's 1812 Overture Dehn and Bergek found themselves recording the cathedral bells and real cannons on location. People who thought they knew identified the bells of Gothenburg's Cathedral. What one hears is actually a mixture of bells from two other churches in Gothenburg.

" We even have Neeme's digital watch on record. That was in the early days of digital watches and they made a noise on the hour and half-hour. Musically speaking, the take that included the watch was much the best. Instead of swapping the entire section we chose to try and eliminate the sound of the watch as far as possible. If you don't know that it's there you can't hear it. But we know and we'll always hear it every time we play the record."

Lennart Dehn, producer: "No, I'm not going to tell you which record it's on."

Discography– GSO and Neeme Järvi 1983–2003

1983

Wilhelm Stenhammar
Symphony No. 1
(BIS-CD- 219)

Jean Sibelius
Symphony No. 1, Finlandia
(BIS-CD- 221)

Jean Sibelius
Symphony No. 5, Andante festivo, Karelia Overture
(BIS-CD- 222)

Jean Sibelius
Symphony No. 3, Suite from King Christian II
(BIS-CD- 228)

Antonín Dvořák
Cello Concerto, Silent Woods
Frans Helmerson cello
(BIS-CD- 245)

1984

Eduard Tubin
Symphonies Nos. 4 & 9, Toccata
(BIS-CD- 227)

Jean Sibelius
Symphony No. 6, Suite from Pelléas and Mélisande
(BIS-CD- 237)

Jean Sibelius
The Maiden in the Tower, Karelia Suite
(BIS-CD- 250)

Wilhelm Stenhammar
Symphony No. 2, Excelsior!
(BIS-CD- 251)

Jean Sibelius
Symphony No. 2, Romance in C major
(BIS-CD- 252)

1985

Jean Sibelius
Symphony No. 4, Oceanides, Canzonetta
(BIS-CD- 263)

Eduard Tubin
Violin Concerto No. 1, Estonian Dance Suite for Violin and Orchestra, Prélude solennel
Mark Lubotsky violin
(BIS-CD- 286)

Jean Sibelius
Lemminkäinen Legends
(BIS-CD- 294)

Jean Sibelius
Scènes historiques Sets 1 & 2, En saga
(BIS-CD- 295)

Franz Berwald
Symphonies Nos. 1–4
(DG 445 581, 2 CDs)

1986

Eduard Tubin
Symphony No. 10
(BIS-CD- 297)

Wilhelm Stenhammar
Serenade for Orchestra
(including Reverenza)
(BIS-CD- 310)

Jean Sibelius
Symphony No. 7, Night Ride and Sunrise, Music from Kuolema
(BIS-CD- 311)

Jean Sibelius
Tapiola, Pohjola's Daughter, Rakastava, Impromptu for Strings
(BIS-CD- 312)

Jean Sibelius
Kullervo
Karita Mattila soprano
Jorma Hynninen baritone
Laulun Ystävät male voice choir
(BIS-CD- 313)

Jean Sibelius
Finlandia, The Origin of Fire, Sandels and other works for male voice choir and orchestra
Sauli Tiilikainen baritone
Gothenburg boys´ choir
Laulun Ystävät male voice choir
(BIS-CD- 314)

Edvard Grieg
Symphonic Dances, Norwegian Dances, Lyric Suite
(DG 419 431)

1987

Eduard Tubin
Violin Concerto No. 2, Ballad for Violin and Orchestra, Double Bass Concerto, Estonian Dance Suite, Valse Triste
Gustavo Garcia violin
Håkan Ehrén double bass
(BIS-CD- 337)

Johan Svendsen
Symphonies Nos. 1–2, Two Swedish Folk-songs
(BIS-CD- 347)

Jean Sibelius
Suite from Swanwhite, The Dryad, Dance Intermezzo, Pan and Echo, Suite from Belshazzar's Feast
(BIS-CD- 359)

Jean Sibelius
Violin Concerto, Overture in A minor, Minuetto, In memoriam
Silvia Marcovici violin
(BIS-CD- 372)

Jean Sibelius
Spring Song, The Bard, Valse lyrique, Autrefois, Valse chevaleresque, Suite mignonne, Suite champêtre, Suite caractéristique, Presto for Strings
(BIS-CD- 384)

Edvard Grieg
Peer Gynt, complete concert version
Sigurd Jorsalfar
Barbara Bonney soprano
Kjell Magnus Sandve tenor
Urban Malmberg barytone and others
Wenche Foss narrator
Gösta Ohlin's Vocal Ensemble
Pro Musica Chamber Choir
(DG 423 079, 2 CDs)

1988
Eduard Tubin
Symphony No. 7, Piano Concertino, Sinfonietta on Estonian Themes
Roland Pöntinen piano
(BIS-CD- 401)

Alfred Schnittke
Concerto grosso No. 4 / Symphony No. 5
Pianissimo
(BIS-CD- 427)

Nikolai Rimsky-Korsakov
Symphonies Nos. 1–3, Capriccio espagnol, Russian Easter Festival Overture
(DG 459 512, 2 CDs)

1989
Wilhelm Stenhammar
Snöfrid, Lodolezzi Sings, Midwinter, Intermezzo from The Song
Ulrika Åhlén soprano
Gothenburg Concert Hall Choir
(BIS-CD- 438)

Jean Sibelius
The Tempest, Prelude and Suite, Cassazione, Tiera, Preludio
(BIS-CD- 448)

Edvard Grieg
Symphony in C minor, In Autumn, Old Norwegian Romance with Variations, Funeral March in memory of Rikard Nordraak
(DG 427 321)

Dmitri Shostakovich
Symphony No. 15, October, Overture on Russian and Kirghiz Themes
(DG 427 616)

1990
Jean Sibelius
Humoresques Nos. 1-6 for Violin and Orchestra, Serenades for Violin and Orchestra, Overture in E major, Ballet Scene
Dong-Suk Kang violin
(BIS-CD- 472)

Wilhelm Stenhammar
Piano Concerto No. 2, Suite from Chitra
Cristina Ortiz piano
(BIS-CD- 476)

»Intermezzo«
Music by Cilea, Giordano, Leoncavallo, Mascagni and other works
(DG 429 494)

Pyotr Tchaikovsky
1812 Marche slave
Alexander Borodin
Polovtsian Dances, On the Steppes of Central Asia
Nikolai Rimsky-Korsakov
Capriccio espagnol, Russian Easter Festival Overture
(DG 429 984)

1991
Jean Sibelius
Scaramouche, Wedding March from The Language of the Birds
(BIS-CD- 502)

Sergei Prokofiev
The Fiery Angel
Nadine Secunde soprano
Rosemarie Lang alto
Siegfried Lorenz baritone
Bryn Terfel bass and others
(DG 431 669, 2 CDs)

Dmitri Shostakovich
Symphony Nos. 11 and 12, Suite from The Golden Age, Suite from Hamlet
(DG 459 415, 2 CDs)

1992
Alexander Borodin
Symphonies Nos. 1–3, Overture and Polovtsian Dances from Prince Igor, On the Steppes of Central Asia, Petite Suite, Nocturne
(DG 435 757, 2 CDs)

1993
Carl Nielsen
Symphonies Nos. 4 and 6
(BIS-CD- 600)

DISCOGRAPHY

Carl Nielsen
Symphonies No. 1–6, Violin Concerto, Flute Concerto, Clarinet Concerto
Dong-Suk Kang violin, Patrick Gallois flute, Olle Schill clarinet
Myung-Whun Chung and Neeme Järvi conductors
(BIS-CD- 614/616 boxed set. 5 CDs)

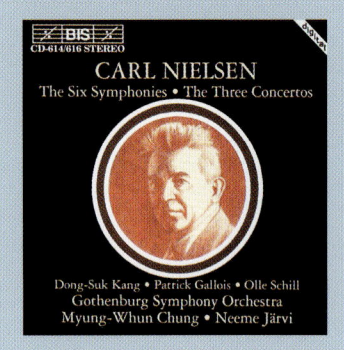

Jean Sibelius
»Sibelius Encore!«
Finlandia, Karelia Suite, Lemminkäinen's Homeward Journey, The Swan of Tuonela and other works
(BIS-CD- 610)

Carl Nielsen
Symphonies No. 1–6
Soile Isokoski soprano
Jorma Hynninen baritone
(DG 437 507, 3 CDs)

Edvard Grieg
Orchestral Songs
Barbara Bonney soprano
Randi Stene mezzo-soprano
Håkan Hagegård baritone
Rut Tellefsen narrator
(DG 437 519)

Edvard Grieg
Holberg Suite, Two Elegiac Melodies, Two Melodies, Two Nordic Melodies, Two Lyric Pieces
(DG 437 520)

Edvard Grieg
Landkjenning, Olav Trygvason, Peer Gynt Suites No. 1 and 2
Randi Stene mezzo-soprano
Anne Gjevang alto
Håkan Hagegård baritone
(DG 437 523)

Edvard Grieg
Piano Concerto in A minor, Lyric Suite, In Autumn
Lilya Zilberstein piano
(DG 437 524)

Dmitri Shostakovich
Symphony No. 14, Songs and Dances of Death
Lyuba Kazarnovskaya soprano
Sergei Leiferkus baritone
Brigitte Fassbaender mezzo-soprano
(DG 437 785)

Jean Sibelius
Symphonies Nos. 1–7, Kullervo
Karita Mattila, soprano
Jorma Hynninen, baritone
Laulun Ystävät male voice choir
(BIS-CD- 622/24 boxed set. 5 CDs)

Edvard Grieg
Complete Orchestral Music
Lilya Zilberstein piano
Barbara Bonney soprano
Håkan Hagegård baritone and others
(DG 437 842, 6 CDs)
Also as budget collection
(DG 471 300, 6 CDs)

1994
Gustav Mahler
Symphony No. 8
Ulla Gustafsson soprano
MariAnne Häggander soprano
Carolina Sandgren soprano
Anne Gjevang mezzo-soprano
Ulrika Tenstam alto
Seppo Ruohonen tenor
Mats Persson baritone
Stockholm Philharmonic Choir, Concert Hall Choir, Gothenburg Opera Choir, Estonian Boys´Choir, Children's Choir, Gothenburg Opera Orchestra
(BIS-CD- 700)

Wilhelm Stenhammar
Symphonies Nos. 1–2, Serenade, (including Reverenza), Lodolezzi Sings, Intermezzo from the Song, Midwinter; Florez and Blanzeflor, Sentimental Romances, Piano Concerto No. 1 (original version), Piano Concerto No. 2, Excelsior!, Snöfrid
Neeme Järvi and Paavo Järvi conductors
Love Derwinger piano
Cristina Ortiz piano
Malmö Symphony Orchestra and others.
(BIS-CD- 714/716 boxed set. 4 CDs)

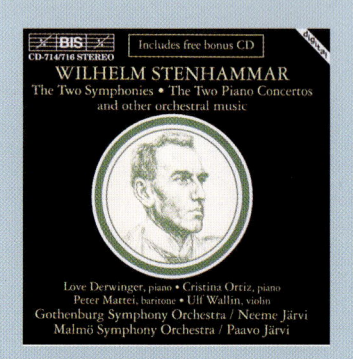

Dmitri Shostakovich
From Jewish Folk Poetry, Six Romances on poems by Raleigh, Burns and Shakespeare, Three Romances on poems by Pushkin, Two Fables by Krylov
Lyuba Orgonasova soprano
Larisa Dyadkova mezzo-soprano
Nathalie Stutzmann alto
Philip Langridge tenor
Sergei Leiferkus baritone
(DG 439 860)

Piotr Tchaikovsky
Mazeppa
Galina Gorchakova soprano
Larisa Dyadkova mezzo-soprano
Sergeij Larin tenor
Richard Margison tenor

Heinz Zednik tenor
Sergei Leiferkus baritone
Monte Pederson bass
Anatoly Kotcherga bass
Royal Opera Chorus Stockholm
(DG 439 906, 3 CDs)

1995
Wilhelm Stenhammar
Symphonies Nos. 1–2, Serenade, Excelsior!
(DG 445 857, 2 CDs)

Dmitri Shostakovich
Michelangelo Songs, Songs on poems by Marina Tsvetayeva and others
Ilya Levinsky tenor
Elena Zaremba mezzo soprano
Sergei Leiferkus baritone
(DG 447 085)

1996
Carl Nielsen
Suite from Aladdin, An Imaginary Journey to the Faroe Islands, Helios Overture, Maskarade Overture, Pan and Syrinx, Saga-drøm
(DG 447 757)

Jean Sibelius
Finlandia, Karelia Suite, Andante festivo, Suite from King Christian II, Luonnotar, The Oceanides
Soile Isokoski soprano
(DG 447 760)

Dmitri Shostakovich
Symphony No. 13 »Babi Yar«
Anatoly Kotcherga bass
Estonian male voice choir
(DG 449 187)

1997
Jean Sibelius
Lemminkäinen Legends and other works
(DG 453 426)

Sergei Rachmaninov
Three one-act operas: Aleko, The Miserly Knight, Francesca da Rimini
Maria Guleghina soprano
Anne Sofie von Otter mezzo-soprano
Sergei Larin tenor
Sergei Leiferkus baritone
Anatoly Kotcherga bass
(Aleko: DG 453 453, The Miserly Knight: DG 453 454, Francesca da Rimini: DG 453 455)

»Entry of the Gladiators«
Marches, overtures and other orchestral pieces by Alfvén, Massenet, Lehár, Delibes, Gounod and others
(DG 453 586)

1999
Maximilian Steinberg
Symphony No. 1, Fantasie dramatique, Prélude symphonique
(DG 457 607)

Arvo Pärt
Fratres, Tabula rasa, Symphony No. 3
Gil Shaham violin
(DG 457 647)

2000
Jean Sibelius
Tapiola, En saga, Spring Song, The Bard, Music from Kuolema
(DG 457 654)

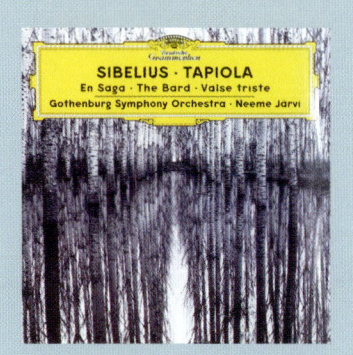

2001
Dmitri Shostakovich
Symphonies Nos. 2–3, Suite from The Bolt
Gothenburg Symphonic Choir
(DG 469 525)

Maximilian Steinberg
Symphony No. 2, Variations for Orchestra
(DG 471 198)

2002
Nikolai Myaskovsky
Symphony No. 6
Gothenburg Symphonic Choir
(DG 471 655)

»Aurora – Music of the Northern Lights«
Nordic orchestral favourites including Alfvén's Midsummer Vigil, Sibelius´ Finlandia and Valse triste, Grieg's Morning Mood and Solveig's Song, Larssons's Romance, Wirén's March from Serenade, Järnefelt's Preludium, Lumbye's Copenhagen Steam Railway Galop and other works
(DG 471 747, 2 CDs)

Rolf Martinsson
Bridge Trumpet Concerto No. 1
Arvo Pärt
Concerto piccolo über B-A-C-H
Eino Tamberg
Trumpet concerto No. 1
Håkan Hardenberger trumpet
(BIS-CD- 1208)

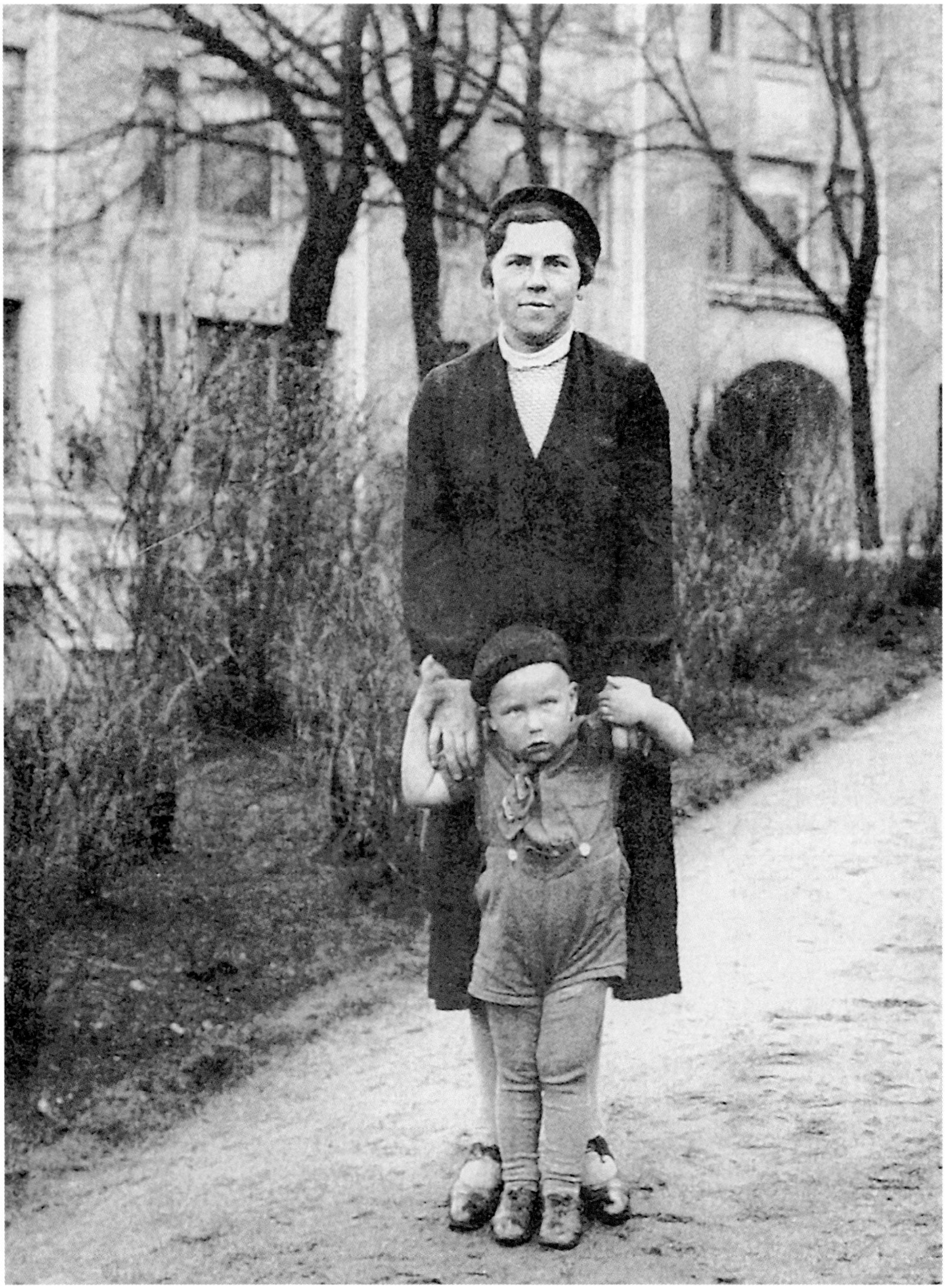

Behind the iron curtain

Neeme Järvi's conducting career can be divided into two: The first was spent behind the iron curtain under a communist regime. The other was spent making a career on his own terms.

He often refers to the destiny of the Estonian people which is also his own. Their history has had a major effect on his artistic development.

Together, we leaf through the thick biography published in Estonia a few years ago, when he was voted the Estonian of the Century. One of the first photographs in the book, which is entitled Maestro, was taken in 1940, the year Russian tanks crossed the border into Estonia. Järvi was three years old at the time and is wearing a pair of long knitted socks. He is cuddling up to his mother Elss. The Second World War was in progress, however this did not prevent Neeme from making his first appearance on Estonian Radio the following year. His performance was no mere game, but was in deadly earnest, he explains. He performed two folk dances on the xylophone.

His elder brother Vallo was also present. Vallo was the first professional musician in the family. 13 years older than his brother, he was a great influence on Neeme. If Vallo played the xylophone then Neeme wanted to play the xylophone too.

When the Russians bombed Tallinn in 1944 the family was living a few miles from the capital. "My mother was

A very young Neeme with his mother Elss in 1940. A photo from Neeme Järvi's collection.

eminently sensible," says Järvi. A year later the war ended, but the Russians stayed.

"Within the official limitations great music was being made in Estonia despite the focus eastwards," he explains.

Estonians were being Russianized but, on the other hand, classical music had a strong position in the Soviet Union. Symphony orchestras were given state support and records were cheap. Neeme Järvi lived in a world of music lovers.

"I was probably about nine or ten years old when I came across a Czech recording of Mahler's fourth symphony," he explains as though it's normal for ten-year-olds to listen to Mahler.

He'd never heard of Mahler at the time.

"I took the record home and played it over and over again."

He became a Mahler fan and had a favourite orchestra to which he would remain loyal for many years: the Czech Philharmonic.

Neeme's school was near his home and he travelled each afternoon to the music school by train and tram into Tallinn. In due course he graduated in music and choral direction. By the age of 16 he was such a skilful percussionist that he was asked to perform a xylophone transcription of the violin part in Khachaturian's violin concerto at a broadcast concert with his elder brother Vallo conducting.

It was 1953, the year of Stalin's death and an important year in Soviet musical life.

Stalin's successor, Khrushchev wanted to increase contact with the West and initiated cultural exchanges. These included invitations to foreign symphony orchestras from Philadelphia, Cleveland, New York, Boston and Munich. They performed in the legendary concert hall in Leningrad with its splendid architecture and magnificent acoustics. Leningrad, or St. Petersburg as it is once more known today, became

Older brother Vallo conducts 16-year-old Neeme on the xylophone in 1953. A photo from Neeme Järvi's collection.

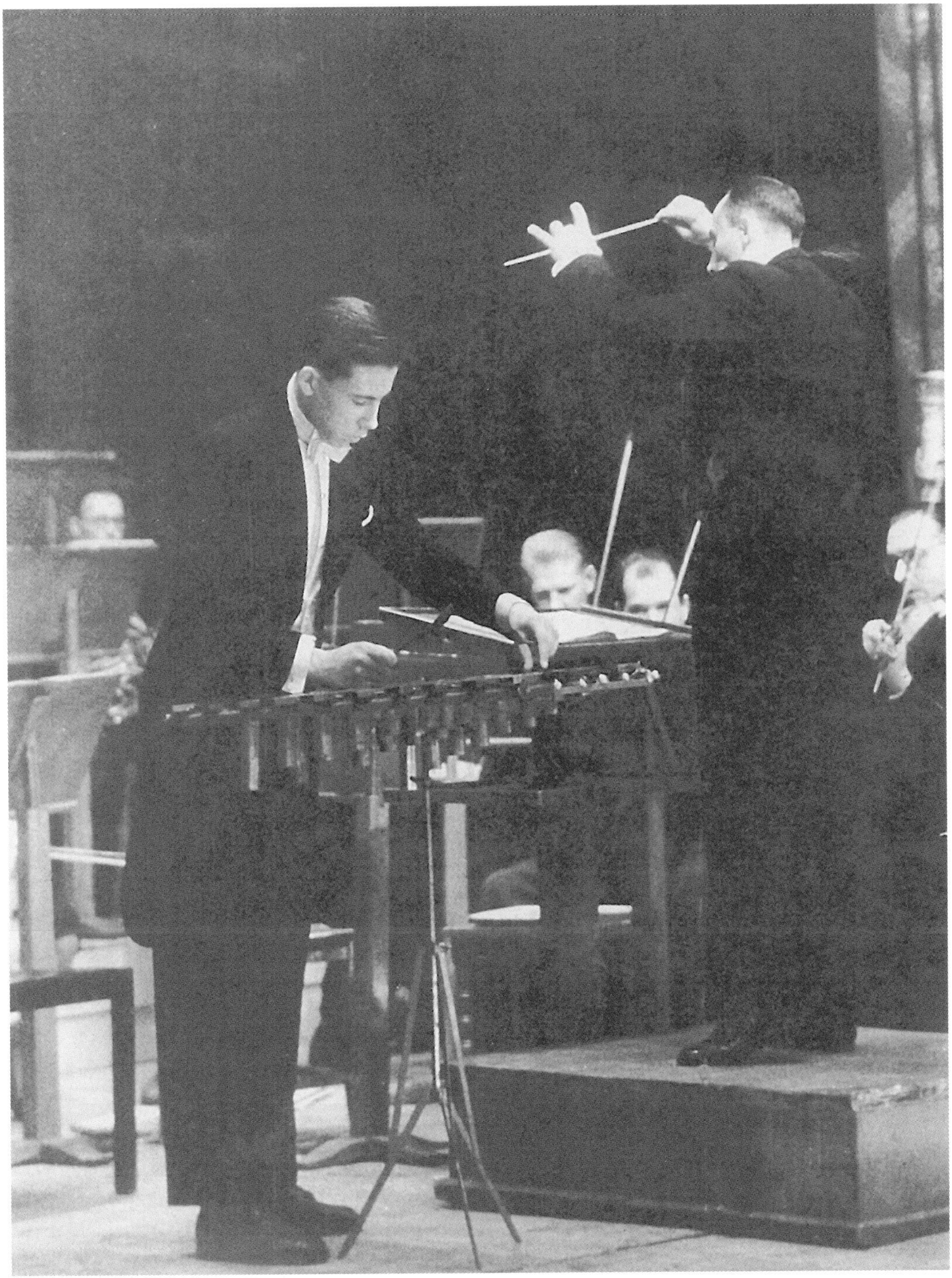

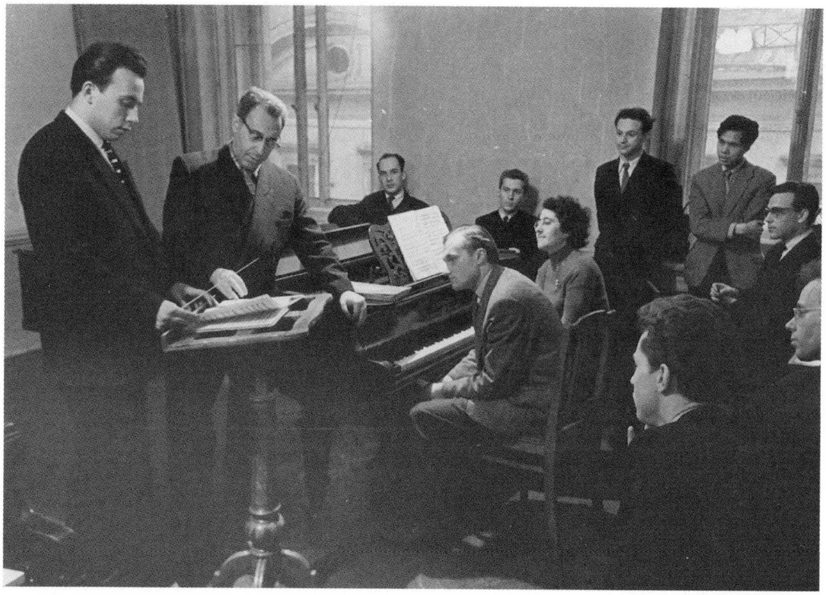

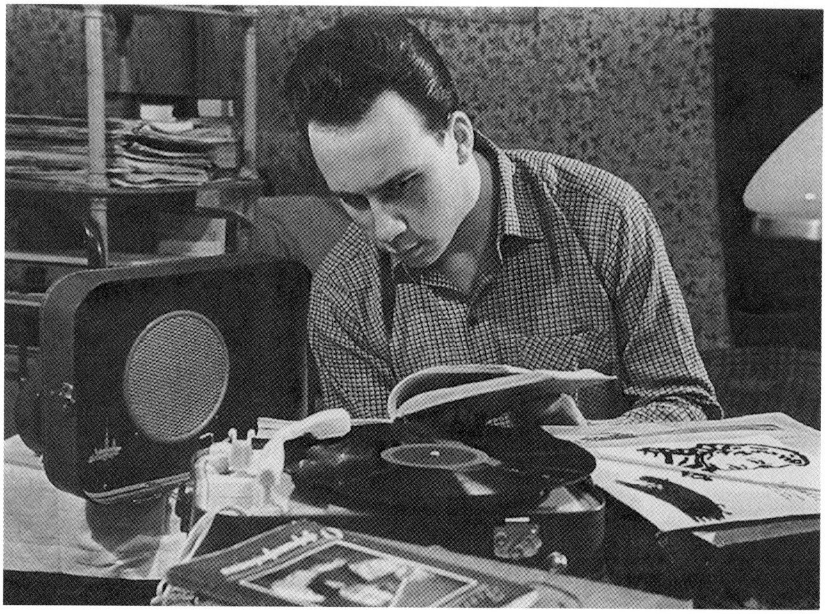

something of a window on the West during the Khrushchev era.

It was to Leningrad, with its famous conservatoire, that Neeme Järvi went to study.

"The Leningrad Philharmonic Orchestra became my second home. I went to concerts every evening, I was fanatic about everything to do with music."

The conservatoire had three symphony orchestras and two student orchestras, and Neeme Järvi was always present. One of the tutors was Evgeny Mravinsky, world famous head of the Leningrad Philharmonic. Other well-known conductors visited, with or without their own orchestra: Sanderling, Stokowski, Bernstein, Karajan, Ormandy and Monteux. His favourite tutor was Nikolai Rabinovich.

"When Rabinovich was tired he usually asked: who wants to conduct? I always wanted to. Sometimes he would cry out no, no that's no good, but I always took the opportunity of having a go. I was happy because I was doing what I loved… music."

Järvi learnt Russian, "street" Russian, as he puts it "because I lived in a dormitory". He has kept his creative approach to languages. He speaks expressive, direct English without unnecessary grammatical diversions. He is famous for greeting the King of Sweden with "Hello King" after a rapturous concert in Munich. The King's response has been kept under wraps. "Hello Maestro" is the hottest tip.

Some people maintain that Neeme Järvi's use of language matches his conducting style. "Speaking with Järvi is like tackling a violent onslaught of words and ideas. They pour out of him," wrote an English reporter.

But let's move back to the 1950s and the Soviet Union. Neeme Järvi and his friends scoured the Leningrad record shops for bargains.

Rabinovich taught Neeme to conduct at the conservatoire in Leningrad. A photo from Neeme Järvi's collection.

Neeme Järvi started his vast record collection very early. A photo from Neeme Järvi's collection.

THE 1985 TOUR OF THE SOVIET UNION

The first tour of the Soviet Union by the GSO in 1985 had to be undertaken without Neeme Järvi because he was *persona non grata* with the Soviet authorities. The Swedish conductor Göran W Nilson replaced him. One of the concerts in Leningrad was magical. Shostakovich's widow sat at the front as Frans Helmerson played Shostakovich's first cello concerto.

"New records were being released all the time. We wrote long lists and shopped like hell."

This was how he began his vast record collection. He probably has the world's largest collection of recordings of Mahler's Fourth Symphony.

"There were plenty of interesting things to learn from old 78s and LPs," he explains. Comparing different conductors' interpretations was a means of gathering know-how. He still searches through record shops for gems from the past when he has time. "But," he mutters, "record shops' classical music sections have shrunk over the years all over the world." This concerns him: "Young people don't acknowledge this kind of music and older people aren't buying discs any more. Record companies are not concerned about trying to promote new talents."

"We have already recorded that symphony, they say, the market is saturated. So what can new conductors and musicians do? How will their interpretations of this music be saved for coming generations?"

When he returned to his home town of Tallinn in 1960 his career took off, and in 1963 he began a 13-year period as chief conductor of the Tallinn Opera. He was also head of the Estonian National Orchestra. Being located at some distance from the Soviet centre of music in Leningrad he decided to test the limits of what was permissible. So Strauss' *Rosenkavalier* and Gershwin's *Porgy and Bess* received discreet Soviet premières in Tallinn under his baton. He performed a great deal of newly written music including many works by Arvo Pärt. Järvi's never ending desire to spotlight and perform new and forgotten pieces has much to do with his years spent under Soviet rule when everything he did was scrutinized. He became a "repertoire expander", which makes him a rarity among international conductors, who, more often than one might imagine, stick to a rather limited number of well known scores.

Szymanowski's second violin concerto, performed at the Gothenburg Concert Hall in January 2002, is an example of rarely heard music that Järvi is determined to tackle.

He sees it as his mission to highlight unknown 20th century composers.

"Nobody really knows about this violin concerto. We play it as though it were a new piece."

During the 1960s and 1970s Neeme Järvi's fame began to grow. In 1971 he won a prestigious conducting competition in Rome and in 1978 received the highest accolade for a conductor from the Soviet Union.

"I made a lot of guest appearances in Moscow, Leningrad and the other major cities. They used to throw me bones, fancy things, like a dog." He performed with "fantastic orchestras", but felt more hemmed in. The fickle Soviet system of control got on his nerves. He was however permitted to visit the USA a few times with different orchestras and in 1979 was able to conduct Tchaikovsky's *Eugène Onegin* at the Metropolitan in New York. But he could only travel when the authorities granted permission.

Järvi's decision to leave the Soviet Union matured gradually. It wasn't easy to get permission to emigrate. But then international politics came to his aid. When the USSR went into Afghanistan in December 1979, relations between East and West soured, and in the diplomatic turbulence that followed Neeme Järvi was suddenly given permission to emigrate to the USA.

A new life opened up – just as the doors to his old life were being bolted.

"It is my belief that not even the most thorough theoretical analysis can reveal the meaning of music or explain a musician's greatness. Despite this one can quickly form a valid impression. Soon after the young Neeme Järvi's first appearance many musicians predicted he would have a future among the world's elite. Even though politics overshadowed Järvi's years in Estonia his actions were fruitful and dynamic. I am convinced that Järvi holds a very significant role for Estonian music. We merely need to look at the number of Estonian symphonic works that have been inspired by him and performed for the first time in many countries, thus establishing them in the repertoire.

It is very pleasing that Estonian music still has a primary place in Järvi's heart."

Jaan Rääts, Estonian composer. 1992.

DMITRI SHOSTAKOVICH

1906–1975

Russian composer and pianist, born in St. Petersburg, died in Moscow. Trained as a pianist and composer at the conservatoire in St. Petersburg. He was a student of Maximilian Steinberg whose Symphonies No. 1 and 2 are available from DG performed by the GSO.

Important works: 15 symphonies, 15 string quartets. Operas *The Nose* (1930) and *Lady Macbeth from the Mtsensk District* (1934), the latter reworked as *Katerina Izmailova* (1963). Ballets: *The Golden Age* (1930) and *The Bolt* (1931). Two piano concertos (1933, 1957), two violin concertos (1948, 1967), 2 cello concertos (1959, 1966). A piano quintet, sonatas for violin, cello and viola and 24 preludes and fugues for piano. In addition, two jazz suites, film and theatre music, and songs with orchestra.

Dmitri Shostakovich

Considered Soviet Russia's greatest and most enigmatic composer. He grew up in poor surroundings, but his talents were soon discovered and at 19, he made his debut with his energetic first symphony. He wrote 15 symphonies in all, which together create a secret history of the Soviet Union. He later dismissed his second and third symphonies as Soviet propaganda and they are not among his best works. In his opera, *Lady Macbeth from Mtsensk*, he presents themes of murder, infidelity and eroticism. It was a great success until Stalin attended a performance. The opera was then publicly denounced in Pravda and Shostakovich was accused of "Western formalism".

From here on Shostakovich composed under constant threat. He was forced to implement stylistic changes, but prior to this he produced one of his most self-critical and original creations: the fourth symphony.

Performing this work remained impossible for many years, and the première had to wait until 1961. The fifth symphony was presented as "a Soviet artist's answer to just criticism", an irony only surpassed by the work itself. Shostakovich had now learnt to write in code and his seventh symphony, *The Leningrad Symphony*, composed during the siege of the city, led to a major international breakthrough.

In 1938 he began his series of 15 string quartets – a succession of personal confessions. Towards the end of the cycle they become dark meditations on death, especially Nos. 7, 8, 10 and 15. Two of the greatest musicians of the last century, violinist David Oistrakh and cellist Mstislav Rostropovich, were among Shostakovich's best friends. He wrote two concertos for both.

No other composer has created works of such genius under threat as Shostakovich. He met the challenge with chameleon-like changes of style but he never compromised. For him, irony became, as it did for Mahler, an artistic necessity, but for Shostakovich it was also a means of staying alive.

○ CD 1.7

Recordings by the GSO on DG: Symphonies Nos. 2 and 3 and Nos. 11-15, Suites from *The Bolt* and *The Golden Age*, Suite from *Hamlet* (film score) and 2 volumes of orchestral songs.

Shostakovich visiting Järvi & family at their summer retreat in Kirbu close to Pärnu in Estonia at the beginning of the 1970s. The boy is Paavo Järvi. Photo from Neeme Järvi's collection.

ENSV RIIKLIK FILHARMOONIA

SÜMFOONIAKONTSERT
СИМФОНИЧЕСКИЙ КОНЦЕРТ

"ESTONIA" KONTSERDISAAL

4. ja 5. SEPTEMBRIL 1989 KELL 19.30

GÖTEBORG'I SÜMFOONIKUD

SOLIST —
HÅKAN HARDENBERGER
(TROMPET)

DIRIGENT —
NEEME JÄRVI

KAVAS:

I
ALFVEN — Sümfooniline poeem "Ja aniõö metsas"
TAMBERG — Trompetikontsert
PÄRT — Sümfoonia nr. 3

II
SIBELIUS — Sümfoonia nr. 2 D-duur, op. 43

Pääsmed müügil filharmoonia kassas alates augustist

Neeme Järvi's return to Tallinn in 1989 was an emotional occasion.

Conductor anonymous

Neeme Järvi has scaled many musical heights over the past 20 years, but none was quite so emotionally charged as the GSO's visit to Tallinn in September 1989. Neeme had spent almost 10 years in exile, was refused permission to enter his native Estonia by the Soviet authorities, and treated as though he did not exist. His name had been erased from every register and the words "conductor anonymous" appended to his recordings. But things changed after the fall of the Berlin wall in November 1989. Järvi, who now had American citizenship, was welcomed back to Estonia.

The tour was triumphant. When his ship docked it was greeted by a brass band and a boy's choir. Old colleagues from the Estonian National Orchestra and The Tallinn Opera assembled to greet their former boss and people on the street cheered him. He was finally able to meet his elder brother Vallo, his only close relative who was still alive.

The four concerts moved everyone involved.

"Järvi was cheered on by the enthusiasm of the audience. He was so touched that he was almost exhausted after the first piece," says Johan Björkman, the GSO's stage manager, who was behind the scenes.

Neeme Järvi's return to Tallinn was an act of symbolic power. Estonia had just begun its struggle for liberation and it was not only music lovers who received Järvi as a hero. The programme was a mixture of Scandinavian, Estonian and Russian music. On 7 September Tamberg's trumpet concerto was performed with Håkan Hardenberger as soloist.

The evening began with the Swedish and Estonian national anthems. Håkan Hardenberger waited for his entrance:

"Nobody in the hall dared to sing the Estonian national anthem because they didn't know how the Russians would respond. But the caretaker behind the scenes sung his heart

The Concert Hall in Tallin was completely sold out.

"We were almost squeezed to death by people who were trying to shake Neeme Järvi's hand. The white-haired president and his elegant wife passed almost unnoticed in the crowd of congratulants."
Camilla Lundberg reporting in Expressen from the Estonia tour

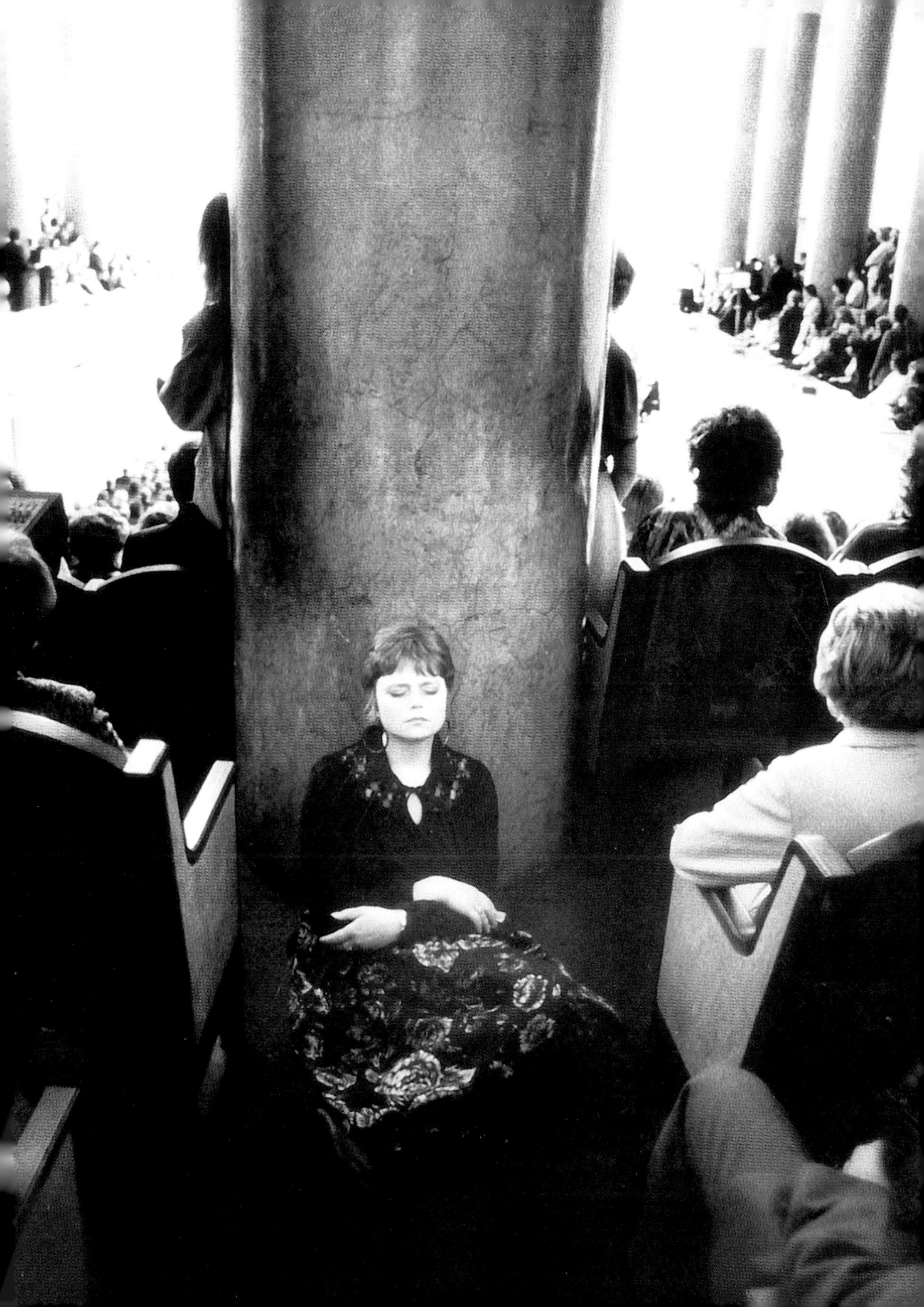

Astrid Lindgren and Neeme Järvi in Tallinn in 1989.

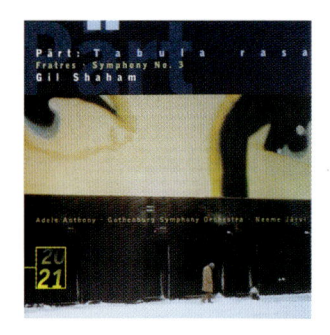

CD 1.11

out with tears running down his cheeks."

Hardenberger summarises the evening in two words: "incredibly moving."

In 1991 the Russian tanks withdrew and Neeme Järvi regained all his civil rights. He now visits Estonia regularly and returns each year to support musical development. Each summer he directs a summer school for conductors in Pärnu, a few miles from Tallinn.

Astrid Lindgren, the famous Swedish author, was in the audience during one of the Tallinn concerts. Her good friend Ilon Wikland, the illustrator of many of her books, had returned home to Estonia to receive an award and Astrid was her travelling companion.

"When we realised that Astrid Lindgren would be there, it was my job to arrange the song *Here comes Pippi Longstocking* to pay homage to her," says Lars-Göran Carlsson, principal trombonist with the GSO.

"There was a grand piano but no score. It was late in the afternoon, a few minutes before the concert, but I somehow managed to make an arrangement for brass and percussion. When we began playing the song Astrid stood up and turned into a little girl who danced and skipped down the centre isle all the way up to the stage where she was presented with a garland of flowers."

"The ovations from the audience were incredible; something I'll never forget."

Arvo Pärt

One of the musical greats of the modern era, Arvo Pärt has reached cult status with his own festivals and selling thousands of records. He experimented with aleatory and twelve tone music, and made friends with Neeme Järvi at the Estonian Radio when Järvi conducted his works. These performances were subject to the whims of the authorities, some were censored while others were later awarded prizes.

Pärt's career falls into four distinctive periods: up until 1968, his experiments were dominated by serial techniques, which were fired off in collage form in the cello concerto *Pro et Contra*, where beautiful baroque-like sections clash with powerful dissonances. After exploring medieval choral music, Pärt departed from 20th century musical idioms in his Third Symphony which looks back to the romantic tradition. He was strongly influenced by orthodox liturgical music and embarked on an inward journey that altered his creative approach completely. His personal synthesis is presented in pieces such as *Tabula rasa, Cantus in memoriam Benjamin Britten* and *Fratres*.

Pärt became a pioneer of European "holy minimalism" with its strong spiritual content and repeated simple triads with hypnotic power. A number of his pieces have reached a wide audience, and for today's stressed city dweller, the quiet and deeply religious Pärt has become the prophet of sincerity. Recordings for ECM featuring violinist Gidon Kremer, the Kronos Quartet and the Hilliard ensemble have sold in vast numbers.

The GSO has performed and toured with the Third Symphony on several occasions. Håkan Hardenberger premiered *Concerto piccolo über B-A-C-H* in 1994 with the GSO and Neeme Järvi at a guest performance in Vienna the same year.

ARVO PÄRT BORN 1935

Estonian composer born in Paide, Estonia. He was a student of Heino Eller at the conservatoire in Tallinn, worked at the Estonian Radio (1958-67), emigrated to Vienna in 1980 and then moved to Berlin where he has lived since 1981.
Important works: Symphony No. 3 (1971) dedicated to Neeme Järvi. *Tabula rasa* and *Cantus in memoriam Benjamin Britten* (1977), *Fratres* (1983) *Johannespassion* (1982), *Berlin Mass* (1991), *Silhouan's Song* (1991) and *Kanon pokajanen* (1998).

Recordings: The GSO and Neeme Järvi recorded Symphony No. 3, *Fratres* and *Tabula rasa* with Gil Shaham for DG, and *Concerto piccolo* über B-A-C-H with Håkan Hardenberger for BIS. Many other works by Pärt are available from ECM and BIS.

Järvi and Pärt

The programme at the Concert Hall in Gothenburg on Thursday, 10 May 2001, included music by Arvo Pärt, Carl Nielsen and Joseph Haydn with Neeme Järvi conducting.

As Pärt's *Cantiques des degrés* came to a close Järvi encouraged the audience to carry on applauding. The otherwise shy Arvo Pärt, who was in the audience, climbed the stage.

Here, in this moment's warm and thunderous applause is the distillation of Neeme Järvi's life; his old friend Arvo Pärt is the link to the music of his native land, to the old days when Järvi and Pärt worked together at the Estonian Radio. The deeply religious Pärt was then a recording engineer. He was forced to compose at night because the Soviet arbiters of taste, not surprisingly, had little interest in sacred music.

The première of Arvo Pärt's *Credo* by the Estonian Radio Symphony Orchestra in 1979 was one of the reasons why Neeme decided to leave Estonia.

"The regulations said that the composers' union had to approve new pieces by Estonian composers before performing them, but this time I didn't bother about the rules," Järvi says.

The quotations from the Bible hidden in *Credo* caused a scandal and people at the radio station were fired.

"But because I was the principal conductor, both of Estonia's Radio Symphony Orchestra and at the opera house, I was in a strong position. They couldn't get rid of me that easily."

"It was a very special concert," he explains.

"We played the piece twice. Both Pärt and I left Estonia the following year."

Arvo Pärt and Neeme Järvi at the concert in May 2001.

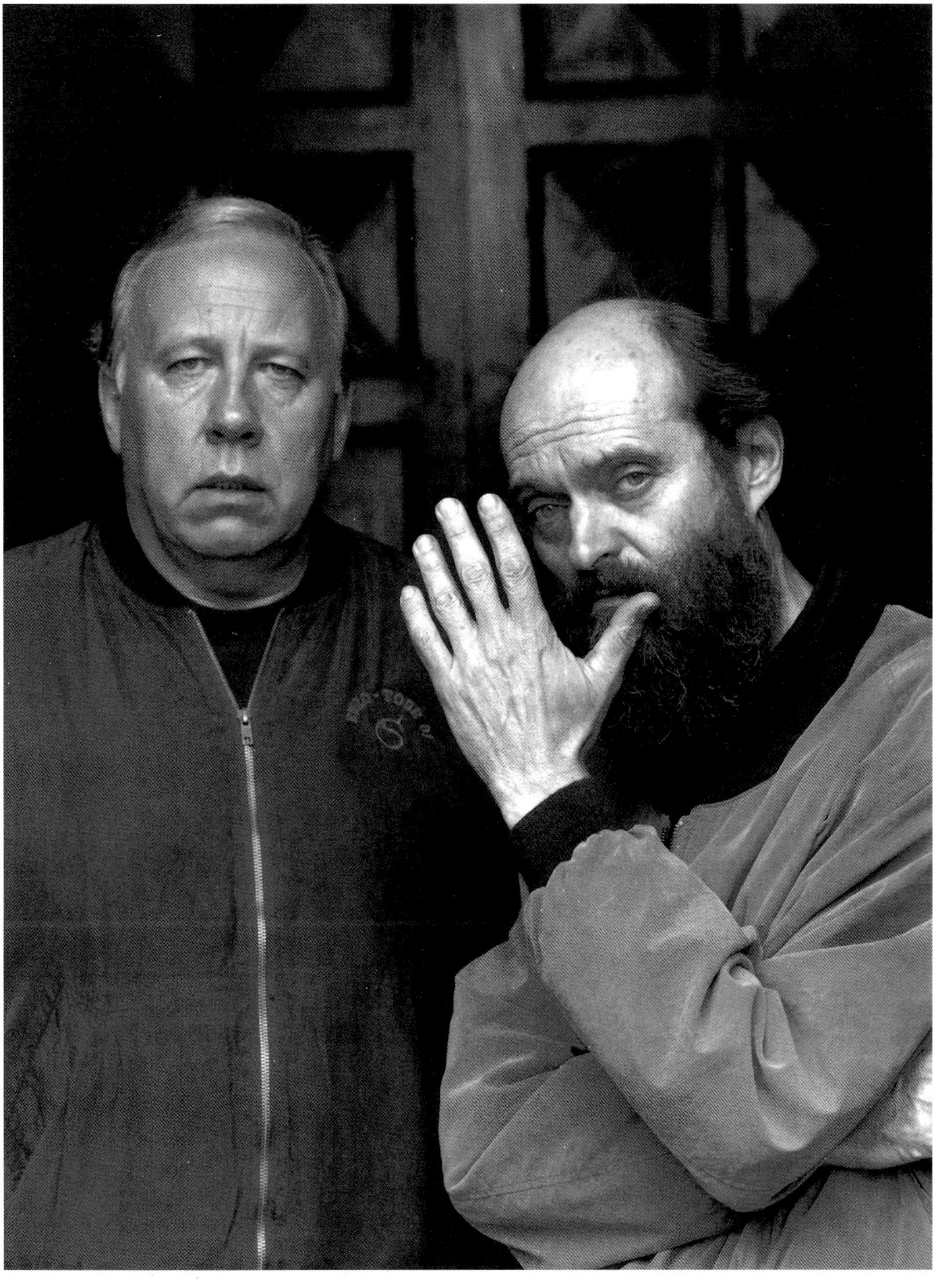

TEATRO DE
La Maestranza

22 de agosto

ORQUESTA SINFONICA DE GOTEMBURGO

Director:
Neeme Järvi

Solista:
Cristina Ortiz, piano

I

La Noche de San Juan
Hugo Alfven

Concierto para piano y orquesta núm. 2
Wilhelm Stenhammar

II

El Pájaro de Fuego
(versión integra)
Igor Stravinsky

El concierto será
comienzo a las
21.00 horas

Citizen of the world and Gothenburg

"We are now in Italy". Neeme Järvi leans forward and studies the photo for a second before he continues: "It rained just before the concert and we didn't know whether we were going to be able to perform, but the weather cleared… and it was a tremendous evening."

The audience was seated in a magnificent garden. The podium and the orchestra were on a terrace high above Salerno Bay and its steep cliffs. Behind the musicians, the Mediterranean regained its azure blue as the rain cleared. It's not difficult to imagine the warm breeze of a July evening blowing the music far across land and sea. This must be among the most beautiful locations for a concert, anywhere.

"We played Wagner," Järvi explains, "Wagner wrote Parsifal not far from here."

The audience was also treated to Grieg, Brahms and Haydn. And Sibelius' No. 2, the orchestra's signature. The Ravello Festival tour is a wonderful memory, but is it his happiest memory? If not, what is?

Neeme Järvi has many to choose from. Somebody has worked out that he has conducted more than 1,100 concerts in 125 cities with 72 different orchestras.

This week however, he is on home ground. He has also been music director in Detroit for the past 12 years and is principal guest conductor of the Japan Philharmonic Orchestra.

Concert with a view. Ravello Italy 1987.

He still has a relationship with the Royal Scottish National Orchestra, where he was principal conductor for many years. But no relationship has been as intense as that with the GSO. Twenty-three years have passed since he arrived at the Concert Hall for the first time. Next to his seat in the conductor's room there is a memento on the wall from an even earlier period, the time the hall was built. A sketch by Sven X:et Erixon illustrating the artist's design of a huge tapestry for the foyer. Järvi has been photographed in front of this painting on numerous occasions over the years.

Neeme Järvi really likes the Gothenburg Concert Hall. He considers it to be one of the finest in the world. And he feels at home there.

This week's rehearsals work out as planned, according to the following pattern:

At 10 am on Tuesday Järvi steps briskly onto the podium, dressed in a burgundy-coloured polo-necked jersey and carrying his reading glasses. Tchaikovsky's *Capriccio Italien* is the first piece. A romantic work with many interpretative possibilities.

Järvi is generally considered to be a notable Tchaikovsky conductor. A quick hello to the musicians, then he begins – ta ta tam, ta tam. The music starts, interrupted by Järvi's brief instructions: correct rhythm, please – no time to pause here, he expresses it with hand and song – la la, la la. Movement complete.

Thank you.

At one point trumpeter Paul Spjuth refers to the score: "That's not how it is written," he says.

"Too bad," Järvi replies. Laughter. They reach agreement. Spjuth tries it again.

Järvi: "Now it's right."

Spjuth: "That was better."

The atmosphere among the players is friendly and attentive. Järvi turns to the violinists: Somebody was lagging behind. As he goes through the violin part, the winds relax. Björn Bohlin who plays the cor anglais, whittles away at one of his reeds. He makes them himself from a bamboo-like plant, which means a lot of fiddly work at the beginning of a concert week.

There's some whispering: Mårten Larsson, who is section leader, has bought cream buns for the woodwinds.

Järvi raises his hand – Morten Agerup's tuba makes a sound. A hand up – stop. Tap, tap, tap with the baton: no, no, no. It should be moderato: ti ta, ti ta, ti ta. This is how rehearsals go, and there are moments when individual quality shines through: when Bohlin inserts the correct reed and plays his solo it sounds really – well what can one say? Fantastic is too flat a word. It is difficult to choose adjectives for describing music. One thing is certain, the *Capriccio Italien* is a very melodic piece.

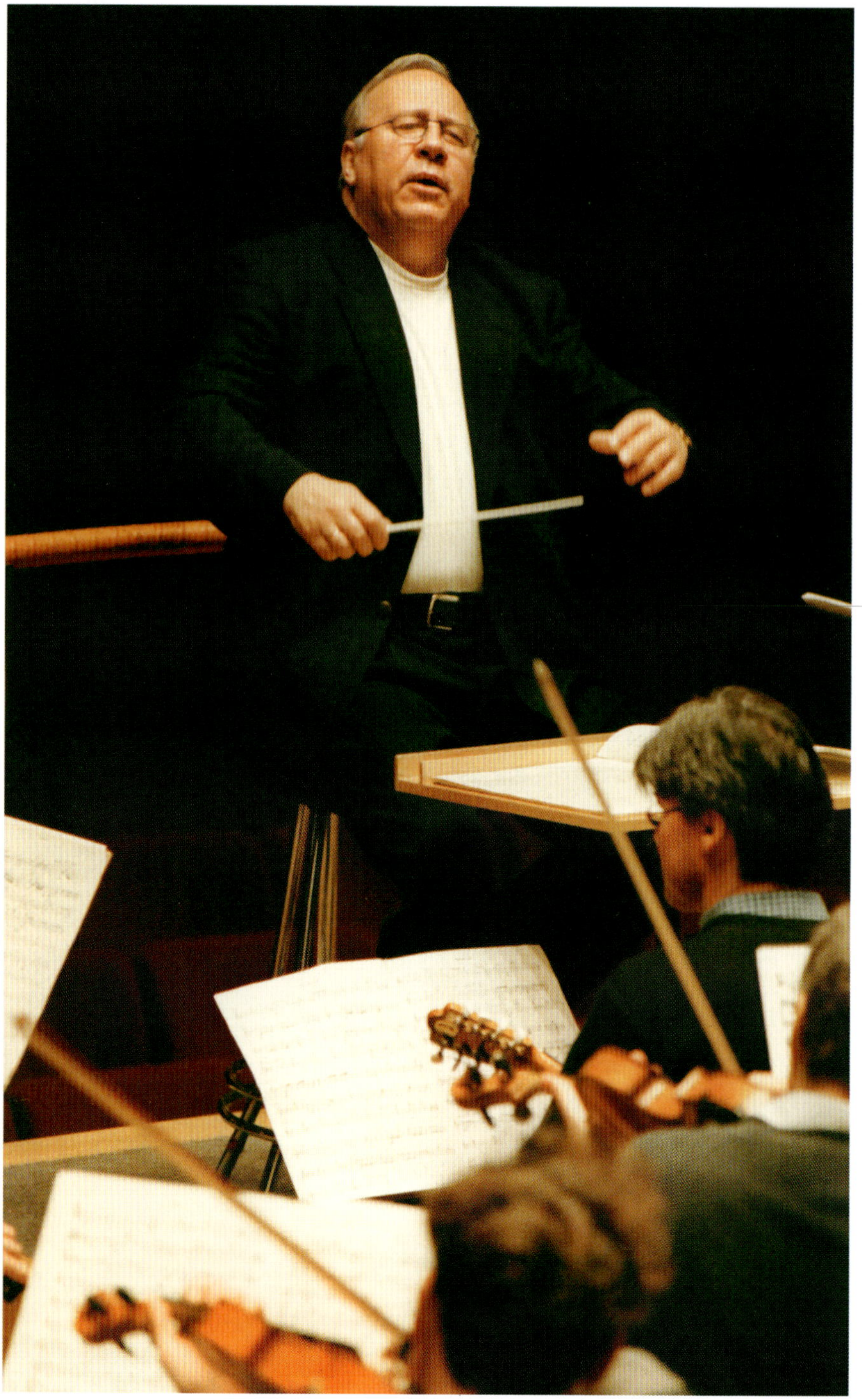

All the sections will be integrated to form a single enjoyable piece by Friday evening. Tchaikovsky's music will then be projected throughout the hall and when everything is let loose the listener can experience how the music moves through the air, as if rising from the floor itself, through the audience's feet up to the roots of their hair.

Each performance is a small miracle; with a magic of its own.

When Järvi is asked about the highlights of his career he reflects on the various tours.

"Japan," he says finally, "is always fantastic because they have such good audiences there. And superb concert halls. They are building new ones all the time." The Japanese perform so well (the GSO toured Japan for the fourth time in November 2002) and if you tour there you really have to work hard." There are other wonderful memories, too, and he has trouble choosing from among them. "Our work is extremely fulfilling…" he explains, "but also very hard. Travelling from one city to another is not easy. Performing the same repertoire time after time can be difficult, because as an artist you need variation. But there have, of course, been special occasions – Ravello was great."

Neeme Järvi is an American citizen. He likes to spend some of his spare time at his house in Palm Beach. "It's always warm in Florida." The panoramic view from his house in Detroit is also marvellous and the apartment in New York is right in the very centre, near the Lincoln Center. From his window at Viktor Rydbergsgatan in Gothenburg he would be able to see the famous statue of Poseidon, if the Concert Hall did not obstruct the view.

When he is in Gothenburg he mainly stays in the vicinity of Götaplatsen. There is little time for anything other than work. But with his sense of humour and his enjoyment of life, the people of Gothenburg see him as one of their own. Indeed they would like to be able to claim him as a native! He has been awarded an honorary doctor's degree by Gothenburg University, and has been named an honorary citizen as well as having a tram named after him.

Where does he feel most at home?

"With my lifestyle," he says with a little sigh, "you don't live anywhere in particular. I'm like a gypsy, travelling from one place to another."

But, quite naturally, he is Estonian and nothing else, "even if I don't have time to go back as often as I would like."

Neeme Järvi left Estonia in January 1980, together with his wife Liilia and their three children, Paavo, Maarika and Kristjan. The family stayed in Vienna and then travelled to the USA. Two major agents offered Järvi their services. He chose Columbia Artists and immediately received engagements as guest conductor in Boston, Philadelphia and New York. "I had refugee status and immediately started earning money so I could start a new life from scratch."

Initially the family lived with Estonian friends. "We had a wonderful friend, Mrs Bostrom, who was born in New York, but whose parents were Estonian. We lived with her until we could afford the mortgage on a house of our own. Kristjan was seven, Maarika sixteen and Paavo seventeen."

The family knew that they would not be able to return to Estonia and decided to invest everything in their new life. Better look forwards rather than backwards now that the Western world finally lay open. But they had not foreseen that they would be severing their roots so completely. The Soviet authorities didn't make things easier. Their refusal to allow Järvi to visit his mother as she lay dying was very painful.

Järvi seeks out his Estonian friends when he visits Gothenburg. Maria and Eero Tarjus, who came to Sweden at the beginning of the 1950s and are his oldest friends here. Eero Tarjus has now been retired for many years. He was once the principal of the Estonian School in Gothenburg and leader of the Estonian Male Voice Choir. The composer Eduard Tubin was the first natural link between the families, since Eero Tarjus and Tubin were friends in Estonia.

Eduard Tubin is one of many composers that Järvi admires and likes to promote. "The 20th century has given us so many wonderful composers," he explains, mentioning Stravinsky, Prokofiev and Shostakovich. But there are others too: "Tubin lived in Sweden for 40 years but the Swedes don't consider him Swedish and the Estonians don't consider him Estonian, because he left the country as early as 1944. He lived in a twilight zone between two nations and, despite being a fantastic composer, he never became really well known."

Maria and Eero Tarjus live in a small, cosy house surrounded by luxuriant countryside in Landvetter just outside

Gothenburg. This is where Neeme and Liilia Järvi relax in the silence of the forest. Bouquets from Järvi's concerts wind up in Maria's flower vases. "We have a lot of laughs and many long chats," says Eero Tarjus, "friendship cannot be manufactured, it must develop naturally."

Järvi considers his performances of Mahler's symphonies to be among his fondest memories of his work with the GSO. "Mahler's time is now, and when we perform his music there is always a full house." That was how it was in November 2001, with extra coverage because Järvi had just recovered after his illness. "Mahler's Third Symphony was the sole work this evening. A very gripping interpretation in every way, loving and balanced," according to music critic Magnus

Haglund, whose review stated:

"Mahler is the music of rememberance, but here I get a strong sense that the sound is reminiscent of the orchestra's own history, just as if it was Stenhammar himself conducting, and that the echoes of bygone concerts from the old concert hall at Heden found their way to Götaplatsen."

He continued: "It's difficult not to exaggerate in this expansive music. Rather than employing grandiose and exaggerated gestures, Järvi lets a sense of intimacy dominate. He trusts the music to speak for itself and conjures up a sweetness in Mahler's art of instrumentation which is difficult to resist."

And yes. Järvi has had ideas about composing himself, and his thoughts drift to Gustav Mahler, when discussing the subject. But, to be able to compose one has to have peace and quiet. And access to beautiful, natural surroundings that encourage contemplation. Composing requires one to be in the same place for a long time, "one must be free, and dedicated to something." It takes days to find concentration. Those days are rare in the constant hustle and bustle of a conductor's diary.

"Only Mahler managed to be a magnificent conductor and composer," he continues. "He lived in Vienna and Salzburg, and in beautiful, inspiring summer retreats in the Alps… He was a genius and wrote glorious symphonies."

Järvi points towards the window; it's 4.30 in the afternoon and dusk is already beginning to fall. January's ice-cold haze begins to settle over Gothenburg. The warm July evenings and the natural beauty of Ravello in Italy seem very far away. But, on the other hand, he reminds himself: Gustav Mahler was a workaholic with a traumatic life. "He was only 51 when he died."

Liilia and Neeme Järvi rarely miss the opportunity to pick mushrooms when they are in season in Landvetter. Especially Liilia, who is from Russia, knows her mushrooms. Some of them are immediately prepared in Maria Tarju's little kitchen; though without cream, because Liilia keeps an eye on her husband's waistline. A top class conductor feels at his best if he maintains a healthy lifestyle.

Postcards from the four corners of the globe regulary drop into the Tarju's letterbox in Landvetter.

Neeme Järvi keeps regular contact with his children through letters and postcards and by phone. Despite constantly being on the road, and even when Liilia Järvi is responsible for the practical management of the family, Neeme has managed to maintain a close relationship with all of his children. His youngest son, Kristjan, accompanied his father on a number of long tours with the GSO. One musician recalls: "Never have I seen Neeme Järvi so exhilarated as the time when he and Kristjan sat alone talking in a train compartment. Neeme was just like a boy."

When Neeme Järvi speaks about Lukas, Kristjan's little son and Neeme's first grandchild, he breaks into a huge smile; just think about all the things that child can do already. Having a grandson means a great deal to Neeme.

Lukas Järvi has a lot to live up to. His mother, Leila Josefowicz, is a violinist. His father Kristjan is a pianist and conductor who, aged 20, started The Absolute Ensemble in New York, a much talked-of cross-over group of musicians who play everything from renaissance music to rock. Kristjan Järvi is known in Sweden as principal conductor of the Norrlandsoperan in Umeå.

Lukas' uncle Paavo has conducted several of the USA's and Europe's best-known symphony orchestras, including the GSO. He has been principal guest conductor of the Royal

Gustav Mahler

One of the major conductors who revolutionised opera performance, and a dedicated perfectionist who schooled the modern symphony orchestra. Mahler was a complex person, a late romantic doubter and a modernist precursor, a despairing egocentric who sought universal truths. He married Alma Schindler in 1901. She was a talented composer who, on her marriage, relinquished her own musical ambitions.

Mahler wrote scarcely any chamber music, no solo concertos, operas or masses, but his symphonies raised the genre to new heights. "My time will come," he said, but only in the 1960s did it do so. Twenty years later his symphonies were among the most popular. But it was as a conductor and opera director that he made his career, famous for his uncompromising faithfulness to the composer's intentions – a sworn enemy to laziness and bad musical habits. Mahler only composed during the summer in the Austrian countryside.

Stenhammar was an early admirer and he performed Symphony No. 4 in 1917 in Gothenburg. The GSO's cycle of Mahler symphonies was completed during the spring of 2002, when Mark Wigglesworth conducted the Tenth symphony. Only with the enlargement of the GSO, it was possible to perform Mahler's grand scores as originally intended.

Except for the fourth, all of Mahler's symphonies are of huge proportions and require very large orchestras. The detailed perfection of his scores is unsurpassed, and they present everything from the intricate rhythms of Austrian Ländler and ghostly waltzes, to lyrical depictions of nature.

A symphony, according to Mahler, should be like life itself. It should contain everything.

GUSTAV MAHLER 1860–1911

Austrian conductor and composer, born in the Bohemian village of Kalist to Jewish parents, died in Vienna. Grew up in poverty with 13 brothers and sisters of which 7 died in childhood. Trained in Vienna, where he got to know Bruckner. Worked as a conductor in Prague, Budapest, Hamburg, Vienna and New York at the Metropolitan Opera and with the New York Philharmonic Orchestra.

Important works: 10 symphonies, the final one posthumous plus *Das Lied von der Erde* (1911), described by Mahler himself as a song symphony. Songs with orchestra: *Des Knaben Wunderhorn* (1892-98), *Lieder eines fahrenden Gesellen* (1885), *Kindertotenlieder* (1904).

Recordings: Symphony No. 8 with the GSO and Järvi (the recording, made at the Gothenburg Opera, is dedicated to the victims of the Estonia ferry disaster) on BIS. Järvi has recorded a number of the orchestral songs and Symphonies Nos. 1, 3, 4, 5 and 6 with the Royal Scottish National Orchestra for Chandos.

A third generation Järvi conducts Beethoven's Ninth in Mahler's orchestration. His name is Lukas Järvi, the year is 2002.
Photo Neeme Järvi's collection.

Stockholm Philharmonic, principal conductor in Malmö and is now head of the Cincinnati Symphony. Lukas' aunt Maarika is a flautist. She made her debut in 1989 at the Gothenburg Concert Hall with her father conducting. Vallo Järvi's son Teet is a cellist in Finland, a professor at the conservatoire in Lahti and married to a pianist. All five children play the piano.

"We weren't expected to become musicians," Paavo has said, "It's something we wanted to be. Dad was so wrapped up in music and we were always allowed to be with him while he was working. I spent as much of my time as I could at his rehearsals."

Music was always on top of the Järvi family's agenda. Neeme Järvi's parents played the mandolin and guitar, and sang. And when he became a father himself and was listening to records at home he let the children follow the score as an educational game.

"Conducting is in our genes," he states. "It is a family disease and I love it."

The three Järvi conductors are close to each other. Paavo Järvi talks to Neeme almost daily and much of their telephone conversations are naturally about music. In 2001 they recorded three Estonian symphonies in Manchester. Neeme Järvi conducted Willem Kapp, Paavo did Arvo Pärt and Kristjan took on Eduard Tubin. The recordings brought them together.

"That's a good recording, I sometimes say when the family is playing CDs at home. Whose is it? It's yours, of course, they say. Many of my recordings are actually quite good. There is a kind of audacity in the interpretation which is different from the ususal run of things. Sometimes I get criticised for it, but that's the way I am."

So far he has recorded around 90 CDs with the GSO.

Does he have a favourite?

"Possibly the Rachmaninov recordings, they were very successful. Or perhaps Prokofiev's The Fiery Angel? Or Tchaikovsky's Mazeppa – very good – and Shostakovich's symphonies and Steinberg of course, Maximilian Steinberg, an unknown composer. Not forgetting Stenhammar, I can't just pick one or two. Each time I play something I think, oh, I really love this music. We performed a marvellous version of

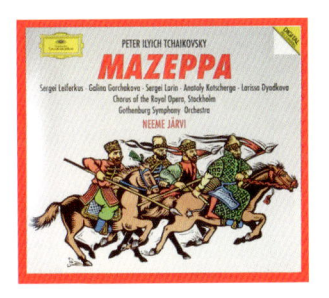

◉ CD 1.8

The three Järvi conductors, Kristjan, Neeme and Paavo, on the cover of the BBC Music Magazine, October 2001.

"I love mp3, I never thought that I would be able to manage such technical things, but now I can download 20 gigabytes of my favourite music."
Neeme Järvi

"Madonna is my secret vice. She is talented, beautiful and she has a great voice."
Neeme Järvi

Sibelius' second symphony last autumn for Deutsche Grammophon …"

During the week of the interview it's time for more recording, a live version of Sibelius' seventh symphony, this time round.

Friday morning. The musicians are prepared and everything is ready in the recording room above the stage.

Will Järvi be able to make the music come alive during the concert? The engineer and producer have to be patient. The opening number is by Szymanowski, then comes Sibelius. After the break they are to perform Tchaikovsky.

The disparate sounds of instruments being tuned is mixed with murmuring from the audience. Neeme walks down the narrow stairs behind the stage. Through the stage door he can see the orchestra.

A deep breath, and total concentration. Stage manager Johan Björkman makes sure that everything is ready for Järvi's entry and opens the door onto the stage. The baton is waiting on the stand along with the score. Applause. A quick bow. He turns his back to the audience, faces the orchestra, raises his baton: "Let's make music".

A place in town

In the past, during the summer, musicians of the orchestra could be heard playing wherever people gathered: at the spa bandstand, in the public gardens and at the beach. Until 1937 the musicians were only contracted for seven months a year and they had to find other means of support for the rest of the year.

When the GSO and Neeme Järvi started annual concerts in Slottsskogen on 3 June 1984, open-air concerts were very much a thing of the past. The combination of a large symphony orchestra and a beautiful park seemed new and exciting. And audiences flocked to the concert with their picnic hampers and pushchairs.

They were treated to popular music of the day: the title theme of the TV series The Onedin Line, a medley from the *Sound of Music*, favourites from *West Side Story*, the most famous Swedish summer hymn, *Den blomstertid nu kommer*, and one of Neeme Järvi's favourite jazz tunes, Duke Ellington's *Solitude* (which he recorded with the Detroit Symphony Orchestra in 1993).

This was the orchestra's first open air concert in a long time. The concerts in the park are now an annual tradition, marking the commencement of summer for the people of Gothenburg.

The concerts are not conducted exclusively by Järvi, though he was a very keen park conductor in the 1980s. He thoroughly enjoys these concerts. They remind him of Tallinn's famous festival, which he directed for many years, and which is also held outdoors.

The concerts in Slottsskogen were an immediate success. "Slottsskogen is the best concert hall I know," Järvi said in 1988 to an enraptured journalist in a typical interview minutes before the concert. ("The next moment he pressed his nose into a lilac bush, 'enchanting,' he exclaimed, and laughed in a world-famous-conductor sort of way.")

It's easy to fall for Järvi's charm.

The concert in Slottsskogen in June 1988 was special because it was a dress rehearsal for the Minnesota Midsummer Festival in Minneapolis, which was part of the large-scale New Sweden Jubilee during which Järvi conducted six concerts with the GSO.

The tour included performances by the famous Swedish male voice choir, Orphei Drängar, Dalecarlian fiddlers, singers Elisabeth Erikson, Elisabeth Söderström and Lill Lindfors and the actor Max von Sydow. The GSO also performed Mahler's eighth symphony together with the Minneapolis Symphony Orchestra and an 800-strong choir, as Mahler intended.

There was also a première during the US tour: Bengt Hallberg's specially commissioned *Glädjens dansande sträng*, a mix of elements of jazz, classical and folk music. This was first played to the audience in Slottsskogen.

That year's concert was also special in another sense. The

Thousands of people from Gothenburg listening to the GSO in Slottsskogen in 1998.

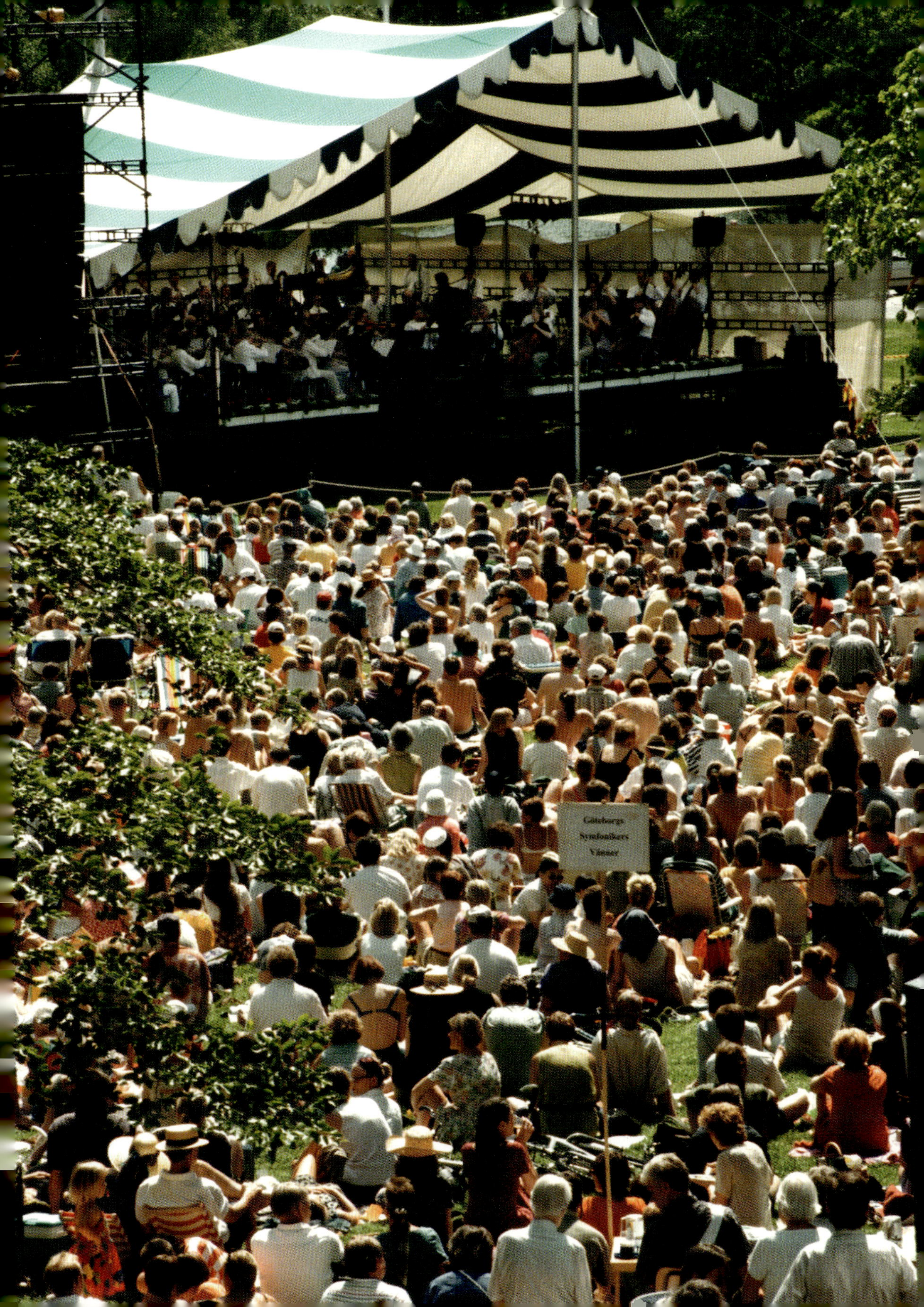
Göteborgs
Symfonikers
Vänner

"I specially remember the first rehearsal for the gala held during the World Athletics Championships in Gothenburg. The Neeme-GSO team were impressive. The musical telepathy between the conductor and orchestra was excellent and all of my musical intentions were read instinctively and as fast as lightning by both Neeme and the GSO. A musical memory that I will carry with me for the rest of my life."
Christian Lindberg, trombone soloist, in June 2002.

The audience at the closing concert during the World Athletics Championships. Götaplatsen 1995.

rain poured down for hours before the concert. Despite this, some 8,000 people turned up to listen. The rain stopped fifteen minutes before the concert and the sun appeared in time for the opening number. As the popular folk tune known as *Gärdebylåten* sounded forth in an unusually powerful orchestral arrangement the sun was shining brightly.

Taking a symphony orchestra, with its expensive, rain-sensitive instruments, outdoors in the climate of western Sweden is risky. But today there is a roof to protect the orchestra. "The date for the concert was chosen scientifically with regard to the weather forecast," says Bjørn Simensen, the orchestra's manager at the beginning of the 1980s.

"I had read about open-air concerts and thought that was something we should do in Gothenburg. On Sundays I scouted for a suitable site. The city park Trädgårdsföreningen was a little too small, so in the end I opted for Slottsskogen. But I was concerned about the weather. I consulted meteorologists who told me that there was least risk of rain at the beginning of June. When I woke up on that first June morning and saw the sun shining I was a happy man."

The concerts in Slottsskogen transported the orchestra from the somewhat overawing Concert Hall and showed it off to the citizens in Gothenburg. When the concerts started in 1984 there were doubts as to whether orchestral music was of interest to blue collar workers. People working for Volvo were asked their views by the newspapers. Volvo, after all, was the sponsor and the money could have been spent on other projects. "There's a guy here on the factory floor who likes this stuff, Lennart in the paint shop. It would be cheaper to send him by plane to Stockholm than to invest millions here," one interviewee said.

The concerts in Slottsskogen changed people's attitude toward the GSO. People who had never bought tickets for a

GÖTAPLATSEN

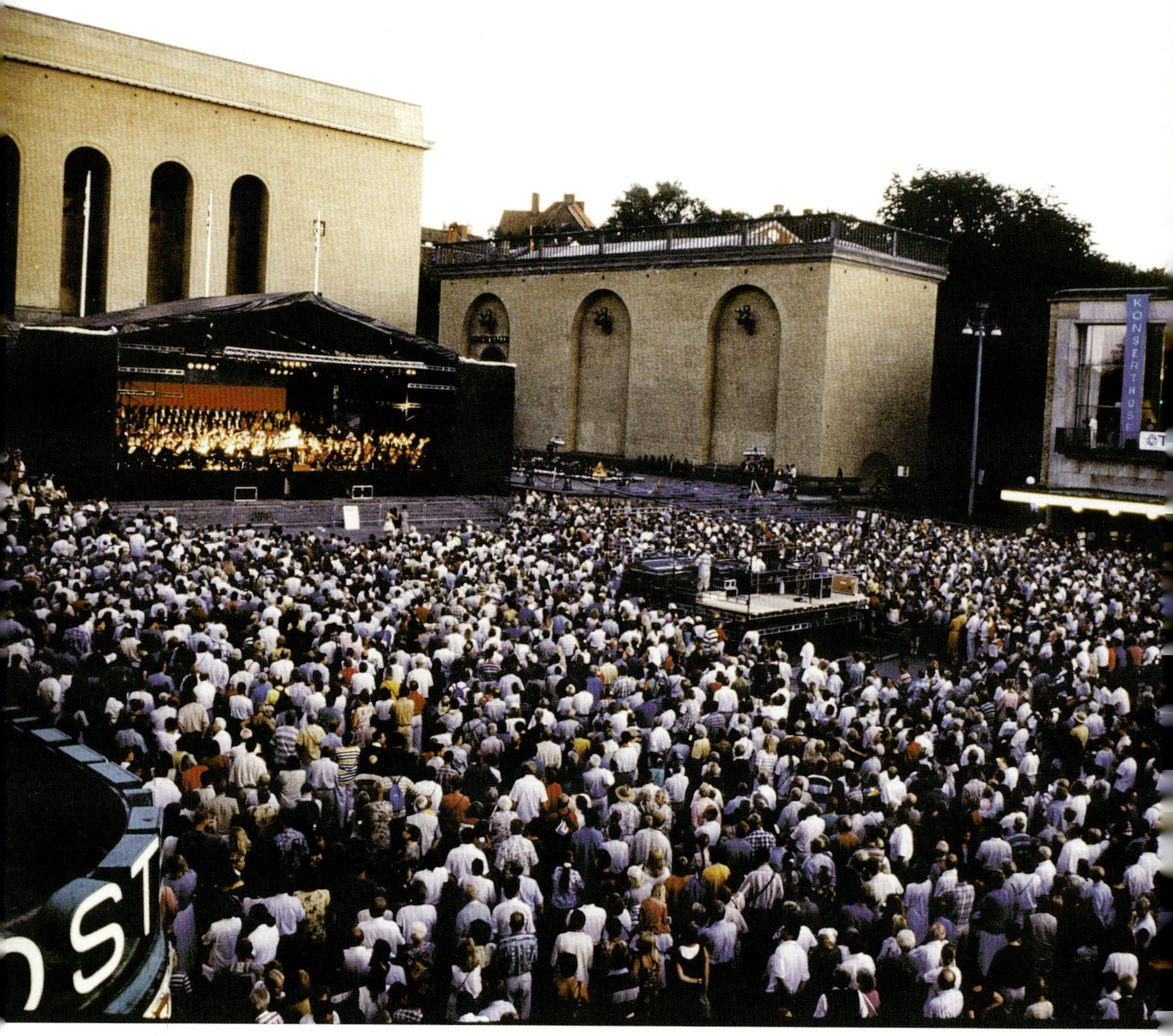
KONSERTHUSE

performance at the Concert Hall suddenly discovered classical music. And even if the abbreviation GSO will never be as well known as IFK, ÖIS and GAIS (Gothenburg football teams), pride of the city's world-renowned national orchestra is apparent, even among people who prefer other kinds of music.

The GSO now plays an active part in the life of the city. Thousands of people began their Millennium New Year celebrations by listening to a performance by the GSO of Mahler's *Resurrection Symphony* at Götaplatsen. When the Liseberg amusement park celebrated its 75th anniversary in 1998, the GSO performed Stravinsky's *Firebird suite* and Alfvén's *Midsummer Vigil*. The concerts on Götaplatsen during the city festival attract large numbers of people. In February 2001 the orchestra introduced the Frölunda – Modo ice hockey match at the Scandinavium ice rink. The largest audience the GSO has encountered so far, was at the opening ceremony of the World Athletics Championships at Nya Ullevi in 1995, which was broadcast all over the world.

Well-known conductor immortalized on a tramcar.

Not a dry eye

When a symphony orchestra plays music that is not part of the standard repertoire, people often talk about cross-over. But this is a realm of difficult definitions. What actually is serious music? Conductor Anders Eljas finds it difficult to pin it down. If you enjoy any music, it's serious. The concerts with Povel Ramel – an icon of Swedish popular music – in the winter of 2001/2002, mixed his own melodies with Mozart, Stravinsky and other composers. After the première there wasn't a dry eye in the hall, and tears of joy were running down the conductor's eyes. They start to flow again as he talks about it:

"It's a wonderful feeling when everything falls into place.

The concerts at Götaplatsen always draw big crowds.

Povel Ramel is one of the musicians that I most appreciate."

The GSO is admired for its classical concerts, but the orchestra has also gained a reputation for its efforts in other areas of music.

"Popular productions are needed, not least for financial reasons. The yardstick is that we should perform quality music," says tour and project manager Lars Nyström.

The *Chess* concerts and the Swedish tour of the musical *Kristina from Duvemåla*, both conducted by Anders Eljas, were great successes. Anders Eljas had previously conducted the orchestra at a concert in Slottsskogen, on a beautiful summer's day.

"Mikael Samuelson sang. There was a crowd of 30 000 people. It was an honour to be a part of it," recalls Eljas.

Povel Ramel with the Amanda Vocal Ensemble and the GSO in 2001.

During the GSO's tour of China in 1999 Järvi and Eljas shared the conducting. Eljas took care of the music by Benny Andersson and Björn Ulvaeus, including the arrangements for symphony orchestra, rhythm section and vocalists. The two conductors enjoyed each other's concerts enormously.

"Järvi is so precise and clear as a conductor that only an arch-idiot of a musician wouldn't understand him," says Eljas. "He isn´t afraid of improvising, even in the middle of a concert. Even his back is charismatic."

Anders Eljas has other fond memories from China, for instance the Orsa folk musicians performing on the Great Wall, and a solitary evening in a Shanghai bar in a nameless alley. "I was a long way away from Gothenburg that evening. A beer, five Chinese men and me, taking a breather together."

While working on Chess he collaborated both with the London Symphony Orchestra and the GSO.

"The GSO concerts in 1993 were so successful that we recorded a live performance," he says. "When performing Chess the GSO are just a bit better than their colleagues in London."

The success is possibly due to the working atmosphere, he says.

"The amicable atmosphere in this house is exceptional.

Life is not always like this in the world of orchestral music.

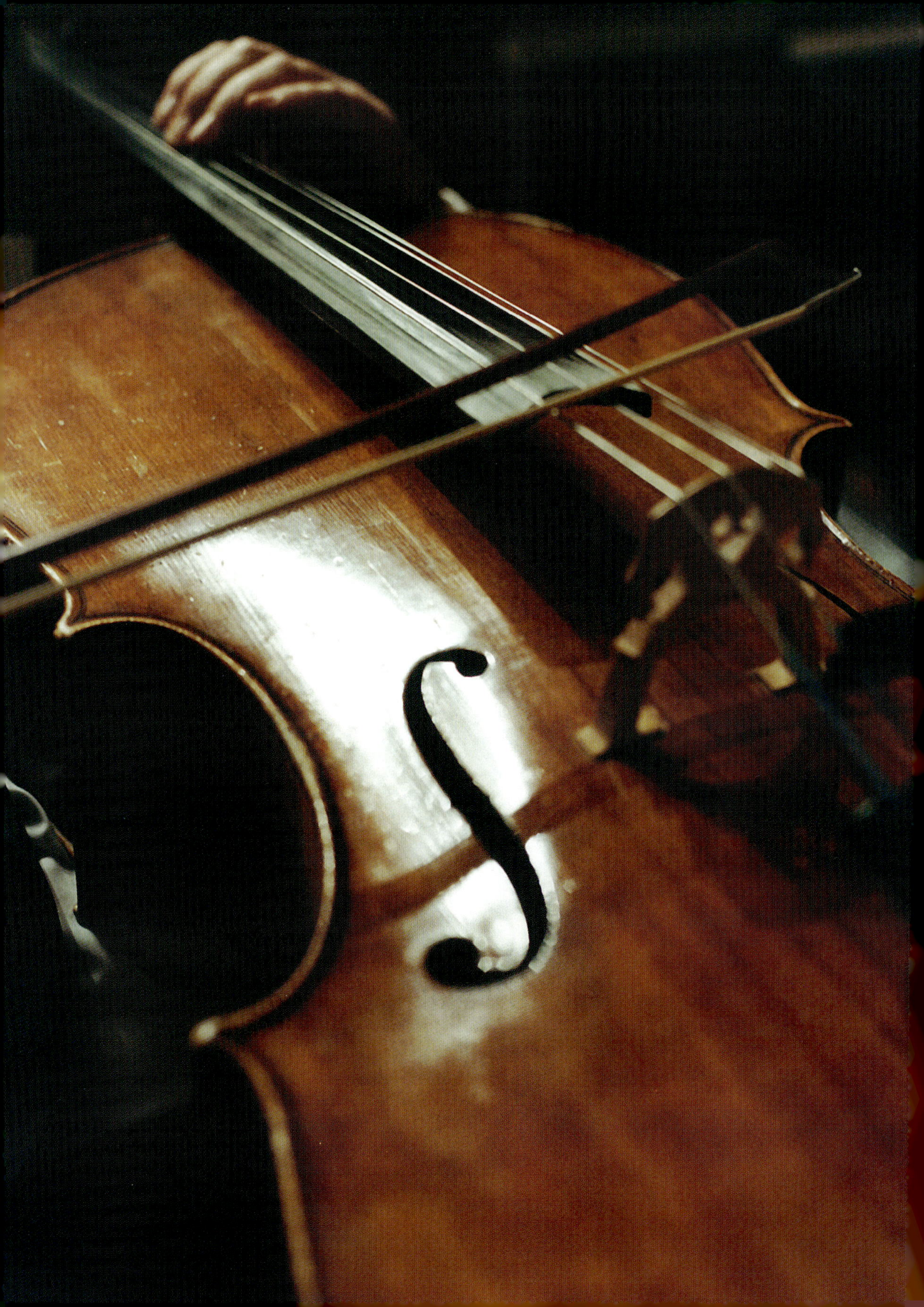

Performing is always risky

Above the reception desk at the concert Hall there is a TV monitor displaying what's happening on the stage. On the left are the first violins and on the right the cellos. Behind them, along the right wall sit the double-bass players.

If you know how a symphony orchestra is seated, and get closer to the TV screen, you will notice that to the right of the first violins are the second violins and in the middle, at the front, are the violas. The string section is like a tower: the double basses form the foundation and in layers above them are the cellos, violas, second violins and then the first violins at the top.

Behind the strings are first the woodwind section: clarinets, flutes, oboes and bassoons and then the brass section: horns, trumpets, trombones and a single tuba. On the left flank is another solitary instrumentalist, the harpist.

Is a musician characterized by the instrument he or she plays? Definitely, according to the musicians. "You can't tell just by looking at us, but if you start discussing music, it becomes apparent that each one of us is focused on his or her area of expertise. A clarinettist has his problems, with breathing and so on, and violinists have their concerns.

When you try repeatedly to create that beautiful tone with a sensitive bow, a very delicate sound, you create tension in your arms.

Horn-player Per Göran takes a different standpoint: "It's more interesting to see how the individual plays the instrument than to analyze how the instrument affects the musician," he says. "The same instrument is going to sound completely different depending on who's playing it. It's like art: no two people paint in the same way."

The TV monitor is showing the percussionists playing drums, cymbals and various kinds of bells. Neeme Järvi played percussion when he was young. The experience left its mark, making him a very rhythm-conscious orchestral conductor.

Working in a symphony orchestra is among the most testing forms of collaboration imaginable. Hundreds of highly qualified, talented instrumentalists have to work together as one unit.

It's the conductor's task to create an ensemble of the players. A single movement of his hand and a flute trills. Rehearsals are a matter of repetition. The artist must subordinate his own will. This is true of much art, but never more evident than among orchestral musicians. Being a talented musician isn't enough, one has to be able to listen to others and adapt.

"The problem is," Per Göran explains, "that you can't quite be yourself, because there is always someone on the podium telling you how to play. In addition we have colleagues playing in their own special way. We have to adapt ourselves to become a team. Being an orchestral musician is an art in itself, in the last analysis possibly a greater art than that of a soloist. There is actually only one way to do things in a symphony orchestra," says Per Göran, "and that's the right way."

"Experienced orchestral musicians," continues principal cellist Leo Winland, "know the rules, but if you want to be a real artist you can not give in every time. That balance is the most difficult aspect of our profession: Having your own opinion and at the same time beeing accepted by the others."

Horn player Per Göran on his way to the podium at the Proms in London in 2001.

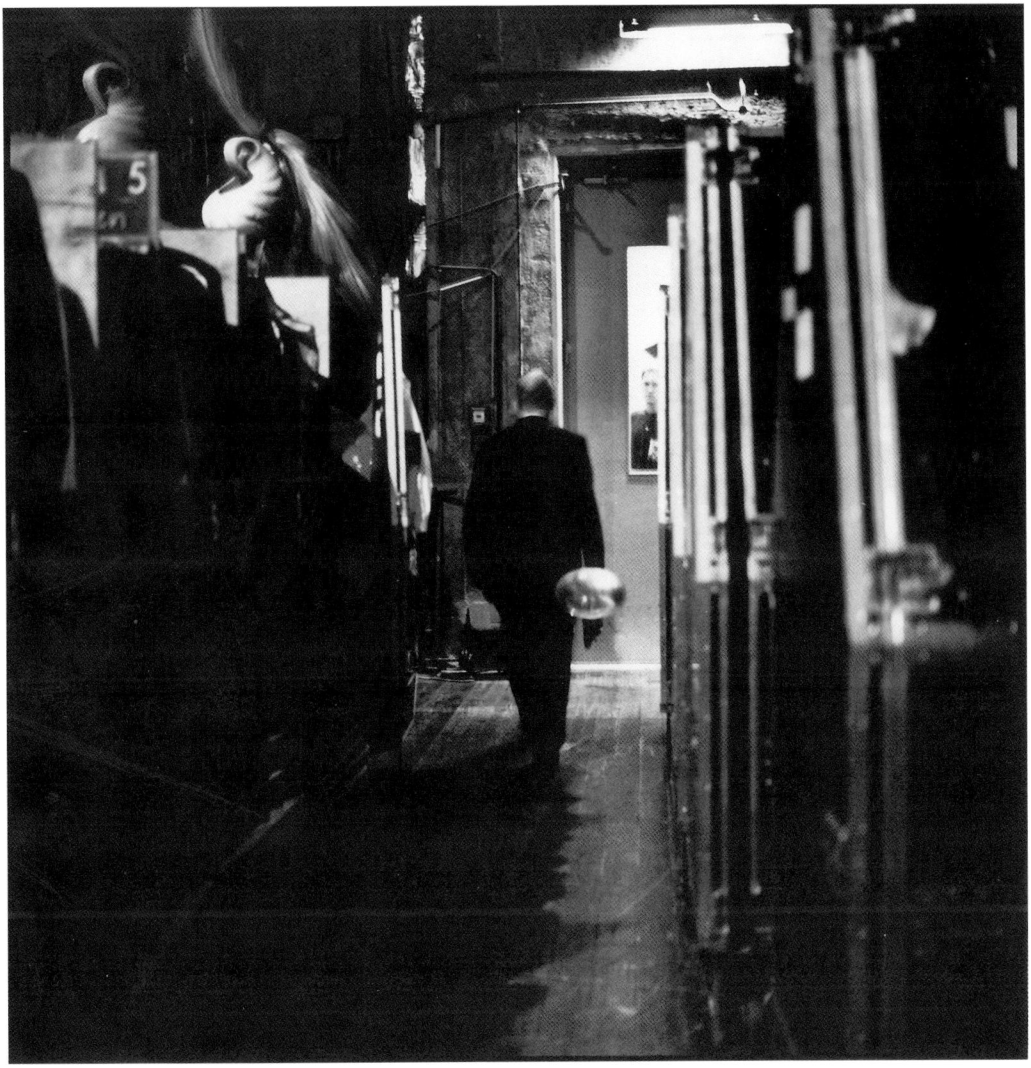

Sometimes it's the principal conductor who is on the stand, sometimes a guest conductor, with his own ideas about the music. The pyramidal structure is maintained by whoever stands in front of the orchestra. The conductor is at the top with the leader of the orchestra next to him and then the section leaders, who are the supervisors for their respective group of instruments.

The music from the TV monitor's speaker echoes in the space between the concert hall's brick wall and the lacquered birch façade of the extension. Through the ceiling high above the reception, light pours in through the glass roof. Everything that takes place here has the purpose of facilitating the main task of making music.

The symphony orchestra's strength is its fantastically rich tonal and dynamic resources.

During a concert the musicians are surrounded by sound. "Music, our profession," someone says quietly, "… is incredible. Being in the centre of all this sound, being part of it, engulfed by it, it's sheer joy."

When you get away from all the difficulties of physically

playing your instrument, the only thing that matters is Music.

Sometimes it's routine. Like every job. Professionalism then takes over. "It's like being an actor. You can´t possibly think it's wonderful to be on stage every night. But a professional copes with that. It's a matter of getting the best possible result, every time. Irrespective of your personal situation that day."

Routine isn't by definition negative, routine is also a sign of experience. To do one's job, you need to be able to get a sense of the structure of the piece, and the conductor's intentions: "but you should never sit back and feel that you could do this in your sleep."

Nerves can sometimes take over. Music, like all other creative occupations, sometimes calls forth stage fright. Alarming words. It can prove contagious: "imagine that you are in the Musikverein in Vienna and is going to play a solo. If someone near you stiffens and starts to tremble the anxiety spreads like ripples on a pond. And the strange thing is that this can happen even when you are feeling comfortable: boom! It just explodes; really strange."

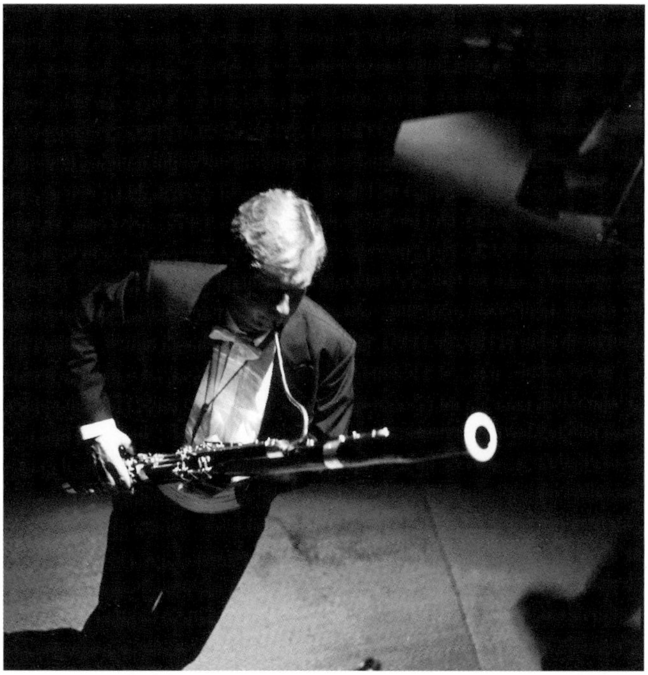

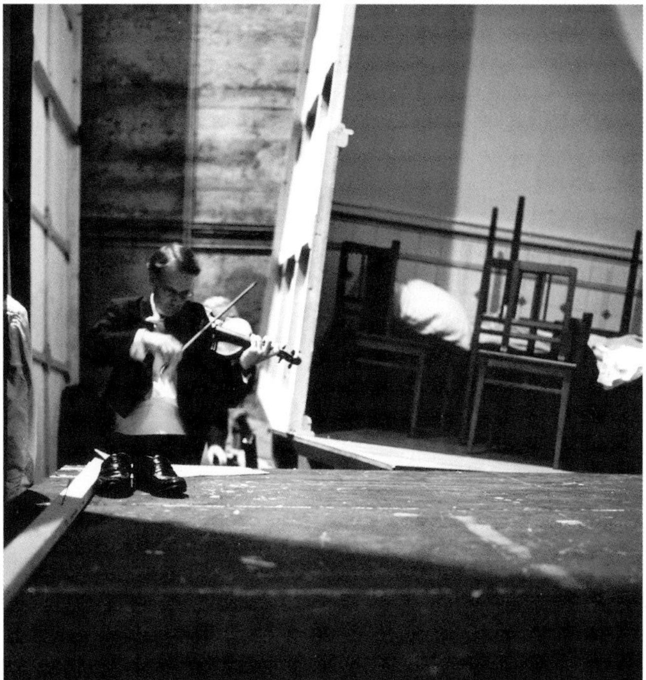

Can't you just hide in the crowd, as you're not exactly alone on stage? Sometimes it's possible. The tension is a natural part of making music. Necessary for giving edge to the performance. But nevertheless, one day the unpredictable happens, "there could possibly be a musical derailment, when something goes horribly wrong … you're sitting there and you can't even lift the bow, if you are a violinist of course. You are holding on tightly and trembling …

"Once you have experienced this you are afraid it will happen again. You must learn to gain control of it. There are as many solutions as there are musicians, but it's also a question of corporate healthcare. We've even had sports psychologists here to lecture to us. Musicians and sportsmen have a lot in common. Both are required to perform at their maximum, physically and mentally at any given moment.

"We have a physiotherapist for strained muscles, seminars about mental training and how to protect your hearing. Meditation exercises are common and breathing exercises of different kinds are also practised, but this doesn't always help."

"I have been to many good breathing exercise classes and know what happens to the body when I panic. It's the same reaction as standing face to face with a grizzly bear. But I'd rather stand in front of the grizzly than perform a concert, or rather that's the way it feels sometimes."

Some people find that it helps, when stressed, to take beta-blockers to control blood pressure. "The beta-blockers stops your heart from racing and the trembling disappears. It's a way of making sure you live longer. That you don't die on stage next week of a heart attack."

Visitors in the reception see nothing of this drama, when watching the monitor during rehearsals. The music is heading off in all directions and they think it sounds wonderful.

Arne Nilsson, bassoon and Håkan Sjönnemo, violin warming up for the Proms concert in London 2001.

154 PERFORMING IS ALWAYS RISKY

They probably have a romantic view of the music profession, possibly thinking: lucky devils. To be able to work in this wonderful building, and to do what you care deeply about.

"That's how it is," says one of the musicians. The times that things go well outweigh the rest. "It's as if you're floating. That's how it felt for me last Thursday during the last piece. That feeling of – ah, this is it. It's wonderful. That's what you live for, and it's worth it."

"Performing is always full of risks," Christer Thorvaldsson explains.

Christer Thorvaldsson is the leader of the orchestra. As such he is the principal violinist in the symphony orchestra. He is the section leader for the violins and the middleman between orchestra and conductor. He plays the first violin's solo parts.

The leader or concertmaster in a symphony orchestra is a central figure. If he or she doesn't do the job properly then the whole ensemble can come adrift. GSO has two principal concertmasters, Thorvaldsson and Per Enoksson, while Sara Trobäck is concertmaster. Thorvaldsson joined the orchestra in 1973 and has 26 years' experience. For many years he worked a few weeks each season at the Helsingborg Symphony Orchestra, alongside his duties in Gothenburg. "I have spent a lot of energy on orchestral playing throughout my professional life."

Christer Thorvaldsson has been on all of Järvi's tours. How does such an experienced musician master nerves?

"There are no tricks," he says. "But with time comes experience, you know you have done this before, and you're not a novice. Nobody who has got as far as to a symphony orchestra is a novice. You learn by experience, and that is helpful. Despite that, a few concerts, even for the routine performer, can be dizzying, like going into the woods and not knowing what

Johan Stern, principal cellist and Christer Thorvaldsson, concertmaster.

lies ahead; is there a steep drop or what? You can't just keep plodding on."

"As a musician you must also dare to let go and risk the fact that something might not be completely perfect. Only then can you give your all. Music that's played safely, held back, to avoid mistakes, won't captivate an audience."

"In these days of perfection," he continues, "this is not actually that simple."

Nowadays playing has to be insightful and technically perfect. These increased requirements are probably due to the many recordings released on the market. Digital technology means that we can edit and polish until we have reached the ultimate result.

The Concert Hall's main auditorium is reached from the rear through the side door at reception, after a certain amount of wandering along the stairs, corridors and other back-stage areas. These parts of the building are the musicians' territory. This is where they have their practice rooms, lockers for dress suits and dresses, and the café with a door leading to the newly-built balcony on the corner of Viktor Rydbergsgatan. A caricature of pre-Järvi orchestra members, or 'mountain owls' as someone called them, hangs in the smoking room.

'Before and after Järvi' is how time is calculated.

How did the musicians manage earlier? Requirements weren't the same of course. There were no records with which to compare the orchestra's previous performances, and no 'national orchestra' title to defend. The repertoire was less comprehensive. GSO musicians currently have to be able to play music from four centuries, the 18th, 19th, 20th and 21st, which places great demands on their abilities.

Christer Thorvaldsson dismisses nostalgic ideas about a better past.

"It wasn't better back then. Maybe discipline was a little slacker. There were people who were a bit mischievous. We are more straight-laced nowadays."

It's a marvellous feeling for a talented musician to be taken on by a symphony orchestra. Competition for jobs is tough and auditions can be hellish. There are 20 – 30 applicants for each post, sometimes more.

They are all formally qualified with many years of training behind them. Applicants perform behind a screen for a jury. Your previous merits at that moment are no use.

The best players are accepted and then comes a probationary period, usually one year. If after that year they are approved, they have managed to maintain their standards. As a full time musician you have employment security just like other people. But this doesn't mean that you can rest on your laurels. Your place in the orchestra must be maintained with

"It's a matter of discovering each part of the composition, the placing of each part and the relationship to the other parts, but the actual starting point for this intellectual process must be a more comprehensive overall appreciation. During this process you need to be highly alert and able to maintain a high level of concentration. During a concert I need to – this may sound pompous – be able to move to another dimension, where I am one with the music. The line between awareness and intuition in this instance is fluid. It is a blessing that is both difficult to achieve and capricious."

Frans Helmerson, cellist, in the book Om kreativitet och flow (On creativity and flow), Brombergs 1990.

constant personal development. (Practice, practice, practice.) People who come to a standstill will not keep up, because the orchestra is constantly developing.

Minute preparation by the musicians is the basis of successful concerts. Every musician knows his or her music when the conductor arrives. No emotion is allowed to blossom until all the details have been covered first.

This is why it's never quiet at the Concert Hall. Sounds constantly penetrate the practice room walls. There is a warble from a clarinet, a violin is heard through a door ajar. There is always something going on here. A quiet concert hall is probably a frightening experience. It's as if its heart had stopped beating.

It is usual for conductors to want to be part of the recruitment procedure. Neeme Järvi has instead left that responsibility in the hands of the orchestra, which has given the GSO the ability to control its own development. The jury is made up of section leaders and other players nominated by the orchestra. They know the exact requirements that make up the GSO's musical environment.

Orchestras differ in sound and intention, just like individual musicians. The Swedish symphony orchestras are all "like different worlds". None sounds like any other because of the individual players, the conductors who lead them and the repertoire they perform.

The GSO's sound is said to be "blond" with central European "warmth". The string sound is credited as being "intensive, concentrated, vigorous."

"The GSO has developed a particular way of performing with Järvi," Christer Thorvaldsson explains. "This is marked by the orchestra daring to take risks. That's something we've been allowed to do with Järvi. We have been taught not to hold back, but to take a few risks and possibly make a few

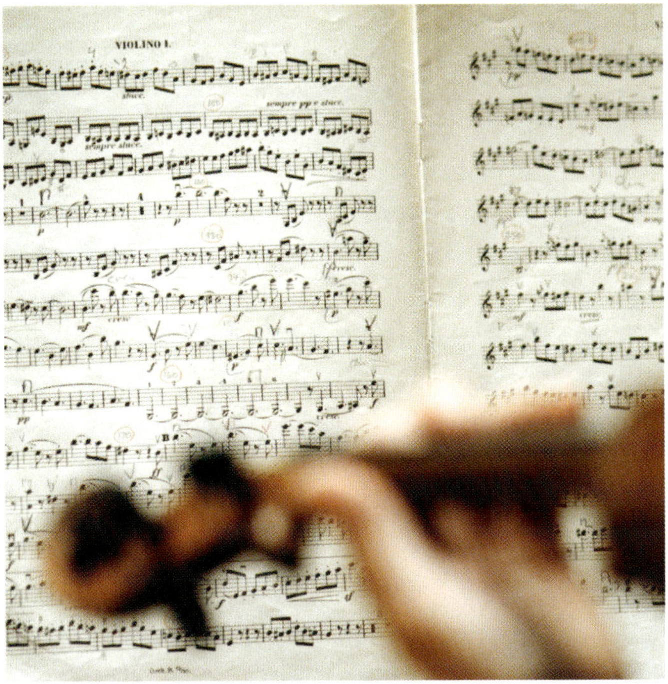
VIOLINO I.

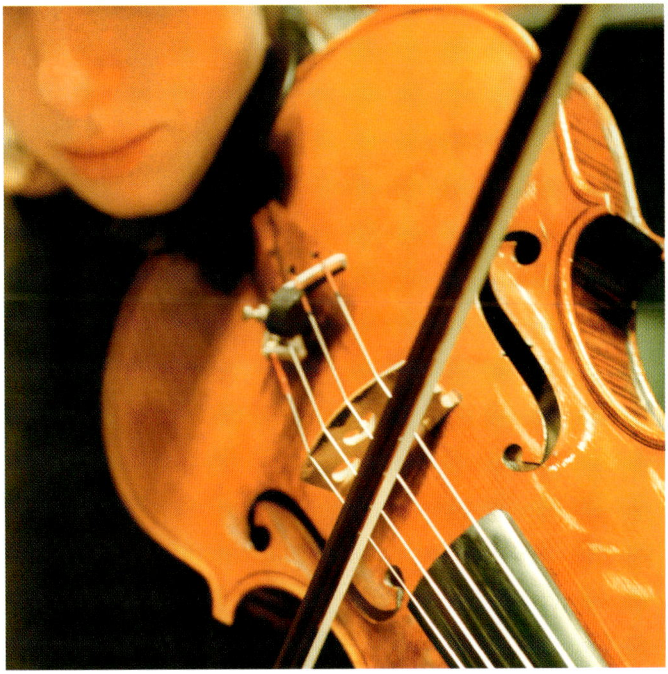

mistakes, because we do sometimes make mistakes during our concerts. The result can also be extremely good, and generally it is. And we've staked our reputation on this for many years."

As concertmaster he stands with a foot in two camps, being both an orchestral musician and a soloist.

"Personality is very important for a soloist," he says. "A soloist must have character for the performance to be interesting. Just standing and performing notes, semi-quavers and quavers, is mechanical – like a typewriter. You have to possess technique, but it's personality that crosses the Ts and dots the Is."

"The small minority of players who have a great deal of personality as well as technical ability are those that become the major stars and tour the world."

Is Thorvaldsson able, with all the music that surrounds him on the podium, to differentiate between individual musician's performances?

"It depends on the kind of music," he says. "If we're performing Mozart or Haydn, then almost everything is heard. One needs to have a very clear and slender tone. That tone is difficult to produce and needs to be worked on."

The Gothenburg Concert Hall is a great place to work. It has the reputation of being maybe the most well-organised cultural institution in the country.

"The attitude to musicians is fantastic," says Leo Winland, "you never get a no, instead it's, 'let's see what we can do for you'. That alone allows you to accept a no when it comes."

Leo Winland is principal cello. That title means that he is section leader for the cellists, a task he shares with his colleague Claes Gunnarsson. Winland commutes between Gothenburg and the Opera in Stockholm and is also active abroad.

Like many orchestral musicians he is also involved in other

musical activities such as chamber music. The friendly atmosphere in the Concert Hall is possibly due to Gothenburg being a small city. The relationship between musicians is better here than in Stockholm, where there are several different kinds of orchestras to choose from. If things don't work out they just go somewhere else. You can't do that in Gothenburg, so you make sure you look after one another.

About my violin, "it's a living entity, believe me"

When the famous Russian violinist, Maxim Vengerov performed in Paris with the GSO in 1994, the French newspapers wrote about his magical instrument. He played a Stradivarius violin and had the Paris audience spellbound. Even the bow was unique – said to have belonged to Jascha Heifetz, one of the 20th century's greatest violinists.

Maxim Vengerov's violin was made in 1727. The Stradivarius that the GSO owns is even older, made in 1697. It is not known for certain whose hands it has passed through over the centuries but one thing is definite: it was brought to Sweden by Helga Hussels.

Here's the story: Helga was nine years old when the second world war broke out. She was living in Berlin and her mother, who had a subscription to the Berlin Philharmonic Orchestra, often took her to concerts. The musicians and the music were glimmers of light in a difficult time and they made a great impression on her.

She wanted to become a violinist and after the war she studied at the Mozarteum in Salzburg and elsewhere. She was very talented and often appeared as a soloist. But she was excluded from becoming an orchestral musician because German symphony orchestras didn't allow female musicians.

Her parents decided that Helga needed a good violin to survive and sold their house to finance the purchase. Helga

Revenge in Amsterdam

From a diary entry in November 2000, Martin Hansson

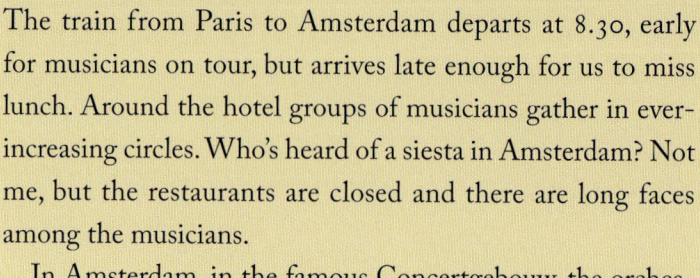

Nikolaj Znaider, a regular performer with the GSO.

CD 2.10

The train from Paris to Amsterdam departs at 8.30, early for musicians on tour, but arrives late enough for us to miss lunch. Around the hotel groups of musicians gather in ever-increasing circles. Who's heard of a siesta in Amsterdam? Not me, but the restaurants are closed and there are long faces among the musicians.

In Amsterdam, in the famous Concertgebouw, the orchestra once performed one of its rare, less successful concerts. This may have been twelve years ago but many of the musicians were present then, and the occasion is not easily forgotten. The acoustics of the Concertgebouw are among the best in Europe, but they are different from the Gothenburg Concert Hall and not easy to master without an audience.

The sound is thrown back and forth making it difficult for the musicians to hear each other.

The atmosphere is tense. Last night's success in Paris belongs to the past. But Neeme knows exactly how to tackle the situation. He is relaxed, joking, allows time for everything spreading an air of security. The musicians rehearse some of the more difficult sections of Shostakovich's sixth symphony and the evening's soloist, violinist Nikolaj Znaider runs through his part. An hour before the concert is due to begin the rehearsals are over.

In the corridors under the hall, where the musicians' changing-rooms are, conditions are cramped and far from glamorous. The huge boxes for freighting the players evening wear act as portable wardrobes. The air is stuffy.

"Whose idea was this?" A voice pierces the atmosphere and I jump.

"How are we to perform at our best under conditions like these? It's just not possible. Surely they understand that?" the same musician laments.

Here I am, on my first foreign tour after two months on the job. I have to say something.

"Well, I, you understand we have to, to solve…"

"You don't understand anything", he interrupts. Nerves are frayed and I discreetly slip away. Will everything go wrong now? Time for the concert. My pulse is racing as Neeme walks onto the platform. He strikes up Stenhammar's Excelsior! and starts off at an uncompromising tempo. Are the musicians going to hate him for this? I am incredibly nervous the first few minutes. But the orchestra is following him. Järvi's make or break tactic works. Excelsior! is a virtuosic and merciless piece that challenges the musicians' capabilities to their limits. The slightest mistake will be spotted, but the performance couldn't have been better.

Nikolaj Znaider then goes on to perform Sibelius' Violin Concerto. His performance is almost hallucinatory, inspired, as if he were sleepwalking. He can hold a note just that extra split second that creates incredible excitement. Znaider's interpretation has a sensuality all of its own. The audience is carried away. After the concert, back stage, it's a completely different orchestra talking. The energy has returned, and the mood is one of elation. The same musicians, yet not the same!

Shostakovich's Sixth Symphony after the interval. A remarkable piece of music, and difficult, for everyone involved. The orchestra performs fantastically well, each solo is perfect and the woodwinds are superb. The audience is in a trance. I fret for a moment that we didn't record the concert. Encores and the success is complete. At the right place exactly at the right time.

travelled around Europe in search of an instrument. In Switzerland she found a Stradivarius that she fell in love with. With the violin in one hand and her seven-year-old son in the other she emigrated to Sweden. It was in 1969 and she had just been battling with the Berlin Philharmonic Orchestra. Wasn't it time to allow women to join? No it wasn't, despite the fuss that broke out in the press.

The musical press considered her as "invaluable to the music scene in Gothenburg" the year she arrived. She soon became section leader of the second violins in the GSO and she also performed chamber music.

The GSO now owns the violin that Helga Hussels brought to Sweden. She sold it in 1989, when she was forced to reduce her solo commitments due to her back trouble. At the time the orchestra could not afford to buy the instrument, which was sold to an anonymous collector who promised that it would remain with the orchestra for four years. After that it was bought by the Municipality of Gothenburg for almost half a million dollars and leased to the GSO which still couldn't afford to buy it. The instrument is said to have been worth much more on the open market but the seller wanted to show the orchestra his appreciation. At the same time a collection was under way. P G Gyllenhammar began the collection by donating 100 000 Swedish crowns in conjunction with the orchestra's 90th anniversary in 1995 and following a secret donation a few years later the orchestra was finally able to buy the instrument.

What is so remarkable about a Stradivarius?

"It has a soul," explains Helga Hussels, who still longs for it sometimes.

"It forces you to play better than you think possible, purely, articulately and beautifully. And it doesn't allow you to have bad moods because then it sounds awful. In addition it

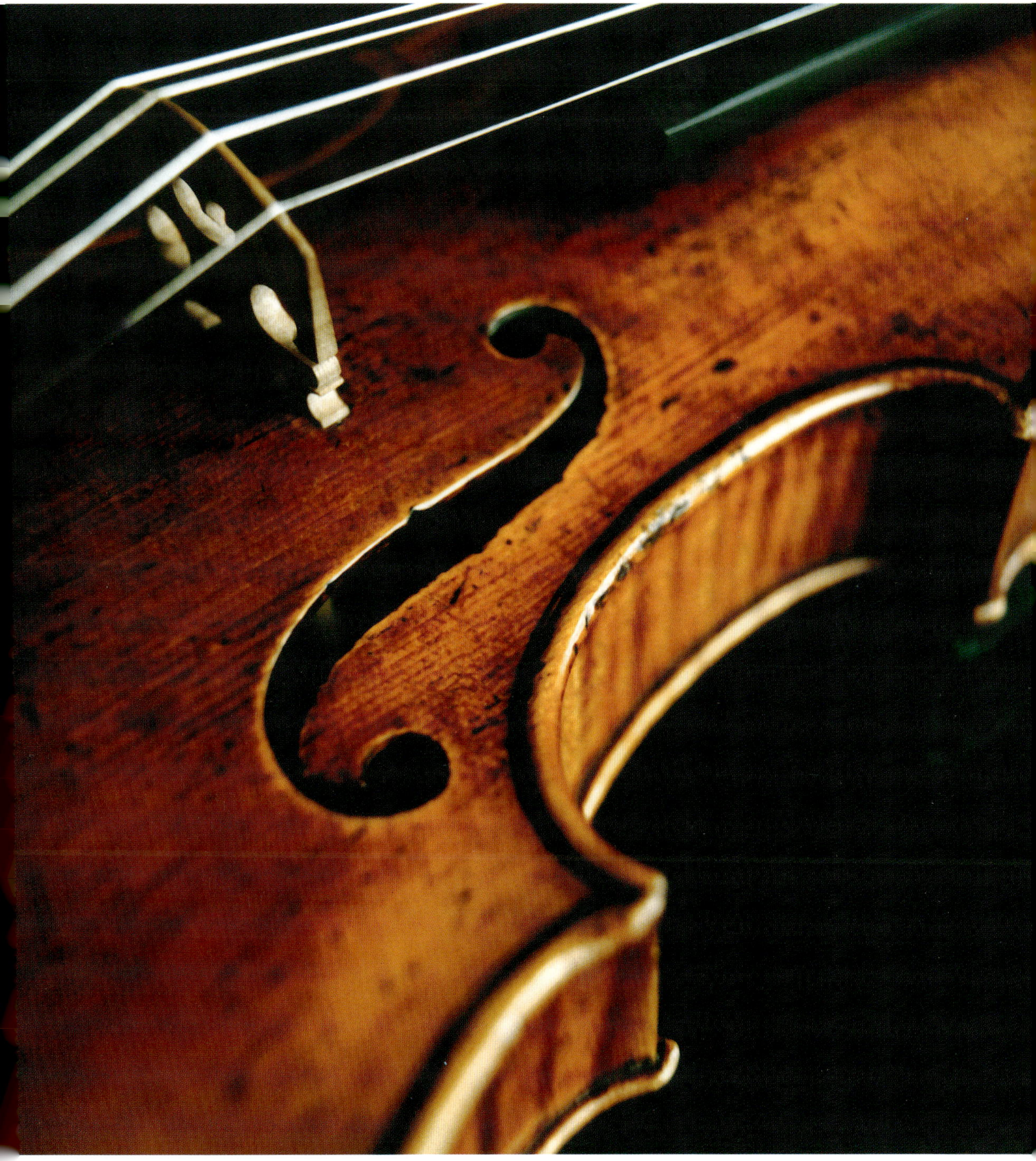

doesn't only affect the person who's playing it, it also affects the surroundings, and it colours the orchestral sound."

She is proud to have contributed to the "Gothenburg Sound."

"My old aim of playing in the Berlin Philharmonic Orchestra faded away as the GSO developed."

A Stradivarius is like an Arabian stallion, strong willed and difficult to handle. You must have patience with it, and try to live up to its strength.

What does it actually sound like? You can't nearly describe it. But as soon as you have learned the instrument, you can produce a sound that no other violin can match.

Violin maker Antonio Stradivari (in Latin Antonius Stradivarius), worked in Cremona in Italy, and was a pupil of the equally famous Nicola Amati. Stradivarius' instruments are "unrivalled in form and tonal beauty", the experts explain, and they command tremendous prices when they come up for sale.

Most violinists obviously can't afford a Stradivarius. But other violins are often very expensive as well. A good violin for professional use will cost around 250 000 kronor. Musical instruments are a heavy financial burden, not only for violinists, but also for other orchestral musicians who have to bear the cost of the instruments themselves.

The Stradivarius, or "Strad" as its called in the profession, is played by Per Enoksson, one of the GSO's two concertmasters. Christer Thorvaldsson plays his own Pietro Guarneri (II), made in 1742. The Guarneri family also worked in Cremona. Paganini played a violin made by Giuseppe Guarneri in 1742. (Violins are often just as famous as musicians and composers. Paganini's violin was given the name del Gesu from the initials IHS on the label, Iesus Hominum Salvator, or in English Jesus, Saviour of man.)

How does a violinist feel about his instrument?

"It becomes a part of you," Christer Thorvaldsson explains. "You have it so close to your body. You fight with it for your entire life, you are friends with it, but also enemies. It is like a living entity, believe me."

"Violins and string instruments in general take time to mature. That's why instruments of the old masters are so attractive," Thorvaldsson explains.

"It takes years before an instrument acquires its final tone, and if its not played it suffers. Violins mature as they are played." The GSO's Stradivarius is over 300 years old. If it's looked after well it should last quite a bit longer. There are centuries of music locked into the wood in these old instruments. "There is something to that actually," says Thorvaldsson. "The fact is that the violin vibrates in every little corner when being played. But the fact that the Cremona violins are so sought after has more to do with the expertise of the Italians at the time they were made. The art of violin making was peaking. The wood was carefully tested: spruce on the front and maple on the sides and bottom. The trees should be felled on north facing slopes where growth was slower. They were selected with great care. When the tree had been selected and felled the timber would be allowed to dry slowly for many years."

Christer Thorvaldsson is very sceptical of new violins such as the ones made in Japan.

"They copy all of these fantastic instruments, with exact measurements, exact everything. But they still sound like cigar boxes when all is said and done."

What do we do when all the Amati, Stradivarius and Guarneri violins are worn out? There are fine instruments around, good violins from the 19th and 20th centuries. These instruments, around a hundred years old, are beginning to make their way into the market. Christer Thorvaldsson always carries his Guarneri himself when he is on tour: "There are special instrument carriers, who will transport your instrument but I think I've only used that service once.

Is it good to have the violin close to you?

"Yes, I'm used to it. Sometimes I want to practice a little between stops."

Personifying traditions

In 1980, on that evening in June when Järvi and the GSO made their breakthrough at the Royal Albert Hall, the 13 year-old Nicola Boruvka sat with her ear close to the radio listening to a live broadcast from London. Mum and dad and friends in the orchestra were touring England. As Nicola heard the Sibelius symphony moving over sea and land she understood that something special was happening, "I felt such a strong bond with my parents. I wished that I could have been there."

Now she can. She is one of the GSO's first violinists and like many other young musicians she lives her life between the two poles of music and family. It's a question of balance. "Music may not really be a matter of life and death but for the person performing it, it has to be. Otherwise you can just pack up and go home," she says.

Every musician in the orchestra has a story to tell, and each is worth its own book. The talent for music seems to be hereditary. Nicola Boruvka is a fourth generation musician and can be said to embody the orchestra's almost 100-year history.

She protests against this description. It sounds demanding and pretentious, "I am me, Nicola Boruvka, and not just somebody's daughter," she says. "So sometimes it's nice to deputise in other orchestras where they haven't a first clue about my heritage."

Because she does have a GSO heritage.

Her father's mother's father, trumpeter Magnus Jensen Senior was among the 52 musicians who gathered for the first rehearsals in 1905, when the orchestra was founded.

His son, Magnus Jensen Junior, became a cellist.

In their day the orchestra was a male preserve. Now, in the 21st century, when great granddaughter Nicola is part of

Nicola Boruvka 2002. Fourth generation GSO musician.

The musicians making up the GSO are relatively young. The average age of the men is 46 and of the women 40. There are 109 musicians (29% are women) who make up the living entity that is Göteborgs Symfoniker– The National Orchestra of Sweden. Together they make an instrument that can play anything and is infinitely flexible. If, for example, justice is to be done to a Mahler symphony, then every member of the orchestra must be involved. In other cases the strength of the orchestra can be reduced. Symphonies by Beethoven and Brahms, for example, only require 60 – 70 musicians and a piece by Bach perhaps 30.

the symphony orchestra, there are still more men than women but among the younger members women are in the majority.

When Nicola Boruvka places her bow against her violin you hear Swedish folk music as well as Central European czardas. Her mother's father was a musician from Dalecarlia and her father's father was a pianist and conductor from Prague. He went to Germany to conduct. There he met a harpist who was so pretty that he went up to her and asked if she would like to go out for a meal, "he then received a slap on the face from my grandmother. That's how their relationship began."

There was a period when Nicola Boruvka didn't really know what she wanted to do, she says.

"I first decided to go to an ordinary sixth-form college. If I wasn't allowed to go straight to music college then who cares, and the application time for music college had just expired. And I realised that I just had to play. I called Christer Thorvaldsson and asked if we could practice really hard for three months, because I had one more school to apply to, the Edsberg School run by the Swedish Broadcasting Corporation. We practiced like mad, and I was accepted. So I left home when I was fifteen."

Nicola's father Magnus Boruvka was a cellist with the GSO for many years and her mother, Elsie Börjes, is a first violinist who has just finished her 42nd season. Elsie Börjes was the first woman in the orchestra, which is history in itself. You can keep on counting: One of Nicola's brothers is a percussionist, the other brother an amateur pianist, her mother's husband Peter Svensson is a cellist in the GSO, her sister-in-law is a singer… her husband Morten Agerup plays the tuba in the GSO, and their daughter plays the violin. The fifth generation. Her sons on the other hand are lying low. So far. Nicola Boruvka was given her first violin when she was six years old.

"My childhood memories of home are full of the conductors and other musicians and managers. I vividly remember when Neeme arrived, it was quite a thing, and everybody was talking about it."

The Concert Hall was an exciting place in which to grow up. There was music in every corner and there were lively discussions. "It was so vibrant. Everyone was really kind and asked how my playing was improving. I tried theatre as well, and played violin at a theatre in a suburb of Gothenburg when it opened. But I wanted to come to this place. My dream was to come here as concertmaster."

At the age of 18 and pregnant she auditioned for a place as a second violinist in the orchestra. The order in which the applicants play is drawn by ballots.

"I got No. 2 in the first round. And I made it to the next round."

In the first round the applicants had to play a Mozart concerto, an obligatory piece that revealed a great deal about the sound and intonation. After that round there were ten or eleven hopefuls left. In the second round she played last, then the jury began to deliberate. As the auditions are anonymous she didn't have any advantage to the other applicants; rather the opposite, she felt the extra burden of her family heritage. The wait was long.

"I felt as if I hadn't lived up to the expectations. I just wanted to get away, but I couldn't. In the end I asked one of the jury members out on the street and he said "congratulations Nicola". I called my mother and my father straight away and they just started crying because they know how difficult it is, and I was pregnant as well. So that was the little train, that I managed to catch." Her plans were to go to Berlin to study, but instead started her career by taking maternity leave.

"This weekend the audience of the Stockholm Concert Hall will again have the pleasure of listening to the GSO and their conductor Neeme Järvi. It is an occasion one shouldn't miss, just as much as one shouldn't miss the Oslo Philharmonic Orchestra (with whom the GSO are closely related in terms of sound) when they perform here. The artistic standard of the GSO is at the highest European level."

Thomas Anderberg, Dagens Nyheter.

> "The fact that things have gone so well are due to many factors. The main reason is probably that we are on the same wavelength musically and emotionally. I like allowing the orchestra to inspire me into making each concert a special occasion. The orchestra has many fantastic musical personalities, who have given me an awful lot through the years."
> **Neeme Järvi**

Sometimes she feels that she has not been able to utilize her full potential "But then many of my colleagues who are my age haven't even started having children yet. I have three and it feels great."

The intense touring hasn't always been easy to combine with parenthood. At the GSO debut in Vienna in 1994 her husband Morten Agerup represented the family. Nicola Boruvka sat by her radio and listened longingly.

"Morten called home afterwards. Oh, it went so well," he said. "Oh yes," I said.

But at the Berlin debut it was she who was there and it was "fantastic, unbelievable".

"In the music profession there is equality between the sexes," she says.

"I never get the impression of anything else on the platform, or from male colleagues, never."

After a few years as second violinist she had further auditions, for a place among the first violinists.

Younger concertgoers also have a place at the Concert Hall. Open House 2000.

On that occasion there were ninety applicants and things went well that time, too.

Music hasn't just been a profession, but a way of life, for better or for worse. The worse part is the nerves. It's a stressful profession, far too stressful at times. But when it works, when positive stress is the driving force, when the music flows, it's all worthwhile. She has also been playing in a string quartet for a few years now. She will always be a musician. That's who she is. It's in her blood. What about the violin? It's Italian, made in 1820, not a really well-known make.

She bought it a few years ago for 30 000 dollars and pays the loan off every month. The bow cost more than 4 000 dollars.

So you shouldn't drop it?

"It just doesn't happen. Many things are dropped, but not one's violin. It's part of your body."

"Being a musician is a very free job, apart from the fact that one can never relax."
On musicians' working hours

"One can only admire the ability to be able to recruit top talent in all sections, but even more amazing is the ability to jointly listen, communicate and express a collective strength…"
The Las Palmas newspaper, La Provincia, reviewing the GSO's guest appearance at the music festival on the Canary Islands in 1995.

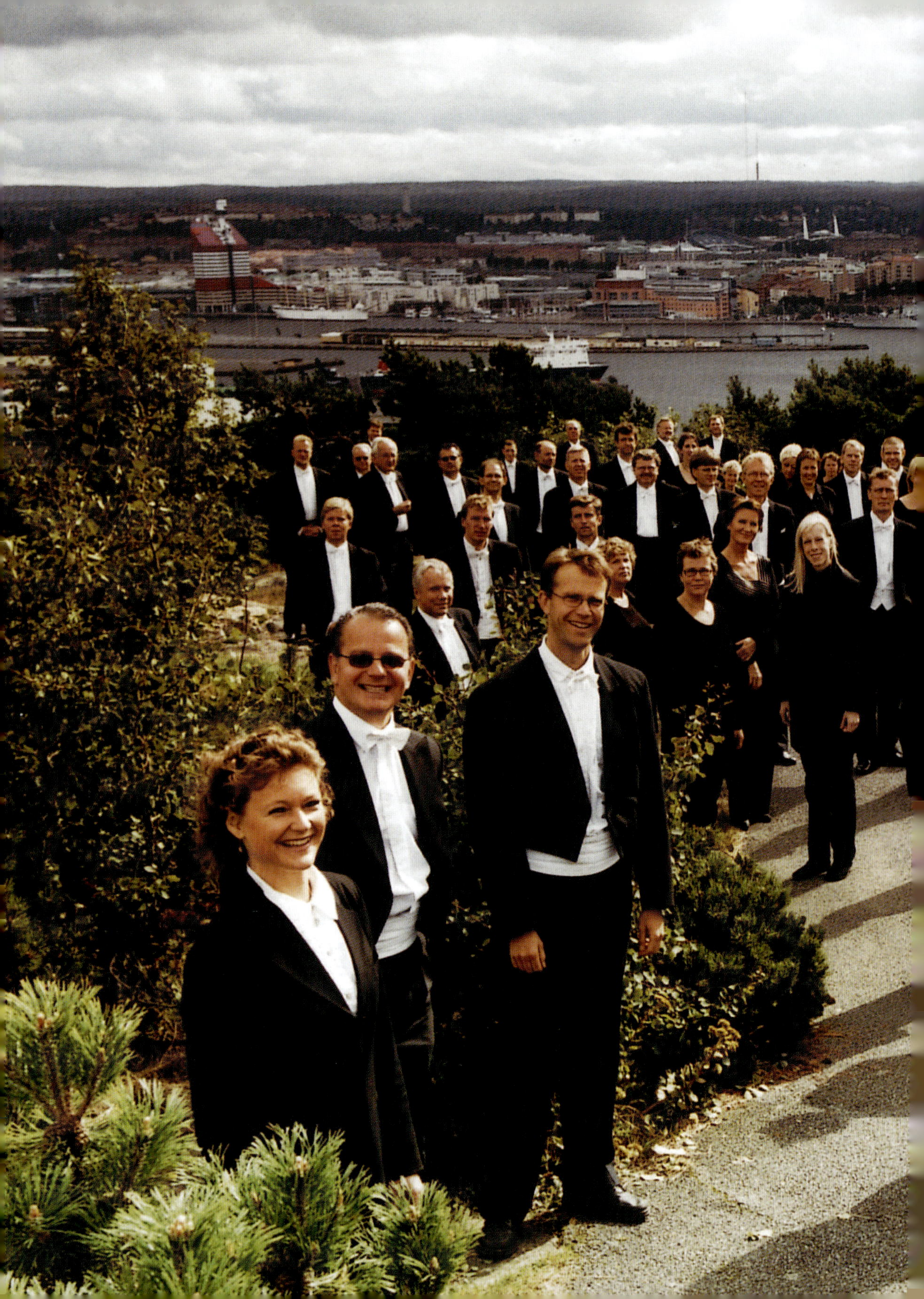

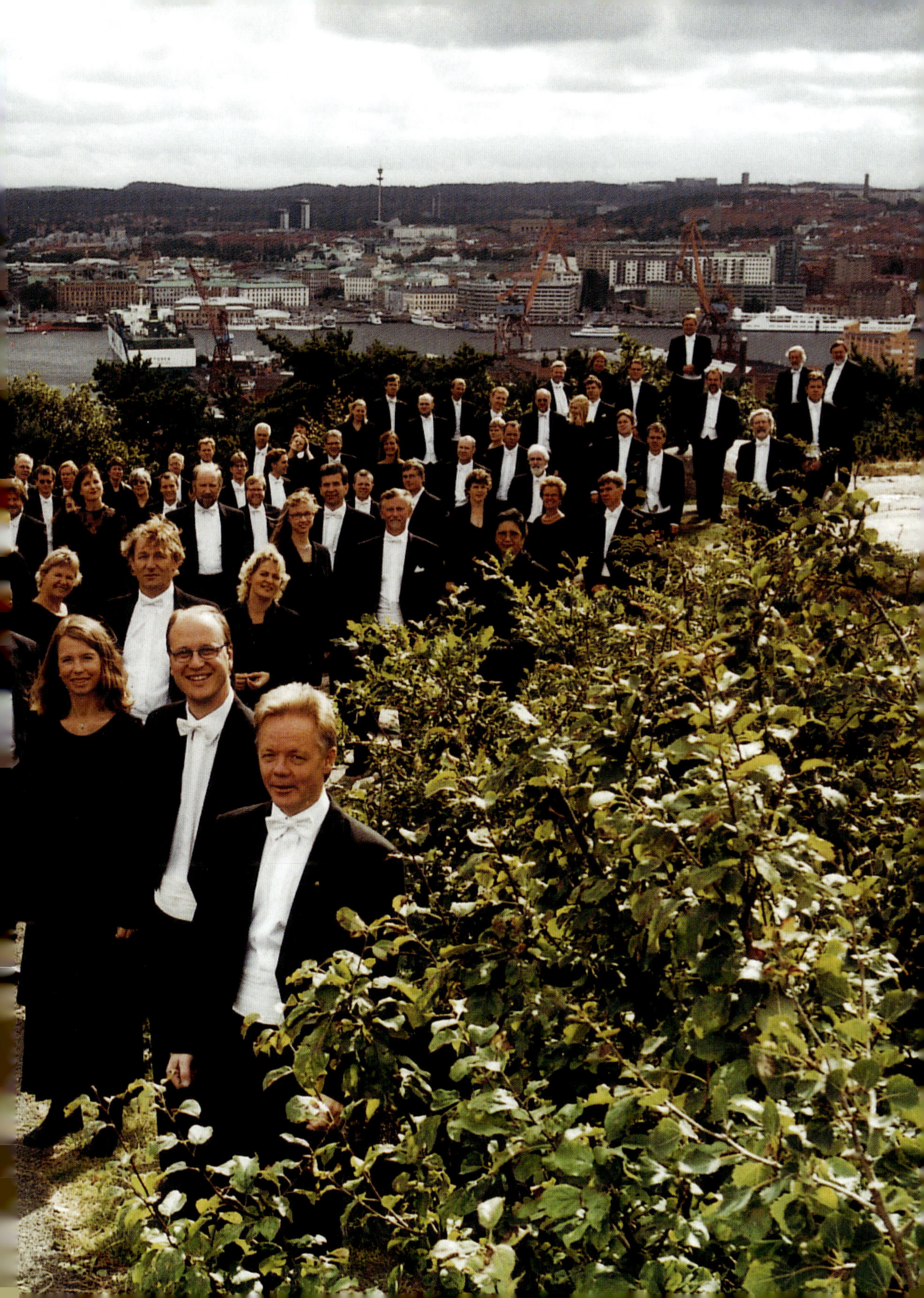

Göteborgs Symfoniker – The National Orchestra of Sweden 2003

PRINCIPAL CONDUCTOR
Neeme Järvi

PRINCIPAL GUEST CONDUCTOR
for classical repertoire
Christian Zacharias

PRINCIPAL GUEST CONDUCTOR
for modern and contemporary repertoire
Peter Eötvös

PRINCIPAL CONDUCTOR DESIGNATE
2004 / 2005
Mario Venzago

LEADERS
Per Enoksson 87
Christer Thorvaldsson 73

DEPUTY LEADER
Sara Trobäck 2002

SECOND DEPUTY LEADER
Michael Karlsson 79

THIRD DEPUTY LEADER
Ingrid Sjönnemo 84

VIOLIN 1
Nicola Boruvka 86
Mats Enoksson 90
Helena Frankmar 88
Bengt Gustafsson 78
Vaclav Herclik 66
Annika Hjelm 84
Helena Kollback 92
Bertil Lindh 77
Lotte Lybeck 2002
Hans Malm 75
Ann-Christin Raschdorf 99

Kristina Ryberg 78
Ryszard Sobis 72
Duncan Taylor 67

VIOLIN 2
Marja Inkinen* 98
Håkan Sjönnemo* 86
Åsa Rudner** 92
Lars Alexandersson 78
Maria Andersson 76
Per-Olof Appelin 76
Catherine Claesson 90
Jan Engdahl 88
Leonard Haight 85
Britt-Louise Johansson 70
Per Ove Jonsson 70
Kerstin Karlsson 69
Annica Kroon 77
Jan Lindahl 79
Elin Stjärna 93
Ingrid Sturegård 84
Thord Svedlund 83

VIOLA
Per Högberg* 92
Lars Mårtensson* 88
Ane Lysebo** 98
Karin Claesson 94
Nils Edin 88
Henrik Edström 98
Björn Johannesson 78
Magnus Lundén 85
Kejo Millholm 75
Bo Olsson 81
Josef Pavlica 75
Laszlo Sziranyi 71
Jan Åkerlund 84

CELLO
Leo Winland, solocellist 95
Claes Gunnarsson, solocellist 2000
Johan Stern* 99
Paula Gustafsson 95
Erik Hammarberg 76
Göran Holmstrand 74
Leif Johansson 68
Karin Knutson 88
Anders Robertson 81
Peter Svenson 71
Lidia Turestedt 78
Grzegorz Wybraniec 85

DOUBLE BASS
Hans Adler* 91
Bo Eklund* 80
Jan Alm** 84
Marc Grue 2001
Jan Johansson 66
Erik Mofjell 92
Ida Rostrup 96
Jenny Ryderberg 2001

FLUTE
Anders Jonhäll* 92
Håvard Lysebo** 97
Linda Taube 2001
Kenneth Wihlborg 79

PICCOLO
Kenneth Wihlborg 79

OBOE
Mårten Larsson* 89
Niklas Wallin** 86
Björn Bohlin 78
Wincent Lindgren 71

COR ANGLAIS
Björn Bohlin 78

CLARINET
Urban Claesson* 86
Selena Markson-Adler** 95
Henrik Nordqvist 99
Åke Schierbeck 66

E FLAT CLARINET
Selena Markson-Adler 95

BASS CLARINET
Åke Schierbeck 66

BASSOON
Arne Nilsson* 79
Anders Engström** 87
Ylva Holmstrand 79
Christer Nyström 77

CONTRA BASSOON
Christer Nyström 77

HORN
Lisa Ford* 93
Per Göran** 74
Dick Gustavsson 87
Ingrid Kornfält Wallin 87
Krister Petersson 89

TRUMPET
Bengt Danielsson* 89
Paul Spjuth** 84
Börje Westerlund** 85
Rolf Tilly 75

TROMBONE
Lars-Göran Carlsson* 81
Ingemar Roos** 78
Jens Kristian Søgaard 94

BASS TROMBONE
Peter McKinnon 72

TUBA
Morten Agerup 81

HARP
Masayo Matsuo 72

PIANO/CELESTA
Erik Risberg 88

TIMPANI
Hans Hernqvist* 91
Daniel Norberg** 94

PERCUSSION
Roger Carlsson* 80
Fredrik Björlin 2000
Kenneth Franzén 85
Daniel Norberg 94

* principals
** co-principals

Violinist Elsie Börjes, member of the GSO 1959–2002. She was the first woman in the orchestra and has recently finished her 42nd and last season.

Age	Number	Percentage
Women		
–19	0	0 %
20–29	6	19 %
30–39	13	40 %
40–49	7	23 %
50–59	5	17 %
60–69	1	1 %
70–	0	0 %
Men		
–19	0	0 %
20–29	2	3 %
30–39	14	18 %
40–49	35	45 %
50–59	20	26 %
60–69	6	8 %
70–	0	0 %
Total		
–19	0	0 %
20–29	8	7 %
30–39	27	25 %
40–49	42	39 %
50–59	25	23 %
60–69	7	6 %
70–	0	0 %
Women	33	30 %
Men	76	70 %
Total	109	100 %

Average age women	40
Average age men	46
Average age total	44

The digits after the names indicate the first year of employment.

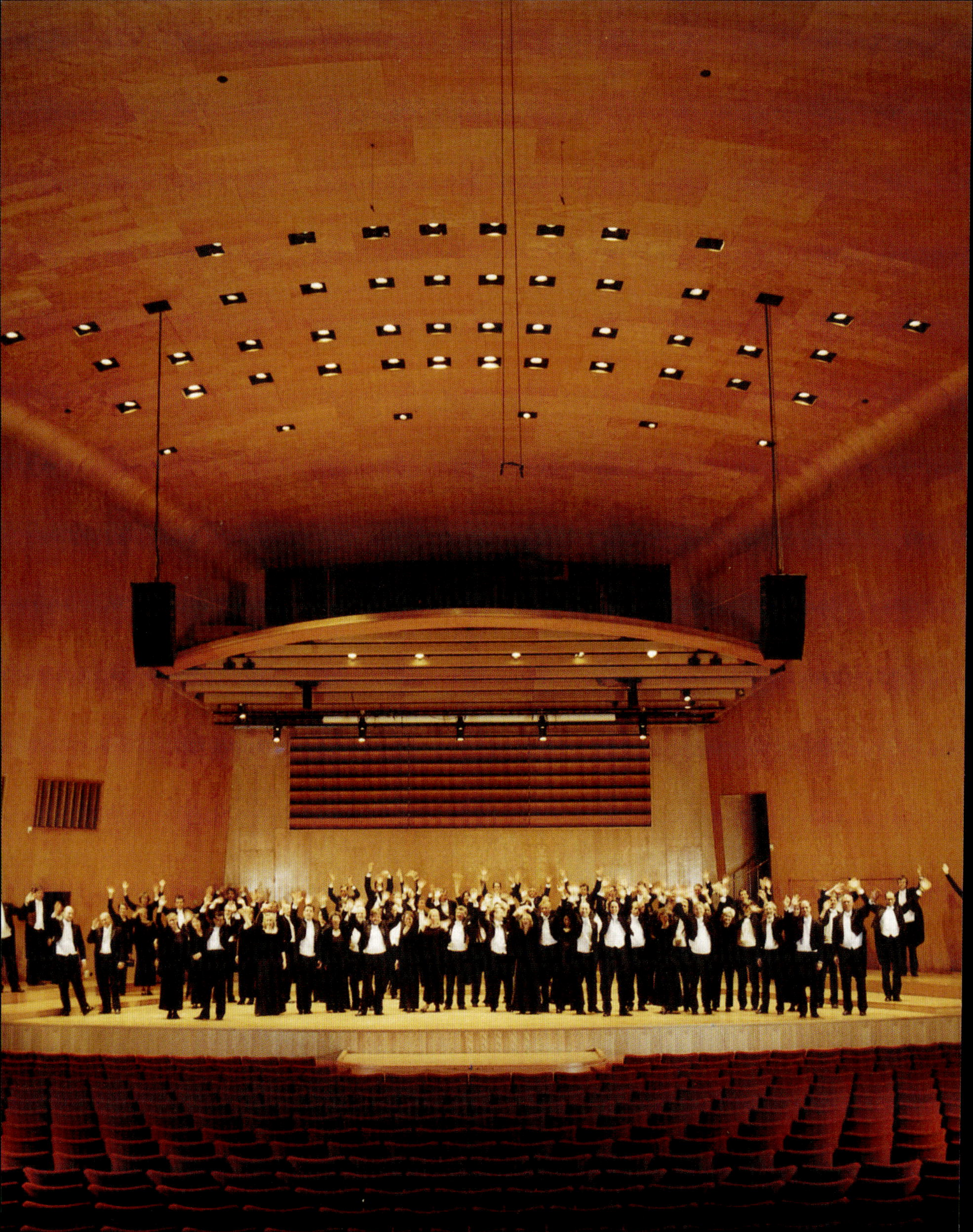

The National Orchestra of Sweden

At last the 7th of May arrived and the manager of the Concert Hall, Sture Carlsson, was finally able to step onto the stage. He vividly remembers his words: "Ladies and Gentlemen, may I introduce the National Orchestra of Sweden."

There was uproar on stage and in the hall, everyone was treated to sparkling wine, after which the Wednesday concert continued with Debussy's *La Mer*.

Despite tough opposition from the capital, Göteborgs Symfoniker the GSO had finally been awarded the title National Orchestra of Sweden by the government.

That was in May 1997. But the GSO really received the title in December 1996, when parliament made the final decision. During the early months of 1997, there was much public discussion. If Sweden was to have a National Orchestra, which wasn't a foregone conclusion, why should the honour go to the GSO?

National institutions of this kind have a long history in opera, theatre and art, but not within classical music. In other countries one, if not two, national orchestras are common. There was a niche here for the GSO to fill, Sture Carlsson thought.

Nominating the GSO as the National Orchestra would be a way of paying recognition for incredibly hard work and considerable artistic success.

> "The committee concludes that good reasons have been put forward in the motions for the GSO to have the right to bear the title of National Orchestra of Sweden. The committee further concludes that the government has the right of decision in this matter. The committee therefore proposes that parliament should inform the government that, in the opinion of the committee, the GSO should be granted the right to the title of National Orchestra of Sweden."
> **From the Parliamentary Committee's report 1996/97:Kr U1.**

> "I remember that Erland Waldenström (Chairman of the Stockholm Concert Hall) said that he once learnt that the government intended to increase funding to the orchestras of the country. Hjalmar Mehr and I then went up to Finance Minister Gunnar Sträng and spoke to him for 20 minutes. When we came out we had made sure that all the new funding ended up at the Stockholm Concert Hall!"
> **Sture Carlsson remembers his time at the Stockholm Concert Hall, from a letter to Anitra Steen 2 December 1997.**

The title would also benefit in the PR-strategy. Promoting an orchestra from a little known city in a small country on the outskirts of Europe is not easy. Few people in the world can place Gothenburg on the map, but everybody understands what a National Orchestra is.

The report from the government commission on culture in 1995 gave Sture Carlsson the chance of making his idea a reality. Institutions in the cultural sphere could be given national responsibilities even if they were not located in the capital. The rhetoric argued that "the whole country should be alive."

The orchestras in Stockholm already had other national connotations. The Swedish Radio Symphony Orchestra has all the country's radio listeners as its audience while the Royal Stockholm Philharmonic stresses the word Royal in its publicity as does the Royal Swedish Opera Orchestra. Their geographic location is to their advantage. It is easier to attract international stars to a capital city than to the provinces.

Gothenburg's local politicians now proposed that a new national institution for music be located in Gothenburg. However, the government bill resulting from the report did not raise the issue.

Spokesmen for the GSO, politicians and lobbyists of different kinds had to find a new impetus. Informal contacts with the parliamentary standing committee on cultural affairs were made and a number of motions were drafted emphasizing the GSO's elevated musical standards.

The "National Orchestra" title would be of "significant importance to the orchestra in international circles and with regard to those who sponsor it", it was explained.

It was a matter of prestige. The claim in one of the motions, that the GSO was "unquestionably Sweden's leading symphony orchestra", further aggravated the Stockholm orchestras.

The chairman of the friends of the Swedish Radio Symphony Orchestra, Dag Henriksson, probably summarised many people's anger in his letter to the Department of Cultural Affairs: "This comment by laymen caused raised eyebrows among active musicians in Gothenburg and Stockholm. Selecting one artistic institution among many to be the leading one in the country would be considered irrational. The musical world in Sweden has many nuances, this proposition has none."

If the title was to be bestowed at all it should be considered from a basic view of which orchestras have, or should have, national assignments, and which were of a sufficiently high standard to be able to represent Sweden abroad, said the critics.

The appointment was not about money. The parliamentary committee could not, at this point, make any changes to the proposition's financial content. But a title would not cost the taxpayer any money and the committee was open to the demands of regional politics. Here was a chance to highlight a major cultural institution not based in Stockholm.

The result of the discussions and motions was that one day at the beginning of December 1996, the manager of the Concert Hall was able to interrupt rehearsals of Shostakovich's Third Symphony and announce: "The parliamentary committee has gone against the government and proposed to parliament that the GSO should have the right to call itself the National Orchestra of Sweden".

The picture in the local paper the next day showed a smiling Neeme Järvi raising his baton. The five column headline reads: The GSO is to become the National Orchestra of Sweden.

But things weren't so simple. More letters arrived at the ministry and the parliamentary committee. Jan Lennart

"When I visit the major cities of Europe, I unfortunately get a feeling that Scandinavia isn't really considered part of Europe, it's somewhere up there in the north, and do they really have orchestras there? And composers? Oh, how nice to hear!"
"Our task is to present Swedish and Scandinavian music, both the new and the old. We not only have to play well, we must also present the music that otherwise wouldn't be heard."
"Listen to this. This is excellent music too! We should perform music in such a way that we convince the world."
"Perhaps Stockholm wasn't pleased with our nomination, but why on earth shouldn't the National Orchestra of Sweden be in the country's second city? Sweden is far more than just Stockholm."
Neeme Järvi speaking of the centre and the periphery, and of the National Orchestra title.

Höglund, orchestra producer at the Swedish Broadcasting Corporation in Stockholm with responsibility for collaboration with the country's government funded symphony orchestras, was not happy:

"If there are any reasons other than regional chauvinism for the government and parliament to reward an orchestra with a national title, then this should be awarded to the ensemble or ensembles that have shouldered the greatest responsibility for stimulating native music."

The Swedish Radio Symphony Orchestra had presented more new Swedish music, which statistics would back up. The Swedish Radio Symphony Orchestra also had the biggest audience, and for good reasons. "But neither the orches-

Glädjebud under repetitionen
Göteborgssymfonikerna blir Sveriges första nationalorkester

tra nor its board has seen any reason for it to use the title of National Orchestra of Sweden. That the Royal Stockholm Philharmonic Orchestra would also have just cause – if it so wished – to fight over the title of National Orchestra should also have been clear from the figures," wrote Jan Lennart Höglund in a submission to the parliamentary committee.

The parliamentary debate on 19 December was heated. "Total confusion in parliament" was the summary by journalists of the Gothenburg daily, Göteborgs-Posten. But customarily, parliament votes in accordance with the findings of the committee, and this is what happened. The nomination was final. Parliament backed the orchestra outside the capital. It is also customary for the government, within a relatively brief period, to follow parliaments' decision. But perhaps the government might make an exception, or at least postpone the decision by calling for a new report? The opposition was hoping for this and continued its petitions.

In a letter to Anitra Steen, chairperson of the board of the Stockholm Concert Hall, Sture Carlsson appealed for calmness and reflection: "Being in opposition to both Stockholm institutions would indeed be a miserable fate. We are not out to get you! On the contrary, we want to be able to strengthen the status of orchestral music in Sweden. A Royal Orchestra in Stockholm and a National Orchestra in Gothenburg should be able, between them, to promote and develop musical life which now seems to be threatened from all directions."

Thus far the GSOs development from provincial orchestra to internationally successful symphony orchestra had neither received any support nor been recognised by any of the governments that had been in power over the previous 15 years. The award of the title of National Orchestra of Sweden was perceived, locally and especially by the GSO itself,

Headline in Göteborgs-Posten: Göteborgs Symfoniker named the *National Orchestra of Sweden*.

as recognition for the constructive work carried out within the orchestra and for the success it had achieved.

Time was passing however and in February 1997 the orchestra was still awaiting the government's letter of confirmation.

Sture Carlsson was interviewed by Dagens Nyheter, the leading Swedish daily, and explained that the nomination was recognition of symphonic art in Sweden. "The orchestra has a special lustre," wrote DN and stated that "The GSO will be named the National Orchestra of Sweden."

In March the GSO was to make a three-day guest appearance at the famous Musikverein in Vienna. Stenhammar's *Serenade*, one of the greatest Swedish orchestral works and one of the most difficult to perform, was on the programme. Being able to use the new title on the tour was important, Sture Carlsson realised and wrote a long letter to the secretary of state for culture where he once again explained the GSO's position. But the government took time to decide.

A petition was sent from Gothenburg to the secretary for cultural affairs signed by a number of influential persons with a view to presenting local opinion and pushing the case. The petition was registered at the Department of Cultural Affairs on 8 April. In an interview in Göteborgs-Posten a few days later the department explained that the delay was due to the need to wait for more submissions, including one from the Royal Swedish Academy of Music.

The letter from the Academy arrived on 14 April. It regretted the decision of parliament and asked for a more in-depth discussion "with representatives from interested parties in musical life regarding national status, duration and actual content; concerning the criteria of the decision as well as an analysis of the consequences and discussion of how the issue had been dealt with so far and the competence of the decision-making body." Did the Academy not consider Parliament to be a competent decision-making body?

The questions piled up and further time passed.

"Preparations are under way" was still the department's answer when journalists pressed for a response.

What exactly persuaded the secretary, Marita Ulvskog, to sign the letter of confirmation is not clear, perhaps the delay was becoming a political embarrassment, or perhaps she considered time to be right.

In the first week of May the signal was finally given. The GSO received government confirmation that it was permitted to use the title of *National Orchestra of Sweden*. The secretary was quoted in the press as saying: "The decision has no formal or financial consequences. The most important thing for Gothenburg and the GSO is the recognition of the orchestra's high artistic ability and its importance in the community, both regionally and internationally."

Life at the Gothenburg Concert Hall continued as usual after 7 May. A long tour of Japan was planned for the summer. The schedule also included the musical Jesus Christ Superstar at the Scandinavium arena and two Prom concerts at the Royal Albert Hall in London. Rachmaninov's rarely performed one-act operas were to be recorded for Deutsche Grammophon as well as tone poems by Sibelius and works by 20th century Russians Miaskovsky and Steinberg. A visit to the Stockholm Concert Hall was also planned. "It will be just a little bit more exciting," Sture Carlsson told Göteborgs-Posten, adding in a conciliatory tone, "we have wonderful audiences there, and we always receive a very warm welcome".

The GSO has kept its old name. But the new title has been of great value for the orchestra on international tours.

The gala concert on 4 June 1997 was a euphoric celebration of Neeme Järvi's 60th birthday. A number of favourite pieces were performed, famous favourite artists contributed, the conductor's sons Paavo and Kristjan alternated on the conductor's stand and daughter Maarika performed Reinecke's Flute Concerto in D major for her father. Estonia's Prime Minister, Mart Siiman, was present to honour his country's famous son.
The hall was full and Järvi himself was radiant despite the fact that he didn't get to conduct until the encore.

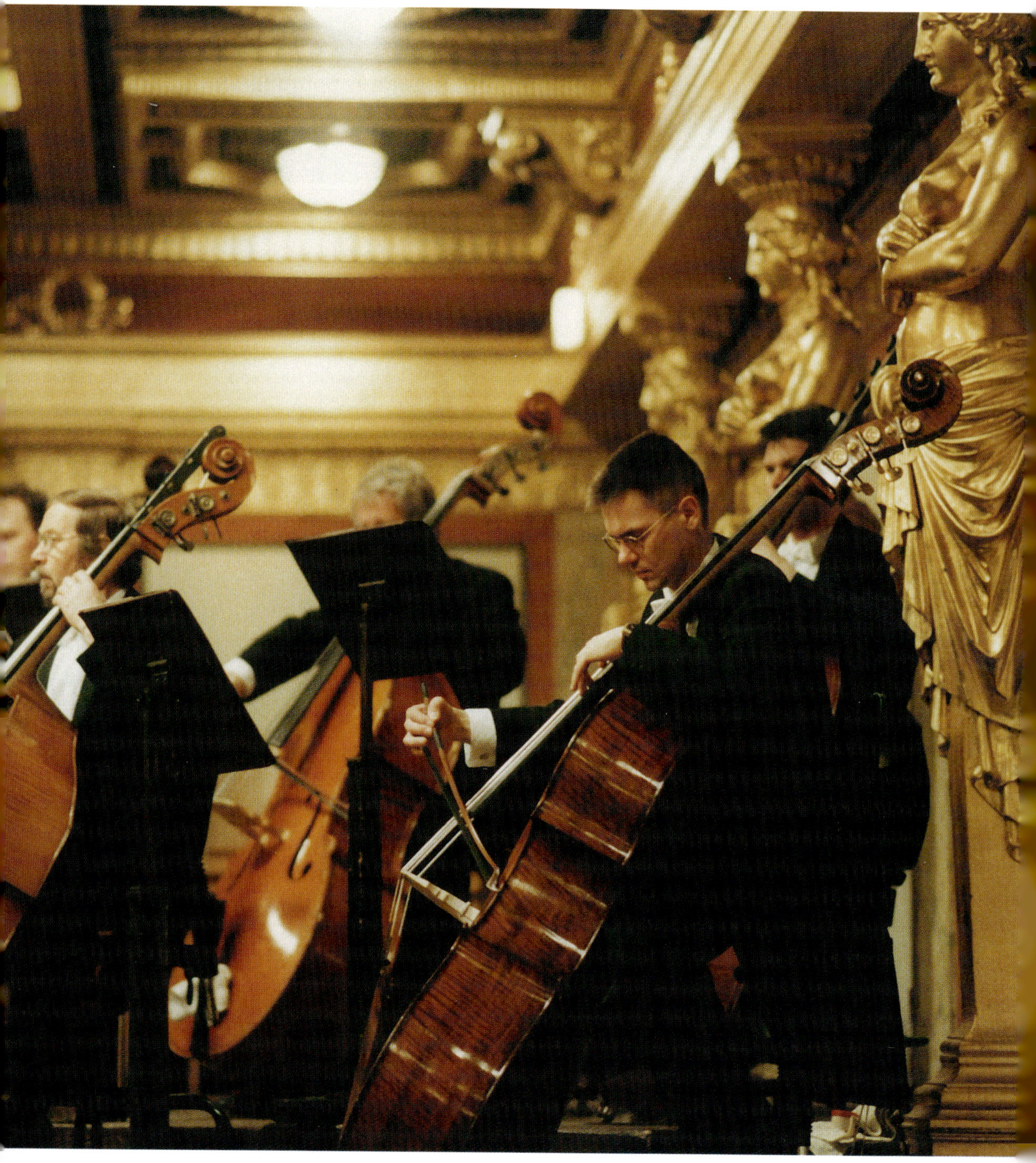

The orchestra on tour

The international tours have resulted in contacts with other cultures, not always of the musical kind. Members of the orchestra were eating a fiery Chinese dish when stage manager Johan Björkman announced: "We have a big problem unloading the instruments." The dish, pieces of meat simmered in a very hot spicy, peppery broth, is served during the winter in China in order to raise body temperature. Central heating is rare and the restaurants are not usually heated.

It was in the middle of the night in Beijing, at the beginning of the Chinese tour in 1999. The Chinese composer Guo Wenjing had invited Neeme Järvi and the GSO management to dinner. The première was a success and Guo Wenjing's piece, *Concerto for Bamboo Flutes* was well received, which was cause for celebration.

Meanwhile Johan Björkman was directing the transportations of all the GSO's equipment on small trucks from one concert hall to another in the huge city. The orchestra was scheduled to take part in an ABBA concert the next day.

"On arrival we realised that there wasn't a ramp to the stage. The Chinese said that we would have to lift the heavy chests off the trucks and carry them along in this huge building. The stage entrance doors were locked. We are talking about five tons of equipment. It was questionable whether we were going to be ready in time for rehearsals by ten the next morning."

CD 2.8 + 2.9

The GSO at Musikverein in Vienna 1994.

Somewhat concerned, Johan Björkman called Sture Carlsson to explain the problem and told him that they would probably be there all night. The dinner guests were ready to return to the hotel in the car that Volvo had placed at their disposal. Sture Carlsson proposed a plan: Neeme Järvi would be quickly taken back to the hotel, and then Sture Carlsson would go straight to Johan. China is an authoritarian country so there was a chance that the unloading might go a bit quicker if the "head man" was there and began shouting orders. "No way," said Neeme Järvi. "I won't go to hotel. If Johan has problem, I come."

The driver realised that time was short and drove like a thief. The car arrived skidding on two wheels in front of the building where the Chinese hired hands – underpaid and bored – were milling around. Shouting at them was useless. The foreman was approached, but the language barrier soon became obvious.

Neeme Järvi then took charge of the situation. He stepped onto a box and began directing the unloading. "One two, one two". The helpers didn't understand one word, but his expressive body language worked as well as during the concert earlier that evening. The protests subsided and everyone got on with things, the missing key to the doors all of a sudden appeared out of nowhere and everything settled. The rather tired concert management wanted to leave, but Neeme Järvi refused. "I'm staying here until Johan has the last trunk inside," he said. "Johan has helped me over the years, now it's my turn to help him."

"China was a profound experience," Johan Björkman explains. He has worked at the Concert Hall and been on tour with Järvi and the orchestra for almost twenty years.

"A surprise was lurking around every corner."

The next day, in the concert hall where Björkman and his

helpers had finally managed to prepare for the concert, the Chinese were rocking away with the GSO and the ABBA band. The company continued on to Shanghai where the pressure was even more intense. The orchestra, conductor Anders Eljas and the singers delivered a mix of ABBA songs and symphonic hits from Benny Andersson's and Björn Ulvaeus' musicals *Chess* and *Kristina from Duvemåla*.

The GSO and the Gothenburg Symphonic Choir were part of the huge "Sweden Goes to China" export drive. The event began purely as a venture for Gothenburg but grew into a national event.

The week in Shanghai was the largest Swedish investment to date in China. Around 500 people with Gothenburg's political leader Göran Johansson at the forefront were part of the delegation. The visit was a display of what western Sweden could offer in the fields of business, culture and sport. Musicians and artists, around 270 people, made up the major part of the delegation.

Thus the GSO made its debut in China. That same year the orchestra also made its Lucerne debut, another remarkable event. The Lucerne Festival is among the finest in the music world. To be invited to perform there is almost as prestigious as performing at the Musikverein in Vienna.

"The Musikverein in Vienna at 11 am on a Sunday is one of my greatest concert memories," says principal cellist, Leo Winland. "We performed Sibelius' Second Symphony…" He interrupts himself: "When were we there Wincent?" Wincent Lindgren, oboist, searches through the tour memories. "When was the debut in Vienna? There have been so many tours over the years."

They arrived in Vienna in October 1994. It was one of the most important concerts in the orchestra's history.

"It was difficult at first," says Wincent Lindgren, "because

The double bass tour dressing-room. Shanghai, China 1999.

Neeme Järvi has a soft spot for big vehicles.

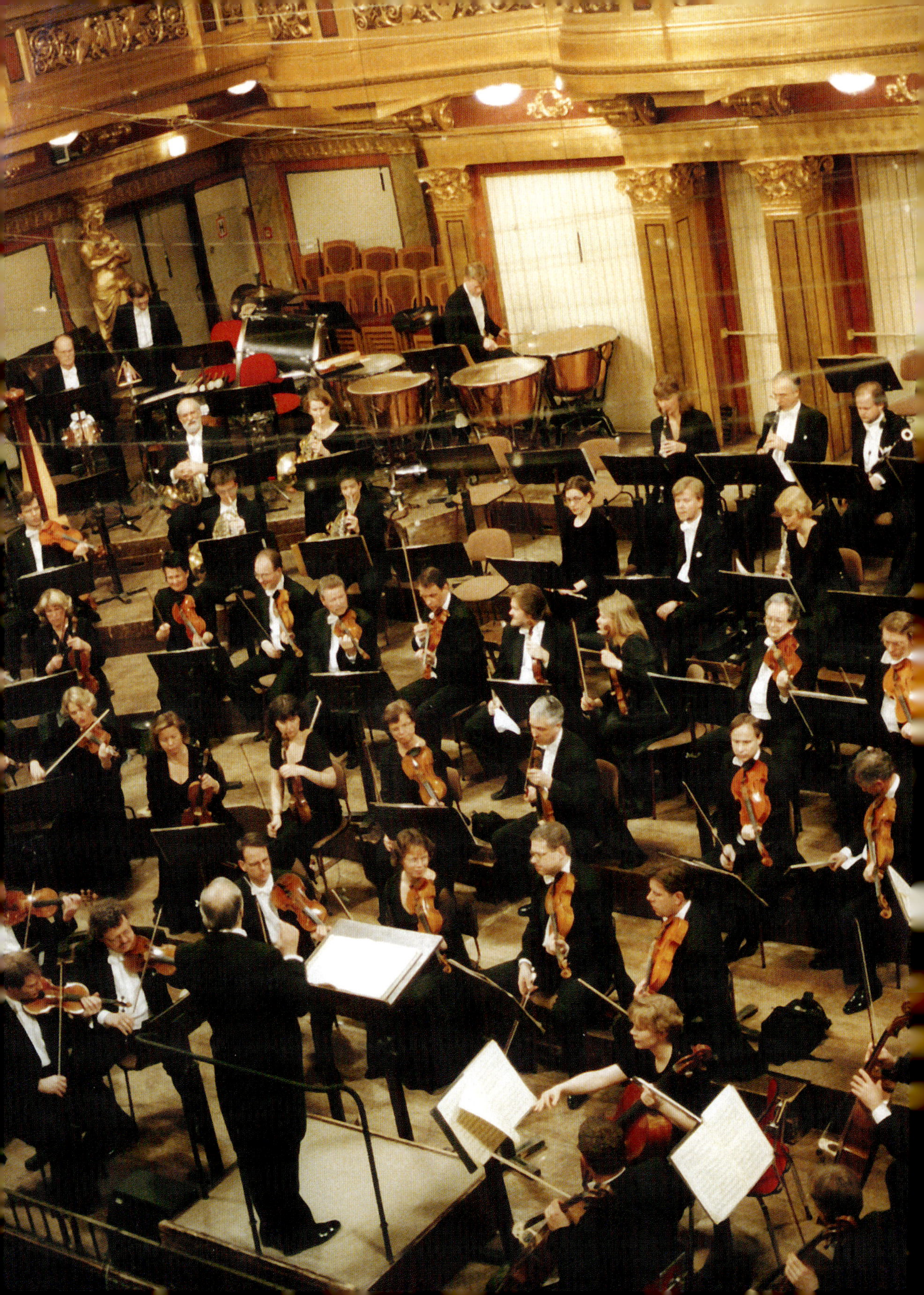

Järvi wasn't pacing things the way we'd rehearsed."

"It was also an unusual time of day for performing, so we had to be on our toes," Leo Winland continues –" And then wow! Afterwards we wondered what really happened? He did the same trick during the tour of the US a few years ago, in Ann Arbor. When the Shostakovich symphony began falling to pieces he suddenly started doing some kind of wild dance up front, which alerted us as well as the audience, and in the end it was quite a success…"

"He surprised the orchestra early on," says Wincent Lindgren, who has been on the tours from the beginning, "by conducting the most important concerts very clearly and articulately, supremely musical with nothing out of place. And the next evening he painted with a completely different brush."

Some reviews are cited more often than others. The following by Christian Heindl of the Vienna Zeitung beats them all:

"People in Musikverein's great hall must for the first time be doubting whether the Vienna Philharmonic's position as 'best' orchestra in the world is truly unchallenged. Those who are familiar with the GSO and their many recordings under Neeme Järvi will not at all be surprised at this 'revelation'. It was a great delight to find that the live concert not only lived up to the impression from the recordings, but in fact exceeded it."

A few hours after the 11 am concert on Sunday 23 October 1994 it was obvious that the Vienna debut had turned into a great success. Some time later Sture Carlsson began to cry; possibly during Sibelius' Second Symphony, he doesn't quite remember, only that "it was so wonderful, it was such a success, and the audience was jubilant."

In Vienna, an orchestra can't ask for more than being compared to the Vienna Philharmonic Orchestra.

And on their home ground as well. The golden hall of the Musikverein is ranked as the musical heart of Europe. But

"Playing Sibelius, the Swedish orchestra revealed all its qualities. Conductor Neeme Järvi is a controlled man with a great amount of concert experience. He performs the music to suit the hall, with plenty of volume…the orchestra, with its mid-European sound, is very well equipped and acts in a disciplined and musical manner. The audience was elated after Sibelius' Second Symphony."
Die Presse, Vienna 24 October 1994.

Neeme Järvi, Maxim Vengerov and Sture Carlsson in Paris 1994.

◉ CD 2.3

The GSO and Neeme Järvi. Musikverein, Vienna 1994.

> "I got a stamp from Hong Kong with a little blue rabbit on."
> **Six year-old Stina, daughter of double bass player Jan Alm, giving an interview at the airport while waiting for her daddy to return after a six-week world tour in 1987.**

> "The orchestra seemed to have calmed down, and it was evident that the curiosity to explore wasn't as strong in Tokyo as in Hong Kong and Singapore. This was probably due to the cold weather. Most members of the orchestra stayed at the hotel and practised in their rooms. You could hear the notes echoing down the corridors. There were the sounds of oboes, bassoons, violins, cellos, flutes, various brass instruments, the tapping of drum sticks which combined to make a pretty remarkable sound in the corridors. Unsuspecting hotel guests gazed somewhat bemusedly at the closed doors."
> **From Benny Hellberg's book Göteborgs Symfonikers världsturné (The GSO's world tour) off art 1987.**

to claim that the GSO equals the Vienna Philharmonic Orchestra, though tempting, would be boasting, say the experts.

The GSO certainly ranks highly among the orchestras of Europe, but the Vienna Philharmonic Orchestra is in a special league (which includes the Berlin Philharmonic Orchestra and the Concertbebouw in Amsterdam... and a few more, which they are is always a matter of opinion.)

The GSO and Järvi travelled from the Austrian capital to Paris, bolstered by the knowledge that they now had a permanent invitation to return to Vienna for series of concerts of their own.

The orchestra performed in Paris for the second year running at the Théâtre des Champs-Élysées. (This was where Stravinsky's *Rite of Spring* was premièred in 1913 and where Josephine Baker danced in her bunch of bananas in the 1920s.) French newspapers recalled the previous year's tour and this brought full houses and rapturous audiences. In November of the same year (1994 was an excellent year) the orchestra travelled to Glasgow – "An absolutely sensational interpretation of Sibelius", was the headline in the Glasgow Herald. Straight after that, the GSO, choir and actors performed a concert version of Sibelius' music to Shakespeare's *The Tempest* at the Shakespeare Festival at London's Barbican Centre. "Intelligently presented and beautifully performed interpretation," said the Times' critic.

There have been many similar tours. Some of more importance to the further development (and reputation) of the orchestra than others, the Autumn Tour 1994 and the Sibelius Festival in 1996 were among the hight points.

The concert at Carnegie Hall in 1983 was also a classic. On that occasion the New York Times critic described the GSO as "a world class orchestra," flattering words for a provincial Swedish orchestra.

The GSO and Neeme Järvi in Berlin 1991.

One member of the audience at Carnegie Hall was viola player Lars Nyström, then a young stand-in orchestra manager and tour manager. As the orchestra performed Sibelius' Second Symphony he shivered with joy and got goose bumps, a reaction not uncommon on the many tours. "I started thinking about my own role in things. Perhaps they played so well because they felt so good. Because everything was well organized? It was at Carnegie Hall that I decided to step down as a musician and to concentrate on the manager's job."

Henry Kissinger and Pehr G Gyllenhammar were also in the audience that day. Volvo had financed a large part of the tour expenses.

Bjørn E Simensen, manager of the Concert Hall in 1983, remembers the hectic time before the tour: "I signed the USA contract without a penny in my pocket, and Volvo at first said no. There wasn't going to be any more money because they had recently promised to donate millions of crowns for 20 new musicians. I then wrote a long letter to Volvo's Ernst Knappe in which I explained the whole situation; that the orchestra

SIBELIUS

12 - 14 April 1996

Symphony Weekend

Gothenburg Symphony Orchestra • Neeme Järvi *conductor*
Concerts and talks exploring Sibelius' seven symphonies

Barbican Centre
The Home of Great Music

Box Office 0171 638 8891 (9am-8pm daily)

Owned, funded and managed by the Corporation of London

gained confidence and status through tours and recordings – that everything is part of a circle. In the end I managed to negotiate a few hundred thousand Swedish crowns."

Touring is expensive. More than one hundred people need to travel and tons of equipment must be shipped. This is where major sponsorship enter. They pay for these activities. Ten percent (2002) of the Concert Hall's funds, nearly a million dollars, come from sponsorship. Of that, around half comes from Volvo.

Without sponsors – no tours. It is not difficult to work out that, as soon as a sponsor pulls out, things quickly become difficult. Replacements must be found quickly.

To return to Carnegie Hall: the young Annika Hjelm standing-in as a first violinist, is also present. "The head of Volvo made his way back stage and thanked us for such a great concert," she recalls. The following year, Annika Hjelm became Sweden's first orchestral musician to be employed and payed by corporate money. She was the first to play on the auditions, and her performance of Bach's D minor partita won the jury over. She was one of several hundred musicians who had applied for the 20 new posts on offer in Gothenburg, with four musicians being hired the first year. The remaining 16 were added slowly but surely. Five years later the GSO was a full-size symphony orchestra.

Annika Hjelm is still with the GSO. She also has a "best tour" memory: "The Proms debut in London in 1989. We performed Nielsen's fifth. There was an amazing atmosphere. A real thriller."

The GSO and Järvi were invited to participate in the Albert Hall's famous series of promenade concerts, the Proms, which attract huge audiences. Best known outside the UK is the Last Night of the Proms, where Edward Elgar's *Pomp and Circumstance No. 1* is performed with the audience singing the

● CD 2.2

Carl Nielsen

CARL NIELSEN 1865–1931

Danish composer, born near Odense on Funen, seventh child of a painter and decorator and village musician. Worked in Gothenburg 1918-1922. He taught at, and was later head of, the Conservatoire in Copenhagen.

Important works: Six symphonies, the operas *Saul and David* (1901) and *Maskarade* (1906), solo concertos for violin (1911), flute (1926) and clarinet (1927), the concert overture *Helios,* a wind quintet, and *Commotio* for organ.

Recordings: The GSO and Neeme Järvi have recorded all the symphonies and other orchestral music on DG. There are also solo concertos and symphonies Nos. 1-3, 5, the *Aladdin Suite* and other orchestral works with Myung-Whun Chung on BIS.

Denmark's most prominent composer has had a crucial influence on his country's music and inspired a number of Scandinavian composers through his work and his well-written ideas about music.

Nielsen began his career as a military musician. He studied composition in Copenhagen and worked as violinist and later as conductor at the Royal Danish Opera. He was good friends with Stenhammar and conducted the orchestra in Gothenburg – not least in his own works – on many occasions both as a regular guest and on longer terms.

Nielsen composed in all genres, his symphonies represent him at his best. It took longer for the world to notice him than it did Sibelius, but Nielsen's symphonies are now part of the standard repertoire. They are filled with fresh melodies and dramatic contrasts. With the powerful third symphony *Sinfonia espansiva* he established his position outside Denmark. During WWI his style changed and in Symphony No. 4 *The Inextinguishable* the irrepressible lust for life becomes almost explosive. After the war his world had changed, and this is obvious in Nielsen's next symphony, the fifth. It is not like any of the others and many people consider it the finest of the six.

With humour, austerity and a sometimes biting irony, he makes his own path from Mahler's universalism to Sibelius' refinement. Nielsen also wrote two memorable books, his memoirs *My childhood on Funen* and *Living music*.

The latter is a collection of essays in which Nielsen considers the clarity of Mozart superior to Wagner and romantic programme music.

patriotic hymn *Land of Hope and Glory* to its closing section. The event is shown on a huge screen in Hyde Park and is broadcast to many countries. The GSO has guested at the Proms on three separate occasions. By 1989 the GSO was an experienced touring orchestra.

Everyone knew what to expect: hard work, frayed nerves, new impulses and artistic challenges. At the beginning of the 1980s a tour of Japan would have been considered a sensation. Now it is simply part of the job.

The first tour of the USA in 1983 has a mythical status. "It was hysterical," say those who were present (shaking their heads and laughing). Wincent Lindgren, who for many years was the orchestra's principal oboe, remembers: "We performed Shostakovich … and I had a crack in my oboe. Sibelius' Second was manageable because the part isn't in such a high register, but Shostakovich's Fifth…that was hard."

"The orchestra performed 20 concerts in 27 days, several in tiny halls with dreadful acoustics in the American Midwest. Everybody apart from Neeme Järvi and the soloists Birgit Finnilä and Frans Helmerson travelled by bus. The viola player Björn Johannesson drove the car carrying Neeme Järvi and his wife, and flautist Kenneth Wihlborg drove the soloists. Kenneth Wihlborg recalls: "We drove 200–300 miles a day. And I was constantly worrying about the fact that I must be alert tonight, because of the piccolo solos. Everything simply has to be right."

"Of course it was difficult, but at the same time it was a wonderful experience." He remembers the first time in Chicago "… at Orchestra Hall. To perform in such a place, respected by every orchestra, was magnificent. At times like these you forget how tired you are."

The tour of the USA ended on 25 October 1983 with the final chord ringing in Chicago's Orchestra Hall, home of the

"During a break in the recording of a CD of Carl Nielsen's second symphony, *The Four Temperaments,* Järvi shouted to me and asked me to come to his room. He looked at something in the score, looked up at me and said: What temperament do you have?"
Peter Schéle, former marketing manager, GSO

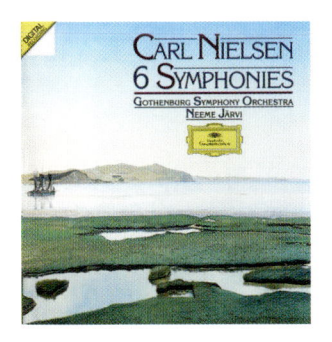

○ CD 1.9

> "The Gothenburg Symphony Orchestra's progress under the supervision of Neeme Järvi has been one of the most notable events on the European orchestral scene."
> **Andrew Clements of the Financial Times after the concert at the Royal Albert Hall in 1989.**

famous Chicago Symphony Orchestra, the audience were on their feet, shouting and applauding. The critics agreed, it was a brilliant debut.

Kenneth Wihlborg has participated on all the tours apart from one, when a gastric ulcer prevented his going. What has been most memorable? He answers without the slightest hesitation: "The fact that I have been part of this fantastic development – that I happened to be around at the right time. What timing! There is an enormous difference between the orchestra today and the orchestra of 20 years ago. Still being able to make the grade is something in itself."

And yes, it's just as much fun after 20 years. Or rather "it's addictive," he says. "We are addicted to it, or at least that's the way it feels. And you have to fight for your victories. In those days I was one of the youngsters, I was a part of the change of generations that everyone said was due. I practised all the time to get better and better. Today I practise to stay on the same level." He explains with an illustration:

"I am always aiming upwards. I'm constantly climbing upwards but I feel as if I'm walking up a down escalator. If I stop climbing up then I inevitably go down."

The US tour opened new doors. An international breakthrough, was what they called it afterwards. The newspapers were perplexed: what had actually happened to the GSO? Neeme Järvi told the press about "the unusually positive situation" at the Gothenburg Concert Hall. "There is a constant creative process going on here, a joint willingness to achieve one's best."

The next high peak was the World Tour in 1987, with a capital W, because there hasn't been anything quite like it, either before or since.

This is the longest tour ever undertaken by a Scandinavian symphony orchestra. Six weeks long, it included visits to

Photos of Shostakovich, a young Neeme Järvi with sideburns and his own grandchildren. Flautist Kenneth Wihlborg's locker door summarises 20 years of life as a member of the GSO.

Singapore, Hong Kong, Japan and the USA and led to future offers from the USA and Japan.

The success of the World Tour of 1987 was sealed at the planning stage. The performance of Brahms' Double Concerto for Violin and Cello in Singapore's Victoria Memorial Hall with soloists Mihaela Martin and Frans Helmerson was a success, as was the second evening when Håkan Hardenberger played Haydn's Trumpet Concerto.

But (as reflected here in the rear-view mirror, say the musicians) history must record the fact that there were some musical lapses. The pressure in Hong Kong was especially great. The tour was also a little too long:

"We are forced to perform as close to perfection all the time in very different conditions. It's not always possible to prepare yourself with enough sleep and food before concerts,

> "The GSO is currently performing in Japan under the supervision of their conductor Neeme Järvi. There have been three concerts in Tokyo, with a great deal of Sibelius, and concerts in Nagoya and Shitzouka. The GSO will be performing this week in Hiroshima and Osaka. The GSO was also in Japan in 1987 and has numerous admirers here since that time.
> The concerts have been sold out and standing ovations have been commonplace, according to communications director Peter Schéle."
>
> **Dagens Nyheter, Friday 15 March 1991. Headline: Sold out in Japan.**

> "Powerful performance by the GSO of Shostakovich's Fifth Symphony. But without going over the top. Previous guest performances have seen Järvi tend to let himself be carried away by the music, but here the conductor was controlled and disciplined.
> A high point was the subtle string performance of the *Largo*, rarely have we heard such controlled perfection by an orchestra."
>
> **Lars Hedblad describing the GSO's guest performance at the Stockholm Concert Hall, Svenska Dagbladet, 6 February 2001.**

as you do at home. It's a risky enterprise. We got ashore, but we could have done better."

A schedule, which is too tight causes problems on long tours. Non-musical events can distract players.

It may be difficult to find time to practice and recharge batteries between events. Tours actually require more practice than otherwise, because muscles can become stiff when travelling.

In retrospect, the world tour was a very valuable experience and it also proved to be a huge endurance-test. Two and a half years' of preparations preceded the adventure. This involved booking countless numbers of rooms in around 30 hotels, as well as assembling huge piles of scores and parts. 60 cubic metres of instruments worth millions of crowns had to be packed. A doctor, a physiotherapist and instrument repairer accompanied the tour. (The Leningrad tour in 1985 was carried out with an entire orchestra suffering from a stomach disorder.)

Preparations for tours of this magnitude are, according to the GSO's Lars Nyström, like a Persian rug. "There are a lot of loose ends to tie up before it's ready. But the end result is often seamless and very beautiful."

During the world tour the orchestra learned all about touring. Every concert hall has its peculiarities, and the orchestra has to be placed accordingly and adapt its sound. Shared experiences like these bring the musicians together. The critics were positive. All concerts were sold out in Japan. The orchestra often played three encores, receiving standing ovations and had 200 people applauding the musicians when they left by the stage door. The final concert in the USA could not have been better. Publicity on arrival in Sweden was enormous and initially, only positive.

The fly in the ointment came when the invoices arrived and the costs proved to be higher than estimated.

Preparations for the concert in Chicago Symphony Hall 1987.

The newspaper headlines were pitch black. The reasons for the losses were discussed. Shouldn't the orchestra have stayed home? Bengt Hörnberg has been both praised and criticised for this on numerous occasions. Praise from people who concidered it right not to cancel at the last minute, despite less funding from sponsors than expected. If the tour, which had been booked for years, hadn't been carried out then the successful development ot the GSO's might have been delayed for years.

Santa Barbara, California 1987.

"Everyone is personally responsible for their own instruments during the entire tour. This means that every instrument to be transported by the instrument bus should be placed in accordance with Johan Björkman's instructions no later than 30 minutes after the end of the concert.
NB! It is important that the number of instruments tallies with the documentation when passing through customs. EVERYTHING not on the carnet will be removed. If the information isn't correct according to the carnet the entire tour may be in danger."
From information to the musicians, Vienna tour 1994.

"As for the music itself, I'm not content to do just what is 'right'. We also have to think of what will excite the musicians in the music they play."
Neeme Järvi in an interview in the International Herald Tribune for the World Tour in 1987.

The losses were covered by private funds connected with the Concert Hall and administered by the municipality.

The city's accountants sighed and their report gave advice on more careful calculations for the future.

New tours were already planned. Later that summer the orchestra travelled to Ravello in Italy. And the next year once again to the USA.

The orchestra's position was further strengthened by its regular subscription series at the Stockholm Concert Hall. Stockholm was, and is, an important tour destination.

There are many more tour memories. The first appearance at Berlin's Schauspielhaus, was a typical hair-raising experience: "You can play just as well at home, but it's that special feeling that arises at unknown halls. Togetherness, suspense, the journey, beeing away from everyday life. You practise intensively and all want to succeed. It's nerve racking. There's an enormous energy. When we arrived, Claudio Abbado sat listening to the dress rehearsal, and even Zubin Mehta I believe… both world class conductors. You feel that you are the centre of attention, and you bring that experience with you to the next concert."

The Berliner Zeitung considered the debut a triumph and stated that one of Sweden's oldest and most famous musical ensemble provided a solid sound to lean on: "Only small gestures were required from the conductor to find the right touch… The musicians were brilliant. Charm, the ability to articulate, deftness of rhythm and secure intonation stay with you. The orchestra, soloists and conductor deserved all their bouquets."

At this stage, Neeme Järvi couldn't find his baton among all the bouquets of flowers when it was time for the encores.

"When this orchestra visits Stockholm there are often standing ovations. It is difficult to say if this is because of the generous nature of the Stockholm audience, the many visiting supporters from Gothenburg, or quite simply because the orchestra is outstanding. The reason could possibly be the latter."
Leo Lagercrantz
Expressen 5 February 2001.

GSO TRAVEL ITINERARY 2000–2001

5 Aug. Trollhättan
3 Oct. Eskilstuna
4 Oct. Linköping
6 Oct. Malmö
7 Oct. Växjö
13 Oct. Jönköping
12 Nov. Paris
13 Nov. Amsterdam
15 Nov. Toulouse
16 Nov. Metz
3 Feb. Stockholm
5–10 Feb. Italy: Turin, Milan, Ferrara
6–17 June Sweden
In addition around 80 concerts were given at the Gothenburg Concert Hall

Tours – GSO and Neeme Järvi on tour 1980–2003

JUNE 1980: Dublin Aldeburgh Festival
London – Royal Festival Hall
Hugo Alfvén Midsummer Vigil
Edvard Grieg Fra Monte Pincio &
The Last Spring
Arvo Pärt Cantus in memory of
Benjamin Britten
Richard Strauss Vier letzte Lieder
Jean Sibelius Symphony No. 2
Elisabeth Söderström soprano

JANUARY 1983: Halmstad
Wolfgang Amadeus Mozart
Overture to Titus
Jean Sibelius Finlandia
Wolfgang Amadeus Mozart
Piano Concerto No. 27
Jean Sibelius Symphony No. 3
Christian Blackshaw piano

OCTOBER 1983: USA
Hugo Alfvén Midsummer Vigil
Lars-Erik Larsson Pastoral Suite
Antonín Dvořák Cello Concerto
Artur Lemba Piano Concerto No. 1
Gustav Mahler Lieder eines
fahrenden Gesellen
Dmitri Shostakovich Symphony No. 5
Jean Sibelius Symphony No. 2
Frans Helmerson cello
Samuel Dilworth-Leslie piano
Birgit Finnilä alto

SEPTEMBER 1984: Oslo
Hugo Alfvén Midsummer Vigil
Johannes Brahms Double Concerto for
Violin and Cello
Jean Sibelius Symphony No. 2
Arve Tellefsen violin
Frans Helmerson cello

NOVEMBER 1984: Stockholm
Franz Berwald Sinfonie capricieuse
Wilhelm Stenhammar Symphony No. 1

MAY/JUNE 1985: Soviet Union
Conductor Göran W Nilson
Soloist Frans Helmerson cello
Leningrad, Tblisi, Moscow
Karl-Birger Blomdahl Sisyfos
Dmitri Shostakovich
Cello Concerto No. 1
Jean Sibelius Symphony No. 2
Hugo Alfvén Midsummer Vigil
Joseph Haydn Cello Concerto
Franz Berwald Sinfonie naïve

JUNI 1985: Marstrand
Hugo Alfvén Festspel
Jean Sibelius Karelia Suite
Johann Strauss II Voices of The Last
Spring
Anonymous Den blomstertid nu kommer
Evert Taube Rosa på bal
Evert Taube Sommarnatt
Johann Strauss II Tritsch-Tratsch polka
Antonín Dvořák Two Slavonic Dances
Jerry Bock If I were a rich man from
Fiddler on the Roof
Hector Berlioz Hungarian March from
La Damnation de Faust

OCTOBER 1985: Flanders
Conductor Moshe Atzmon
Wolfgang Amadeus Mozart
Violin Concerto No. 3
Anton Bruckner Symphony No. 5
Hugo Alfvén Festspel
Hector Berlioz Hungarian March
from La Damnation de Faust
Antonín Dvořák Four Slavonic Dances
Jean Sibelius Karelia Suite
Johann Strauss II Tritsch, Tratsch Polka
Johann Strauss II Voices of Spring
Kun Hu violin

FEBRUARY/MARCH 1986: Linz, Ulm,
Friedrichshaven, Zürich, Frankfurt,
Mannheim, Düsseldorf
Franz Berwald Sinfonie sérieuse
Joseph Haydn Trumpet Concerto
Alessandro Marcello Trumpet Concerto
in C minor
Jean Sibelius Symphony No. 5
Modest Mussorgsky/Maurice Ravel
Pictures at an Exhibition
Maurice André trumpet

MARCH 1986: Trollhättan, Halmstad
Edvard Grieg Symphonic Dances
Igor Stravinsky Concertino for Piano
and Wind Instruments
Antonín Dvořák Slavonic Dances,
Op. 46
Boris Berman piano

SEPTEMBER 1986: Helsinki
Edouard Lalo Symphonie espagnole
Dmitri Shostakovich Symphony No. 10
Mayumi Fujikawa violin

FEBRUARY/MARCH 1987: Singapore,
Hong Kong, Japan, USA
Antonín Dvořák Carneval
Dag Wirén Serenade for
String Orchestra
Edvard Grieg Norwegian Dances
Franz Berwald Sinfonie naïve
Overture to Estrella de Soria
Hugo Alfvén Midsummer Vigil
Antonín Dvořák Cello Concerto
Carl Nielsen Clarinet Concerto
Eino Tamberg Trumpet Concerto
Jean Sibelius Violin Concerto
Johannes Brahms Double Concerto for
Violin and Cello
Ludwig van Beethoven Violin Concerto
Sergei Rachmaninov Piano Concerto No. 2
Sergei Prokofiev Sinfonia concertante
Antonín Dvořák Symphony No. 7
Jean Sibelius Symphony No. 2

Johannes Brahms Symphony No. 1
Sergei Prokofiev Symphony No. 5
Frans Helmerson cello
Olle Schill clarinet
Håkan Hardenberger trumpet
Mihaela Martin violin (J.S., J.B.)
Henryk Szeryng violin (L.v B.)
Harumi Hanafusa piano

JULY 1987: Ravello, Italy
Edvard Grieg Peer Gynt: Suites Nos. 1 & 2
Piano Concerto
Richard Wagner Prelude to The
Mastersingers of Nuremberg
Johannes Brahms Symphony No. 1
Richard Wagner Good Friday Music
from Parsifal
Joseph Haydn Trumpet Concerto
Richard Wagner Orchestral Suite from
Götterdämmerung
Jean Sibelius Symphony No. 2
Richard Wagner Overture to Tannhäuser
Roland Pöntinen piano
Håkan Hardenberger trumpet

MARCH 1988: Concertgebouw–Amsterdam, Cardiff, Eastbourne, Ipswich, Middlesbrough, Bradford, Nottingham, Birmingham, Leicester, Royal Festival Hall – London
Edvard Grieg Norwegian Dances
Franz Berwald Overture to
Estrella de Soria
Johannes Brahms Double Concerto,
Violin Concerto
César Franck Symphony in D minor
Jean Sibelius Symphony No. 1
Kyung-Wha Chung violin
Myung-Wha Chung cello
Boris Belkin violin

JUNE 1988: Minnesota, USA
Carin Malmlöf-Forssling Flowings
Gustav Mahler Symphony No. 8
Hugo Alfvén Midsummer Vigil
Franz Berwald Sinfonie singulière
Irving Berlin There's No Business Like
Show Business from Annie Get Your Gun
Wilhelm Stenhammar Symphony No. 1

Bengt Hallberg Glädjens dansande
sträng
Hugo Alfvén Dance of the Herdmaiden
from The Mountain King
Edvard Grieg Wedding Scene
from Peer Gynt
Carl Orff In Taberna from Carmina
Burana
Birgitta Svendén mezzo-soprano
Elisabeth Erikson soprano
Janis Hardy alto
Karen Williams soprano
Kenneth Riegel tenor
Lena Nordin soprano
Leroy Lehr bass
Magnus Fagerberg baritone
Orphei Drängar
Midsummer Children's Chorus
Midsummer Festival Chorus

AUGUST 1989: Edinburgh Festival, London Proms
Arvo Pärt Symphony No. 3
Jan Sandström Éra
Jean Sibelius Lemminkäinen and the
Maidens of the Island
Lemminkäinen in Tuonela
Violin Concerto, Symphony No. 2
Felix Mendelssohn Violin Concerto No. 2
Edvard Grieg Piano Concerto
Manuel de Falla The Three-cornered Hat
(complete)
Carl Nielsen Symphony No. 5
Cho-Liang Lin violin
Roland Pöntinen piano
Christine Cairns alto

SEPTEMBER 1989: Tallinn, Estonia
Hugo Alfvén Midsummer Vigil
Jan Sandström Éra
Arvo Pärt Symphony No. 3
Manuel de Falla The Three-Cornered Hat
(complete)
Carl Nielsen Symphony No. 5
Eino Tamberg Trumpet Concerto
Jean Sibelius Symphony No. 2
Barbro Marklund alto
Håkan Hardenberger trumpet

MARCH 1990: Turku, Helsinki
Jean Sibelius En saga
Gustav Mahler Kindertotenlieder
Béla Bartók Concerto for Orchestra
Birgit Finnilä alto

SEPTEMBER 1990: Aardenburg – Flanders Festival
Jean Sibelius En saga
Modest Mussorgsky/Dmitri Shostakovich
Songs and Dances of Death
Dmitri Shostakovich Symphony No. 12
'The Year 1917'
Ulrik Cold bass

SEPTEMBER 1990: Brussels, Gent – Flanders Festival
Jean Sibelius En saga
Benjamin Britten Sinfonia da requiem
Wolfgang Amadeus Mozart Requiem

MARCH 1991: Nagoya, Shizuoka, Tokyo, Hiroshima, Osaka
Daniel Börtz Sinfonia I
Jean Sibelius Lemminkäinen Legends
Richard Strauss Don Juan
Felix Mendelssohn Violin Concerto No. 1
Jean Sibelius En saga, Symphony No. 2
Nikolai Rimsky-Korsakov Scheherazade
Béla Bartók Concerto for Orchestra
Reiko Watanabe violin

OCTOBER 1991: Rouen – Festival Octobre en Normandie
Einojuhani Rautavaara A Requiem in Our Time
Edvard Grieg Peer Gynt: Suites Nos. 1 & 2
Jean Sibelius Symphony No. 2

OCTOBER 1991: Le Havre – Festival Octobre en Normandie
Arvo Pärt Cantus in memory of Benjamin Britten
Antonín Dvořák Cello Concerto
Béla Bartók Concerto for Orchestra
Frans Helmerson cello

OCTOBER 1991: Stuttgart, Kassel, Düsseldorf, Braunschweig, Hamburg, Frankfurt, Munich, Rosenheim, Berlin
Joseph Haydn Symphony No. 102
Jean Sibelius En saga
Antonín Dvořák Cello Concerto
Joseph Haydn Trumpet Concerto
Jan Sandström Trumpet Concerto
Béla Bartók Concerto for Orchestra
Pyotr Tchaikovsky Symphony No. 5
Frans Helmerson cello
Håkan Hardenberger trumpet

MARCH 1992: Stockholm, Kalmar
Arvo Pärt Fratres
Eduard Tubin Symphony No. 5
Pyotr Tchaikovsky Symphony No. 5

AUGUST 1992: Kiel – Schleswig-Holstein Festival
Igor Stravinsky Suite from The Firebird
Wilhelm Stenhammar Piano Concerto No. 2
Jean Sibelius Symphony No. 2
Cristina Ortiz piano

AUGUST 1992: Eutin – Schleswig-Holstein Festival
Hugo Alfvén Midsummer Vigil
Edvard Grieg Piano Concerto
Eduard Tubin Symphony No. 5
Bruno Leonardo Gelber piano

AUGUST 1992: Seville – World Fair
Hugo Alfvén Midsummer Vigil
Wilhelm Stenhammar Piano Concerto No. 2
Igor Stravinsky The Firebird (complete)
Cristina Ortiz piano
Manuel de Falla La Vida Breve: Interlude and Dance
Joseph Haydn Trumpet concerto
Jean Sibelius Symphony No. 2
Håkan Hardenberger trumpet

NOVEMBER 1992: London – Barbican Centre, Warwick
Jean Sibelius En saga
Wilhelm Stenhammar Piano Concerto No. 2
Igor Stravinsky The Firebird (complete)
Cristina Ortiz piano

NOVEMBER 1992: Nottingham
Edvard Grieg Peer Gynt: Suites Nos. 1 & 2
Wilhelm Stenhammar Piano Concerto No. 2
Igor Stravinsky The Firebird (complete)
Cristina Ortiz piano

NOVEMBER 1992: London – Barbican Centre
Edvard Grieg Peer Gynt (complete concert version, world première)
Barbara Bonney soprano
Håkan Hagegård baritone
Der-Shin Hwang mezzo-soprano
Simon Callow and other narrators
Tallis Chamber Choir
Knut Buen Hardanger fiddle

NOVEMBER 1992: Cardiff, Birmingham
Edvard Grieg Peer Gynt: Suites Nos. 1 & 2
Richard Strauss Morgen, Meinem Kinde, Wiegenlied, Ich wollt' ein Sträusslein binden, Ständchen
Igor Stravinsky The Firebird (complete)
Jean Sibelius Karelia Suite
Barbara Bonney soprano

MARCH 1993: Oslo
Edvard Grieg In Autumn
Piano Concerto
Wilhelm Stenhammar Symphony No. 1
Sigurd Slåttebrekk piano

APRIL 1993: Stockholm
Franz Schubert Symphony No. 5
Hugo Alfvén Symphony No. 4

MAY 1993: Stockholm
Wilhelm Stenhammar Excelsior!
Ludwig van Beethoven Piano Concerto No. 2
Igor Stravinsky The Rite of Spring
Christian Zacharias piano

SEPTEMBER 1993: Stuttgart
Ludwig van Beethoven Egmont Overture
Antonín Dvořák Cello Concerto
Pyotr Tchaikovsky Symphony No. 5
Bedrich Smetana Ma Vlast: Vltava, Sarka, From Bohemia's Woods and Fields
Antonín Dvořák Slavonic Dances, Op. 46
Wilhelm Stenhammar Symphony No. 2
Mischa Maisky cello

OCTOBER 1993: Munich, Paris, Douai
Carl Nielsen Aladdin Suite
Sergei Rachmaninov Piano Concerto No. 2
Jean Sibelius Symphony No. 2
Wilhelm Stenhammar Symphony No. 2
Hélène Grimaud piano

OCTOBER 1993: London
Edvard Grieg Peer Gynt (complete concert version)
Solveig Kringelborn soprano
Der-Shin Hwang mezzo-soprano
Karl-Magnus Fredriksson baritone
Knut Buen Hardanger fiddle
Tallis Chamber Choir, Actors

NOVEMBER/DECEMBER 1993: Bern, Geneva, Lausanne, St Gallen, Zürich, Basel
Wilhelm Stenhammar Excelsior!
Ludwig van Beethoven Triple Concerto
Carl Nielsen Symphony No. 2 "The four temperaments"

Frans Helmerson cello
Mihaela Martin violin
Roland Pöntinen piano

OCTOBER 1994: Vienna– Musikverein
Jean Sibelius Karelia Overture
Eino Tamberg Trumpet Concerto
Arvo Pärt Concerto piccolo über B-A-C-H
Jean Sibelius Symphony No. 2
Håkan Hardenberger trumpet
Wilhelm Stenhammar Excelsior!
Jean Sibelius Violin Concerto
Hugo Alfvén Midsummer Vigil
Eduard Tubin Symphony No. 6
Maxim Vengerov violin

OCTOBER 1994: Paris
Hugo Alfvén Midsummer Vigil
Jean Sibelius Violin Concerto
Modest Mussorgsky/Maurice Ravel
Pictures at an Exhibition
Maxim Vengerov violin

NOVEMBER 1994: Glasgow
Carl Nielsen Aladdin Suite
Eino Tamberg Trumpet concerto
Arvo Pärt Concerto piccolo über B-A-C-H
Jean Sibelius Symphony No. 2
Håkan Hardenberger trumpet

NOVEMBER 1994: London – Barbican Centre
Jean Sibelius The Tempest (complete)
Susan Gritton soprano
Monica Groop mezzo-soprano
Alan Opie baritone
Tallis Chamber Choir
Alec McCowen, Alexander Hardy,
Andy Rashleig, Dave Hill and other actors

FEBRUARY 1995: Canary Islands
Einojuhani Rautavaara
A Requiem in Our Time
Jean Sibelius Tapiola
Hugo Alfvén Dalecarlian Rhapsody
Igor Stravinsky Psalm Symphony
Alexander Scriabin Symphony No. 1

Carl Nielsen Symphony No. 4
Ilya Levinsky tenor
Irina Tchistyakova mezzo-soprano
Gothenburg Symphonic Choir

OCTOBER/NOVEMBER 1995: Munich, Cologne, Düsseldorf, Berlin, Hamburg, Madrid, Corunna, Valencia
Franz Berwald Sinfonie naïve
Hugo Alfvén Midsummer Vigil
Edvard Grieg The Last Spring,
A Swan, Solveig's Song
Wilhelm Stenhammar I skogen
Richard Strauss Ich wollt' ein
Sträusslein binden, Ständchen
Wiegenlied, Morgen
Wilhelm Stenhammar Flickan kom ifrån
sin älsklings möte, Fylgia
Hugo Alfvén The Forest Sleeps
Carl Nielsen Symphony No. 4
Jean Sibelius Symphony No. 2
Barbara Bonney soprano

APRIL 1996: London
Sibelius Festival at the Barbican Centre
Symphony No. 7
Violin Concerto
Symphony No. 3
Cho-Liang Lin violin

The Oceanides
Symphony No. 4
Symphony No. 1
Tapiola
Valse triste from Kuolema
Symphony No. 2

Pohjola's Daughter
Symphony No. 6
Symphony No. 5

APRIL 1996: Birmingham
Sibelius Festival at Symphony Hall
The Oceanides
Symphony No. 4
Symphony No. 1
Pohjola's Daughter
Symphony No. 6
Symphony No. 2

Symphony No. 7
Symphony No. 3
Symphony No. 5

NOVEMBER 1996: Stockholm, Berwaldhallen
Aulis Sallinen Symphony No. 7
Edward Elgar Cello Concerto
Sergei Prokofiev Symphony No. 6
Leo Winland cello

MARCH 1997: Vienna – Musikverein, Orchestra in residence
Eduard Tubin Suite from the ballet Kratt
Modest Mussorgsky/ Dmitri Shostakovich
Songs and Dances of Death
Jean Sibelius Symphony No. 1
Paata Burchuladze bass
Ingvar Lidholm Toccata e canto
Eduard Tubin Symphony No. 5
Igor Stravinsky The Rite of Spring
Wilhelm Stenhammar Serenade
Eduard Tubin Balalaika Concerto
Sergei Prokofiev Romeo and Juliet:
Suite No. 1
Gennady Zut balalaika

JUNE/JULY 1997: Osaka, Nagoya, Fukushima, Matsudo, Omiya, Tokyo
Eduard Tubin Suite from the ballet Kratt
Jean Sibelius Finlandia
Jean Sibelius Symphony No. 2
Edvard Grieg Piano Concerto
Jean Sibelius Violin Concerto
Niccolò Paganini Violin Concerto No. 2
Hector Berlioz Symphonie fantastique
Yukio Yokoyama piano
Vadim Repin violin

SEPTEMBER 1997: London – BBC Proms
Johannes Brahms Rinaldo
Sergei Prokofiev Violin Concerto No. 1
Jean Sibelius Symphony No. 5
Orphei Drängar male voice choir
Stig Andersen tenor
Cho-Liang Lin violin

Igor Stravinsky Oedipus Rex
Béla Bartók Concerto for Orchestra
Michael Pennington narrator
Anne Sofie von Otter mezzo-soprano
Anthony Rolfe Johnson tenor
Jón Rúnar Arason tenor
Alan Opie bass
Ronnie Johansen bass
Orphei Drängar male voice choir

SEPTEMBER 1998: Stockholm
Gunnar Bucht Symphony No. 12
»Movements sonores et accentés«
Alban Berg Early Songs
Hector Berlioz Symphonie fantastique
Håkan Hagegård baritone

MARCH 1999: China – Beijing, Shanghai
Anders Hillborg King Tide
Lars-Erik Larsson God in Disguise
Carl Orff Carmina Burana
Guo Wen-jing Concerto for bamboo flutes »Chou Kong Shan«
Jean Sibelius Symphony No. 2
Karin Ingebäck soprano
Lars-Erik Jonsson tenor
Mats Persson baritone
Dai Ya bamboo flutes
Gothenburg Symphonic Choir

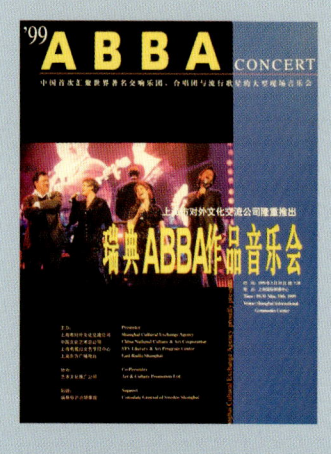

MAY 1999: Tallinn, Riga
Anders Hillborg King Tide
Carl Nielsen Symphony No. 4
Richard Strauss An Alpine Symphony

MAY 1999: Glasgow, Manchester, Birmingham, London
Gioacchino Rossini Overture to The Thieving Magpie
Richard Wagner Overture to The Flying Dutchman
Die Frist ist um from The Flying Dutchman, The Ride of the Valkyries, Wotan's farewell from Die Walküre
Johann Hummel Trumpet Concerto
Rolf Martinsson Bridge, Trumpet Concerto No. 1
Arvo Pärt Concerto piccolo über B-A-C-H
Anders Hillborg King Tide
Richard Strauss An Alpine Symphony
Carl Nielsen Symphony No. 4
Håkan Hardenberger trumpet
Willard White bass

SEPTEMBER 1999: Lucerne Festival, Verona, Merano
Edvard Grieg Peer Gynt: Suite Nos. 1 & 2,
Giya Kancheli Mourned by the wind, liturgy for viola and orchestra
Carl Nielsen Violin Concerto
Gustav Mahler Five Rückert Lieder
Jean Sibelius Lemminkäinen Suite
Pyotr Tchaikovsky Manfred Symphony
Yuri Bashmet viola
Nikolaj Znaider, violin
Anna Larsson alto

NOVEMBER 1999: Frankfurt, Berlin, Braunschweig, Cologne, Düsseldorf, Stuttgart, Vienna, Ljubljana
Anders Hillborg King Tide
Arvo Pärt Symphony No. 3, Tabula rasa
Franz Schubert Unfinished Symphony
Robert Schumann Piano Concerto

Sergei Rachmaninov
Piano Concerto No. 2
Carl Nielsen Symphony No. 5
Pyotr Tchaikovsky Symphony No. 6
»Pathétique«
Liang-Chai violin
Adele Anthony violin
Cristoph Berner piano (R.S.)
Hélène Grimaud piano (S.R.)

JANUARY 2000: Stockholm
Rolf Martinsson
Bridge, Trumpet Concerto No. 1
Gustav Mahler Symphony No. 7
Håkan Hardenberger trumpet

FEBRUARY 2000: USA – Ann Arbor, Washington, New York
Arvo Pärt Symphony No. 3
Edvard Grieg Fra Monte Pincio, The Last Spring
Giya Kancheli Mourned by the Wind, liturgy for viola and orchestra
Dmitri Shostakovich Symphony No. 6
Jean Sibelius The Diamond on the March Snow
Wilhelm Stenhammar Flickan kom ifrån sin älsklings möte
Hugo Alfvén The forest sleeps
Barbara Bonney soprano
Yuri Bashmet viola

JUNE 2000: Hanover – Expo 2000 Conductor Mikko Franck
Hugo Alfvén Midsummer Vigil
Wilhelm Stenhammar
Florez and Blanzeflor
Ture Rangström Kung Eriks visor
Allan Pettersson Symphony No. 7
Håkan Hagegård baritone

An Axel Carpelan.

Symphonie No. 2
D DUR

FÜR GROSSES ORCHESTER

komponiert von

JEAN SIBELIUS

Partitur M. 20.— Orchesterstimmen 25 Hefte je 90 Pf.

Eigentum der Verleger für alle Länder

BREITKOPF & HÄRTEL
LEIPZIG · BRÜSSEL · LONDON · NEW YORK
HELSINGFORS NYA MUSIKHANDEL (Fazer & Westerlund), HELSINGFORS

Copyright 1903, by Breitkopf & Härtel.

NOVEMBER 2000: Paris, Amsterdam, Toulouse, Metz
Wilhelm Stenhammar Excelsior!
Camille Saint-Saëns Cello Concerto No. 1
Jean Sibelius Violin Concerto
Wilhelm Stenhammar Flickan knyter i Johannenatten, Flickan kom ifrån sin älsklings möte
Edvard Grieg Peer Gynt: Suite No. 1
Dmitri Shostakovich Symphony No. 6
Jean Sibelius The Diamond on the March Snow
Hugo Alfvén The Forest Sleeps
Hans Gefors Den Flammande from Lydias romanser
Edvard Grieg A Swan, Fra Monte Pincio
Jean Sibelius Symphony No. 5
Alexander Kniazev cello
Nikolaj Znaider violin
Anne Sofie von Otter mezzo-soprano

FEBRUARY 2001: Stockholm
Italy – Turin, Milan, Ferrara
Benjamin Britten Peter Grimes: Four Sea-Interludes
Gustav Mahler Lieder eines fahrenden Gesellen
Dmitri Shostakovich Symphony No. 5
Karl-Magnus Fredriksson baritone

APRIL 2001: Belgium – Palais des Beaux Arts, Brussels – Conductor Mikko Franck
Hugo Alfvén Midsummer Vigil
Wilhelm Stenhammar Florez and Blanzeflor
Ture Rangström Kung Eriks visor
Jean Sibelius Symphony No. 1
Håkan Hagegård baritone

AUGUST 2001: BBC Proms – London, Salzburger Festspiele
Conductor Manfred Honeck
Edvard Grieg Peer Gynt
(complete concert version)
Barbara Bonney soprano
Bo Skovhus baritone
Ingebjørg Kosmo mezzo-soprano
Joar Skorpen Hardanger fiddle
Sverre Anker Ousdal actor
Wenche Foss actress
Simon Callow narrator
BBC Singers

FEBRUARY 2002: Jönköping
Conductor Mark Wigglesworth
Mahler Symphony No. 10

APRIL 2002: Stockholm Concert Hall
Conductor Mario Venzago
Ludwig van Beethoven Piano Concerto No. 2
Dmitri Shostakovich Symphony No. 4
Boris Berman piano

OCTOBER 2002: Oslo Concert hall
Conductor Joseph Swensen
Richard Strauss Don Juan
Frank Martin Jedermann monologues
Wilhelm Stenhammar Interlude from Sången
Alfvén The forest Sleeps
Edvard Grieg The Mountain Thrall
Igor Stravinsky The Rite of Spring
Håkan Hagegård baritone

NOVEMBER 2002: Japan – Takamatsu, Tsukuba, Yokohama, Osaka, Tokyo Suntory Hall, Sapporo, Tokyo Opera City Hall
Rolf Martinsson A.S. in Memoriam
Jean Sibelius Violin Concerto
Mahler Symphony No. 1
Julian Rachlin violin
Rolf Martinsson A.S. in Memoriam
Edvard Grieg Piano Concerto
Jean Sibelius Symphony No. 5
Hiroko Nakamura piano

FEBRUARY 2003: Stockholm Concert Hall
Anders Hillborg Dreaming River
Gösta Nystroem Sånger vid havet
Sergei Rachmaninov Symphonic Dances
Anna Larsson alto

MARCH 2003: Rotterdam, Dortmund, Cologne, Düsseldorf, Stuttgart, Karlsruhe, Frankfurt
Anders Hillborg Dreaming River
Edvard Grieg Piano Concerto
Sergei Rachmaninov Symphonic Dances
Jean Sibelius En saga, Symphony No. 2
Frederic Chopin Piano Concerto No. 2
Mihaela Ursuleasa piano

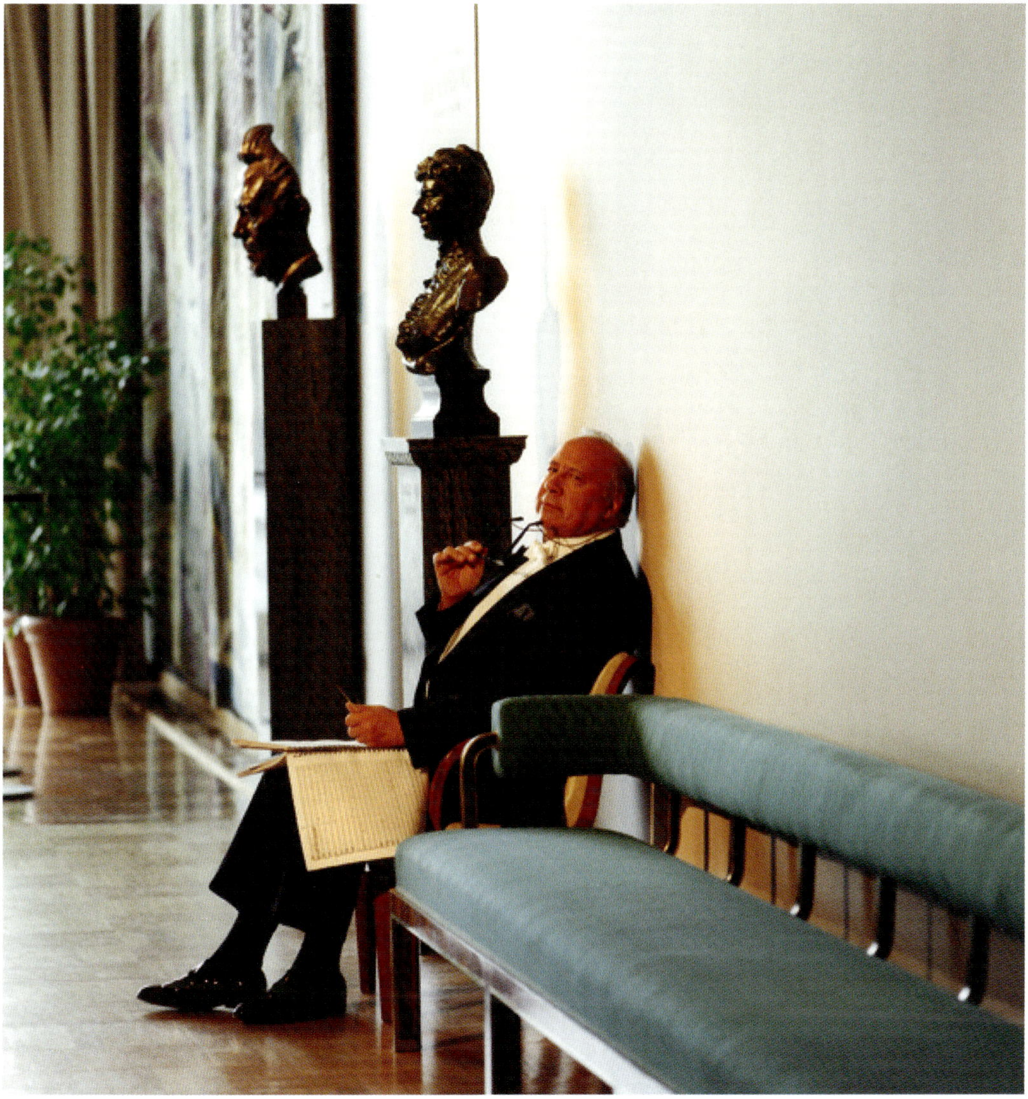

The future

NEEME JÄRVI AT HIS BEST

"It was Järvi at his most inspired standing on the podium. The man who almost magically fills his colleagues with courage, and who creates music with equal parts of technical brilliance and feeling." ... "in a sense it is about clarifying what the composer has laid out in his score. In a positive sense, to simplify, explain and illuminate a musical course of events so that it appears as both full of content, exciting and logical. At his best Järvi is a master at this."

**Review of the subscription concert on 12 June 2002
Håkan Dahl, Göteborgs-Posten**

Orchestral history is often the history of its principal conductors. The difference between good music making and great art often depends on the relationship between the conductor and his orchestra. There are numerous legendary examples and Neeme Järvi's era in Gothenburg will undoubtedly be counted as one of them. Under Järvi, the GSO has developed into a top class orchestra and has become a Nordic icon.

Pride over the orchestra's success is deeply felt. But everyone knows that the serious work is just beginning. Göteborgs Symfoniker – The National Orchestra of Sweden has to maintain the position it has reached in tough competition.

"No matter how well the artists get on with the orchestra and the Concert Hall, we can never escape our geographic location," says planning officer, Karin Tufvesson Hjörne. "If you are sought after in Berlin and Vienna, London, New York and Los Angeles, of course Gothenburg is going to feel a bit far away."

"We work and live in a city that is relatively unknown to the rest of the world," she admits.

"The other major Scandinavian symphony orchestras are all situated in the capital cities. That's why the National Orchestra title is very valuable when marketing ourselves internationally. (We are sitting in the foyer at the Concert Hall talking and, just as the planning director mentions the words National Orchestra, a triumphant trumpet fanfare is heard from the main auditorium. Coincidence of course, but it sounded great.)

The newly printed programme is lying on the table in front of Karin Tuvfesson Hjörne. There is one main topic of conversation. "An era is approaching its end and a new one is beginning." Karin Tuvfesson Hjörne explains: "Neeme will always be a specially honoured guest here. I think that he regards the development of the GSO as his life's most important work."

Karin Tufvesson Hjörne is responsible for planning the concert season. In her job she finds herself with hundreds of unread e-mails at the end of the week. This particular week she has 297 of them, she explains as she looks across Götaplatsen from the enormous foyer windows. On the other side of the square is the Civic Theatre which was reopened on the weekend in September 2002 that the GSO and Neeme Järvi were celebrating 20 years of collaboration.

E-mail is excellent for rapid communication, and it's something she needs. It's part of the job to be constantly updated about artists and news of the music world and to keep in touch with what is going on at other concert halls. What interesting conductors are appearing in Stockholm, Oslo, Copenhagen, what solo artists are performing in Berlin, London or Paris at the moment?

Co-operation is good, even if there is competition for the best artists. Everybody is hunting the same field.

Another reason for the large amount of e-mail is the number of artists now recording CDs themselves. Digital files are then mailed electronically to all kinds of possibly interested parties. "Before, when a recording arrived, we knew that there had been some degree of quality control. A record company had taken the time and money to record it. That control no longer exists. The amount of recorded material has increased enormously, and to that one has to add all the people who contact us wanting to audition, whether they play an

---

"He is well prepared and that means that I must also be well prepared. He is humble which means that I have to be humble too.
He is incredibly knowledgeable, which encourages me to be knowledgeable. He gives his utmost, which means that I also have to give my utmost. Then it doesn't matter where in the world he comes from."
Leo Winland, principal cellist, on the ideal conductor.

"The French talk about repeating the music, répétition. In German you say Probe – testing, trying, training, while in English the delightful term is rehearse – reproducing, listening, performing. I love rehearsing in the English sense of forming the character of the music, and working with the musicians making all of them feel responsible for what they are doing, even if I have the final say."
Christian Zacharias, Mozart expert and principal guest conductor for classical repertoire.

> "The employment conditions we enjoy today would have seemed unattainable to members of the orchestra in the old days.
> What does the future look like for the GSO over the next 90 years? There is a demand for live music, the ability to perform it exists, but is there a willingness among politicians to provide the necessary finance? Let us hope that this is the case, so that our colleagues in 2085 will be able to write something about the wise decisions made during the 1990s, at least with regard to cultural policies."
>
> **Bo Olsson, viola player, at the 90th anniversary in 1995. In 2005 the GSO will celebrate it's centenary.**

instrument, sing or conduct. Unfortunately we neither have the time nor the space to receive them to any great extent."

This season 2003/2004 is Neeme Järvi's last as principal conductor and a tour de force of his achievements, including guest appearances in Vara and Stockholm, a UK tour, continued recordings of symphonies by Sibelius and Tchaikovsky and a Grande finale in May 2004 with performances of major works by Stenhammar, Strauss, Sibelius and Mahler. Järvi will, however, remain an important person in the next step of GSO's development.

In the spring of 2003 the GSO announced their new strategy of a conductors' team and their new principal conductor: the Swiss maestro Mario Venzago, who is taking up his post in the season 2004/2005. Venzago will become the central figure in the future artistic work of the orchestra, leading a team consisting of principal guest conductors Peter Eötvös and Christian Zacharias, and Neeme Järvi in his new position as principal conductor emeritus.

Pianist and Mozart expert Christian Zacharias has been assigned as principal guest conductor. His task is to fine tune the classical repertoire, not just for classical lovers, but because it is good for the health of an orchestra to perform this music. In terms of technique it is often simple, and therefore so difficult to perform well. There is nothing for the musician to hide behind.

The Hungarian composer and conductor Peter Eötvös is principal guest conductor of modern and contemporary repertoire. He is a major personality on the contemporary music scene and he will showcase seminal modern works as well as new international music.

This strategy of working with four international conductors will give the orchestra great possibilities to grow and nurture its unique Nordic identity, while at the same time

Peter Eötvös, principal guest conductor for modern and contemporary repertoire from the 2003–2004 season.

developing the orchestra's command of the Viennese classics as well as of contemporary masterpieces. Venzago was raised in the Central European tradition and is strongly attracted to the music of the 20th century, but is equally at home in the core repertoire. Together with the other conductors in the team, not least Järvi, who will continue to conduct the GSO several weeks each season, Venzago is a strong advocate of the orchestra's commitment to Scandinavian and Swedish music.

"Like Järvi, Venzago inspires the mucicians to surpass their own limits and he has a strong appreciation of the Scandinavian tradition, which is so important to us," says the GSO's head of communications Martin Hansson. "Our tradition is unique and the idea of a conductors' team may be bold, but we are convinced that this is the right path to travel. This is, among other things, what we mean with tradition in transition," Hansson continues.

The main task for the orchesta and their new principal conductor is to build a strong artistic profile and put the orchestra into overdrive so that it can climb even higher up the world rankings.

Järvi has reached a full circle from the days of Stenhammar and Sibelius. Traditions are carefully tended but life has to be lived here and now. As the National Orchestra of Sweden, the GSO also wants to showcase major pieces by contemporary composers. That is the reason why names such as Rautavaara, Ruders, Eötvös, Berio, Hillborg, Lindberg, Sandström, Turnage, Torstensson and others appear on the concert programmes.

The Concert Hall in Gothenburg is the base. From here the orchestra travels to different arenas in Gothenburg, Sweden and the world. At Vara in Västergötland they are building a concert hall where the GSO will perform annually. It will be opened in September 2003 and will further stimulate musical life in the region.

Home and away no longer have clear boundaries. Young artists travel easily between continents. Traditional genre and national borders are erased as different kinds of ethnic music melt together with pop, jazz and classical into exciting new styles.

Conductor and composer Tan Dun, who received an Oscar for the soundtrack for Crouching Tiger, Hidden Dragon and who visited the GSO in the autumn of 2001, is a good example of creative fertilization, explains Martin Hansson: "Tan Dun grew up with Chinese folk music, trained at the conservatoire in Beijing, emigrated to the USA and now lives in multi-ethnic Manhattan."

Giya Kancheli from Georgia is another such example as is Unsuk Chin from South Korea, who has studied in the West and who gets ideas from Greek mythology. Chin's work provides an Asian view of the West European cultural heritage in a modern musical language.

Gothenburg's new musical academy, the National Orchestra of Sweden Academy (SNOA), will be very important for the future of music. The Academy will welcome students from all over the world. Training will be at post-graduate level and after two years the students will qualify for a Master of Fine Arts in Music. The idea is to secure and prepare the next generation of orchestral musicians. There will be an informal network between the Music College and the Concert Hall whose musicians will teach at the academy. The conductors Herbert Blomstedt and Neeme Järvi will be artistic advisors. The programme started at the same time as Neeme Järvi and the GSO celebrated their 20th anniversary.

The anniversary concerts mixed tradition and the present, with a première of the song cycle *Njutningen* by Hans Gefors, composer and professor of composition at the Music College in Malmö. Gefors' song cycle has a special history. It was commissioned by the GSO's sponsor, Göteborgs-Posten, as a present to the orchestra in connection with the nomination as the National Orchestra of Sweden in 1997.

PS – Vienna 1997

The year was 1997 and Martin Hansson, who is now the GSO's head of communications, was then a radio producer with the task of recording the GSO's concert at the Musikverein in Vienna for the Swedish Broadcasting Corporation. Following their successful debut a few years earlier, the GSO was once again in Vienna to perform three concerts.

"This happened during the second concert, which began with Lidholm's *Toccata e canto*," Hansson recalls. "I was present at the first concert in the auditorium of the Musikverein. There was an amazing Russian bass soloist (Paata Burchuladze singing Mussorgsky). It was a really superb concert. For the second concert I was in a small recording studio. It was very basic, in the regions behind the fantastic gilded auditorium. A little chap came in with a small briefcase, the producer from the Austrian Radio. I followed the concert on the monitor in the studio. The final piece was Stravinsky's *Rite of Spring*, which is a complex score that the orchestra knows inside out. It is rhythmically complicated, especially at the end, which must be properly rehearsed.

"All of a sudden the Austrian producer looked up at the screen. Previously he just sat there following the score, but now he was all attention. We had both heard that something was happening."

"I thought, now comes disaster. What had happened was that Neeme had got the bit between his teeth. He obviously felt that things were going so well that he decided to be a bit more creative."

Hansson stands up and starts gesticulating to show us.

"He was doing this kind of underarm motion… cueing the different sections quite artistically. Then, all of a sudden when the music is constantly changing time signatures, Neeme and the orchestra lost contact with each other."

"As luck would have it the percussion was right, and somehow Neeme managed instantly to get control again. The orchestra was back on track. Everything happened in a flash."

"Ninety nine percent of conductors would probably think that he was mad to do such a thing at the Musikverein in Vienna, in the heartland of music. That's probably what some of the players thought as well: putting them through such an ordeal."

"But at the same time that is the charm of the man!"

"He doesn't hold back… I wouldn't call it a lack of respect, but he maintains a kind of healthy distance. He doesn't take things too seriously, and yet he does take things very seriously. He dares to follow the flow of the music, one could say that he improvises…a little like a jazz musician, except with a whole symphony orchestra."

"That for me is greatness."

"It was an awesome feeling. That for a second it wobbled, didn't really mean a thing live, but I didn't want to keep it on the recorded version. I called Jan Lennart Höglund in Stockholm, who was the orchestra producer for Radio P2 in those days. I told him the story, that something had happened in Vienna that I wanted to take out. I've already edited it out of the recording I told him, and it works, but to get it to work I had to make a small cut in Stravinsky's score. I've had to skip a phrase. 'Martin,' Lennart said, 'You can't do that.'

'Can it be that bad?' I said.

'Broadcast it as it is instead,' he said, but I didn't want to, even though I was not working for the GSO at that time. So after pulling my hair out a number of times I managed to fix it by copying a phrase instead of cutting it out, so it now tallies with Stravinsky's score."

"It didn't make any difference; it only confirmed the fact that an all out performance sometimes has a price."

"Genuine musicians know this. It's a part of Neeme's magic."

CD 2.4 + 2.5 + 2.14

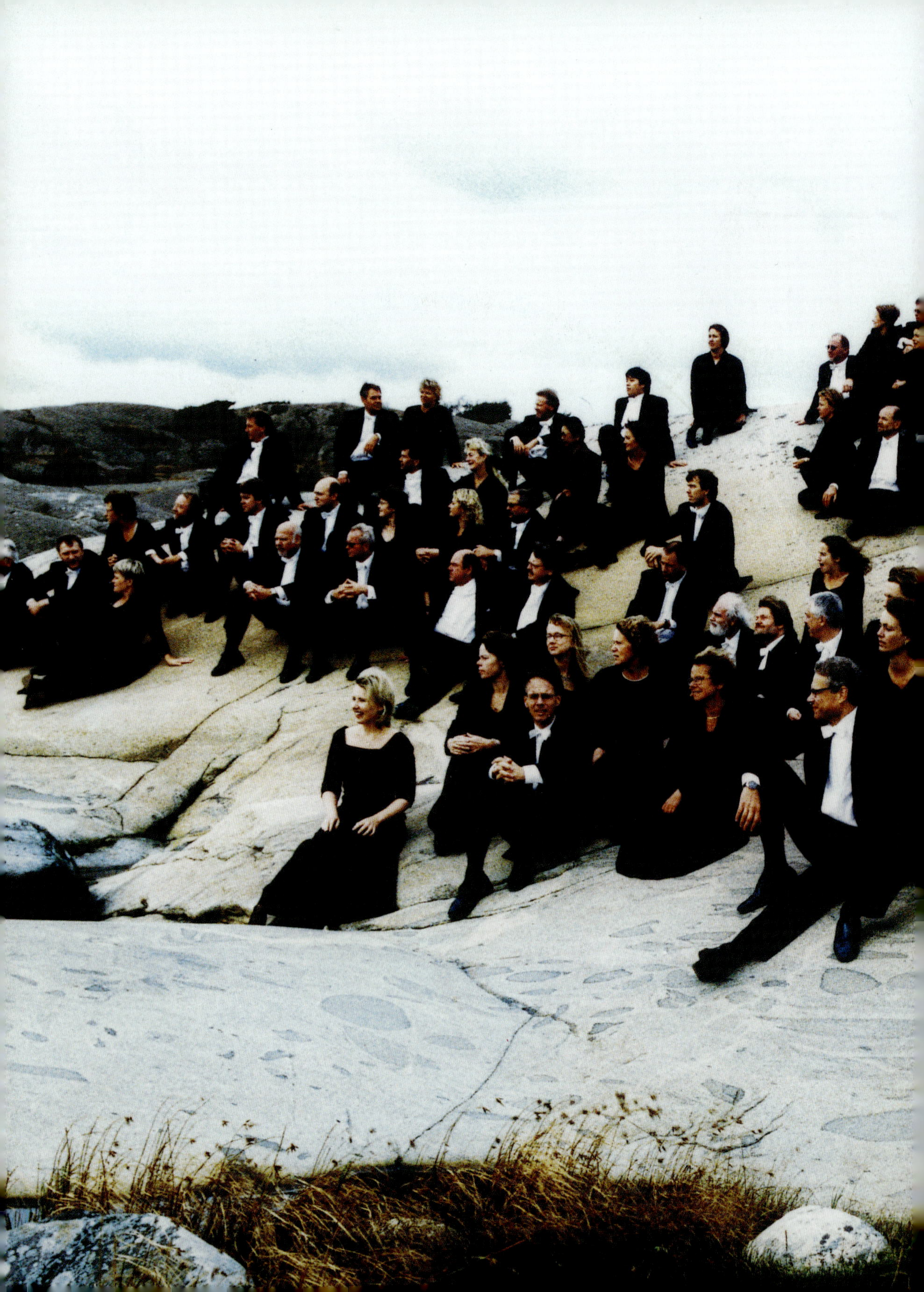

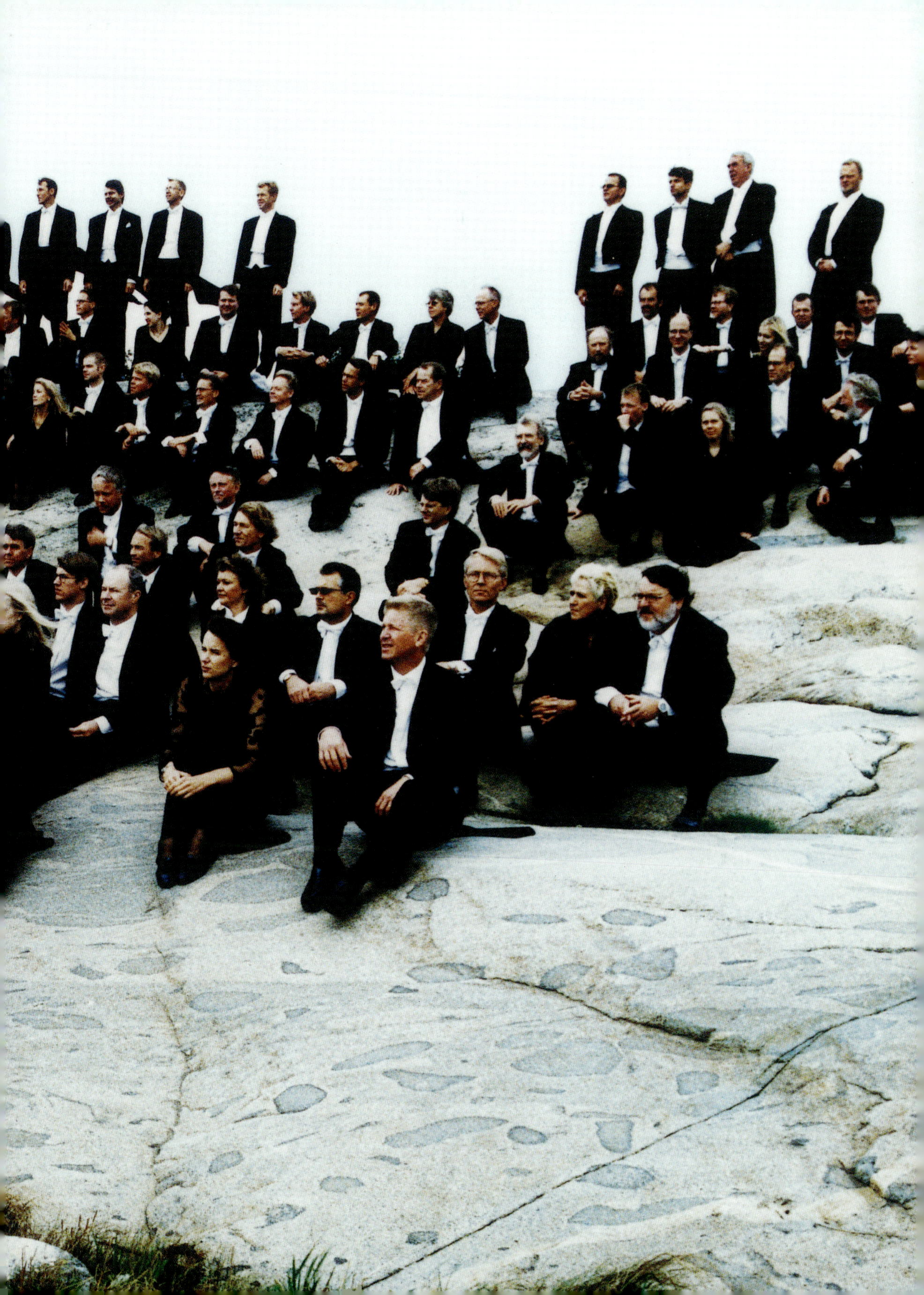

● CD 1 GSO and Neeme Järvi on BIS and Deutsche Grammophon

1. Wilhelm Stenhammar Symphony No. 1, from the first movement **(4.34)**
From BIS-CD-219 (STIM)

2. Jean Sibelius Symphony No. 1, from the finale **(4.13)**
From BIS-CD-221 (Breitkopf & Härtel)

3. Antonín Dvořák Cello Concerto, from Adagio **(5.00)**
Frans Helmerson cello
From BIS-CD-245 (PD=Public Domain)

4. Franz Berwald Sinfonie singulière, from the first movement **(6.10)**
From DG 415 502 (PD, Bärenreiter)

5. Eduard Tubin Symphony No. 10, conclusion **(5.12)**
From BIS-CD-297 (Warner/Chappell Music Scandinavia AB)

6. Edvard Grieg Peer Gynt at the Memnon statue, Peer Gynt's homecoming, Stormy evening by the sea and Shipwreck from *Peer Gynt* **(6.00)**
Toralv Maurstad Peer Gynt
From DG 471 300 (PD, Peters)

7. Dmitri Shostakovich Symphony No. 11 *The Year 1905*, from the third movement **(4.24)**
From DG 429 425 (Sikorski)

8. Piotr Tchaikovsky The battle of Poltava, from *Mazeppa* **(5.44)**
From DG 431 469 (PD)

9. Carl Nielsen Symphony No. 6 *Sinfonia semplice*, third movement **(5.22)**
From DG 437 507 (Wilhelm Hansen)

10. Wilhelm Stenhammar Symphony No. 2, from the first movement **(6.06)**
From DG 445 857 (SK-Gehrmans Musikförlag AB)

11. Arvo Pärt Symphony No. 3, third movement **(9.11)**
From DG 457 467 (Universal Edition)

12. Jean Sibelius Valse triste **(5.37)**
From DG 457 654) (Breitkopf & Härtel)

13. Rolf Martinsson From *Bridge* Trumpet concerto **(5.29)**
Håkan Hardenberger trumpet
From BIS-CD-1208 (STIM)

Released with kind permission from BIS Records and Deutsche Grammophon.

⬤ CD 2 GSO and Neeme Järvi on live recordings from the Swedish Broadcasting Corporation

1. Jean Sibelius Symphony No. 2, end of the finale **(8.49)**
18 June 1980, Royal Festival Hall, London
From Sveriges Radio P2 5462-79/2439
(Breitkopf & Härtel)

2. Hugo Alfvén Finale: Dance from the ballet *The prodigal son* **(3.57)**
18 August 1989, BBC Proms Royal Albert Hall, London. Presented by John Amis
From Sveriges Radio P2 2567-91/5455 (STIM)

3. Eduard Tubin Symphony No. 6, beginning of first movement **(3.15)**
24 October 1994 Musikverein, Vienna
From Sveriges Radio P2 4550-94/7025
(Warner/Chapell Music Scandinavia AB)

4. Igor Stravinsky The Rite of Spring, end of the sacrifice **(4.27)**
20 March 1997, Musikverein, Vienna
From Sveriges Radio P2 4550-97/7001
(Boosey & Hawkes)

5. Jean Sibelius Andante Festivo (encore) **(4.40)**
20 March 1997, Musikverein, Vienna
From Sveriges Radio P2 4550-97/7001
(Warner/Chappell Music Finland Oy)

6. Daniel Börtz Sinfonia I, conclusion **(5.26)**
14–15 September 1990 Gothenburg Concert Hall
From Sveriges Radio P2 3161-90/7024
(SK-Gehrmans Musikförlag AB)

7. Kurt Atterberg Symphony No. 3 *Västkustbilder*, first movement *Soldis* **(7.19)**
20-21 November 1997 Gothenburg Concert Hall
From Sveriges Radio P2 4550-97/70017
(Breitkopf & Härtel)

8. Guo Wen-jing *Chou Kong Shan* Concert for bamboo flutes, second movement **(4.13)**
Dai Ya bamboo flutes
27 February 1999, Gothenburg Concert Hall
From Sveriges Radio P2 4557-99/7001 (M/s)

9. Anders Hillborg from King Tide **(4.18)**
27 February 1999, Gothenburg Concert Hall
From Sveriges Radio P2 4550-97/7001 (STIM)

10. Carl Nielsen Violin Concerto, conclusion **(7.54)**
Nikolaj Znaider violin
3 September 1999, Lucerne Festival
From Sveriges Radio P2 2068-99/3125
(Wilhelm Hansen).
Nikolaj Znaider participates by kind permission of BMG Records.

11. Rolf Martinsson A.S. in Memoriam, conclusion **(3.42)**
4 May 2001, Gothenburg Concert Hall
From Sveriges Radio P2 4557-01/7004 (STIM)

12. Hilding Rosenberg Symphony No. 3 *De fyra livsåldrarna*, from the first movement **(5.10)**
4 May 2001, Gothenburg Concert Hall
From Sveriges Radio P2 4557-01/7004
(Warner/Chappell Music Scandinavia AB)

13. Jean Sibelius Symphony No. 2, end of the first movement **(5.22)**
10 November 2001, Gothenburg Concert Hall
From the Concert Hall's own recording
(Breitkopf & Härtel)

14. Jean Sibelius Karelia Suite, Alla marcia **(4.53)**
20 March 1997, Musikverein, Vienna
From Sveriges Radio P2 4550-97/7001
(Breitkopf & Härtel)

Released with kind permission from Sveriges Radio SR P2

PHOTOGRAPHS

Klaus Albrectsen p 52, Stockholms-Tidningen (1983)

Peter Claesson / Camera report pp 79, 89, 144

Jacob Forsell pp 64, 82, 116, 117

Roger Granat p 120

Anders Hoffgren / Kamerareportage p 93

Kent Hallgren / Kamerareportage p 139

Benny Hellberg pp 201, 202

Anna Hult pp 2, 8, 10, 11, 12, 17, 20, 23, 25, 57, 66, 71, 75, 127, 131, 136, 146, 150, 151, 154, 156, 160, 174–175, 178, 211, 220–221

Sören Håkanlind / Kamerareportage p 185

Robert Johansson / Kamerareportage p 182

Neeme Järvi's collection pp 104, 106, 108, 109, 113, 124, 134

Kamerareportage p 141

Bengt Kjellin / Kamerareportage p 45

Gothenburg Concert Hall Archive pp 16 top, 26, 28, 38, 40, 44, 46, 47, 51, 63, 69, 73, 76, 81, 90, 91, 92, 96, 99, 112, 114, 115 bottom, 122, 132, 143, 162, 169, 177, 189 bottom, 194, 196, 199, 208, 209, 217

Toivo Köpllä p 14

Thore Leykauff / Kamerareportage pp 188, 189 top

P.H. Lindberg p 142

Theresia Linke pp 186, 190

Nigel Lockhurst p 121

Mats Lundqvist p 119

Picture Library Herald & Evening Times, Glasgow p 16 bottom

Max Plunger pp 31, 32, 35, 36

Hans Pölkow p 193

Anna Rehnberg / Kamerareportage pp 86, 126, 130

Signaturen JAN p 56, Arbetet (1983)

Magnus Sundgren / Kamerareportage p 159 top

Kalju Suur pp 115 top, 118

Laszlo Sziranyi pp 59, 65

Roger Turesson p 19

Marie Ullnert / Kamerareportage pp 129, 159 bottom

Mark Vuori pp 95, 98, 149, 152, 165, 166, 172

The Concert Hall has taken all possible measures to trace copyright owners.

SOURCES AND PICTURE CREDITS

Konserthuset's archive

Konserthuset's seasonal programmes 1982–2002

Landsarkivet in Gothenburg

Newspaper archives

Interviews

Håkan Edlén: Göteborgs Konserthus 50 år

Phil G. Goulding: Klassisk Musik, Forum förlag, Stockholm 1994

P G Gyllenhammar: Fortsättning följer, Bonniers förlag 2000

Gothenburgs Konserthus: Ett album. In association with White Architects AB 1992

Benny Hellberg: Göteborgs Symfonikers världsturné, Off art 1987

Gustaf Hilleström: Göteborgs Symfoniker 75 år, The Gothenburg Concert Hall, October 1980

Norman Lebrecht: The Complete Companion to 20th Century Music, Simon & Schuster, UK 2000

Lars Sjöberg and Gösta Åberg: Vem är vem i Klassisk Musik, Rabén Prisma, Stockholm 1997

Sohlmans musiklexikon, Sohlmans förlag, Stockholm 1975

Bo Wallner: Wilhelm Stenhammar och hans tid, Norstedts Förlag, Stockholm 1991